The Condominium and Cooperative Apartment Buyer's and Seller's Guide

The Condominium and Cooperative Apartment Buyer's and Seller's Guide

David W. Kennedy

JOHN WILEY & SONS

New York • Chichester • Brisbane • Toronto • Singapore

Library of Congress Cataloging in Publication Data
Kennedy, David W.
   The condominium and cooperative apartment buyer's
and seller's guide.

   Includes index.
   1. Condominiums. 2. Apartment houses, Cooperative.
3. House buying. 4. House selling. I. Title.

HD1390.5.K46 1983   333.33'8   83-6586
ISBN 0-471-09617-2

Printed in the United States of America

10 9 8 7 6 5 4 3 2

To Vi, Max, Harald, Marty, and Bruce

Your encouragement and good cheer
helped to make it all possible

Preface

Buying or selling a condominium or cooperative apartment is a confusing process for most people. There are many reasons for this but the paramount one, undoubtedly, is that few individuals even know what a condominium or cooperative is, much less how to buy or sell one. Since millions of apartments change hands every year, a book taking the buyer and seller through that process is needed. This is the first book that lays out, in a step-by-step approach, how to go about buying or selling a condominium or cooperative apartment.

For example, on the buying side, the book takes the potential buyer through a rent versus buy analysis. Also, the financial and tax advantages of owning an apartment are set out in great detail. Other relevant topics, such as employing real estate brokers, attorneys, and bankers, are similarly dealt with in a comprehensive manner.

All sellers' concerns, such as the tax consequences of the sale, preparing the apartment for sale, and finding a buyer are covered, as are other important topics.

Foremost among the many unique features of this book is the fact that the reader is given actual questions to ask of brokers, lawyers, sellers, and bankers. Sellers are also aided by a series of questions that must be asked of the buyer, as well as of all the professionals involved in the sale of the apartment.

Actual documents used in the sale and purchase of condominium and cooperative apartments are included, as are full explanations of their use and relevance to the reader.

This book has grown out of my many years of experience selling apartments in one of the country's most active real estate markets, New York City. Because I was concerned about avoiding a New York bias in the manuscript, I purposely interviewed knowledgeable, working professionals in other parts of the country, most notably: Texas, California, Florida, Colorado, and Washington, D.C. As a result, this book can be used by buyers and sellers throughout the United States.

It must be emphasized here, as it is in the text, that different states have laws that directly affect the sale and purchase of condominium and cooperative apartments. Therefore local advice should always be sought before final decisions are made.

DAVID W. KENNEDY

New York, New York
June 1983

Contents

PART 2   SELLING

The Condominium and Cooperative Apartment Buyer's and Seller's Guide

PART 1

BUYING

INTRODUCTION TO BUYING

Buying a condominium or cooperative apartment is generally much more difficult than buying a single-family detached home. Most buyers who are looking for a condominium or cooperative have never lived in one before. They are unfamiliar with the terminology involved as well as with the unique problems that they will encounter when purchasing and living in an apartment.

For example, almost every condominium or cooperative apartment imposes certain restrictions on the owner that would not be found with a single-family house. Also, the proximity of neighbors causes a distinct set of problems with which the average individual might be unfamiliar.

The chapters that follow in the section on buying cover these and other problems that buyers are most likely to encounter. After many of the chapters there will be a set of questions that should be studied and asked by the buyer. If the buyer receives satisfactory answers to those questions, he or she can be sure that most of the problems and their solutions have been covered.

Prospective buyers should also read the section on selling, which comprises the second part of this volume. By reading that section the buyer will better understand how the seller thinks, and therefore will become a better and more knowledgeable buyer.

1

Buying a Condominium or Cooperative Apartment—
Step by Step

1. Make the decision to buy.

    a. Do you have enough of a down payment? If not, stop until you do.

2. Start your apartment search—it could take months.

    a. Decide on location(s).
    b. Find an experienced real estate agent in those areas.
    c. Utilize all search outlets.
    d. Comparison shop.
    e. Interview the board of managers of the apartment you decide on.

3. When you find the right apartment, bid on it immediately.

    a. Price negotiation shouldn't take longer than one week.

4. Find financing. Again, comparison shop.

    a. Know all your financing alternatives.
    b. What type of mortgage is right for you? Under what terms?

5. Find an experienced attorney to handle your end of the deal.
6. Pay any binder, if required.
7. Go to contract—normally completed 15–30 days after bid is accepted. Attorneys become heavily involved at this point.
8. Close the deal.
9. Move in.

1

Why Buy a Condominium or Cooperative Apartment at All?

Providing shelter for yourself and your family is one of the necessities of life. Most individuals opt for one of three alternatives when it comes to housing. The first is the "American Dream"—the single-family detached house with a backyard and two-car garage, located (in most cases) in a suburban or a rural area. The second form of housing is the rental apartment, normally situated in or close to an urban locale. The third alternative is the condominium or cooperative apartment.

Owning a single-family home is wonderful, if you can afford it. But there's the rub; many young couples and single people (as well as some older, more established families) just can't seem to scrape enough money together to buy that split-level or ranch house that is such a familiar part of the American landscape. Inflation, of course, is the chief culprit. It is not unusual these days to see a small, two-bedroom house in an upscale suburban area going for $100,000 or more.

On the other hand, renting a house or an apartment has many disadvantages, the greatest of which is that the monthly rent money is gone forever once it is sent to the landlord. You get nothing for your investment. Of course, you are freed from many maintenance chores; however, you are also subject to the whims of a landlord who may be more interested in making a profit than in providing good services to his tenants. Not a particularly happy scenario, but one in which more and more tenants are finding themselves. Also, you are not the master of your own destiny in a rental situation. The landlord normally has the right to raise your rent periodically and, at some point in time, you may be forced to move because you can no longer afford to pay the rent.

This leaves the condominium or cooperative apartment as your only viable housing alternative. There are seven main reasons that a condominium or cooperative apartment may be the answer:

1.   Condominium and cooperative apartments in most parts of the nation are cheaper than single-family homes. Normally the cost is about one third less. This fact alone makes condos and coops attractive to the first-time home buyer, especially young couples and single people. And, if you are lucky enough to be involved in a conversion where you can buy your rental apartment, the cost savings may be far greater than the one third mentioned.

2. Most condominium and cooperative developers (where it is a newly built project) buy a mortgage commitment at a rate significantly below the prevailing market interest rate for single-family homes. For example, it is common for a developer to have arranged with a lending source to give mortgages to qualified buyers in his project at three points under the market rate. So, if rates are generally 16% for a home mortgage, you may be able to get a mortgage at 13% if you discover the right project. This is an excellent incentive for any potential purchaser. Mortgage loan interest rates will be discussed more fully in Chapter 7.

3. Owners of cooperative or condominium apartments normally, within certain limits, can do whatever they want to their apartments in terms of decorating. In some cases they can even alter the structure of the apartment itself by knocking down walls or by adding terrace enclosures and the like. Rental tenants for the most part are forbidden from changing their apartments in any fundamental manner. See Chapter 9 for more on this.

4. Unlike rental housing, a condominium or cooperative apartment can appreciate substantially in value, and you have the opportunity of possibly selling the apartment for significantly more than what you paid for it. This will be discussed further in Chapter 4.

5. As with a single-family house, you also get some significant tax advantages. There are deductions you can take that in effect will provide some tax shelter for you. More about taxes in Chapter 6.

6. The location of condo and coop developments is important to many buyers. Since many of these structures are located either in or on the outskirts of urban areas, residents are often closer to work than if they lived in the suburbs. If you enjoy the amenities of city life, you are closer to those as well.

7. The final and very important advantage of coop or condo ownership for many people is that they are freed from serious maintenance responsibilities, such as cutting lawns and cleaning out swimming pools.

If any or all of these reasons for owning a cooperative or condominium apartment make sense to you, then you should read and study the rest of this volume. Pay particular attention to the questions that follow many of the chapters. You shouldn't proceed with the purchase of an apartment until you get answers that are satisfactory to you.

2

What Are the Differences and Similarities between Condominiums and Cooperatives?

Probably no area leads to more confusion for the average person than trying to ascertain the differences and similarities between the condominium and cooperative forms of home ownership.

CONDOMINIUMS

A condominium is similar to a single-family home in many ways. Condominium buyers obtain a deed, can sublet or sell their apartment to whomever they please, and pay taxes directly to the local taxing authorities. Although a unit owner owns his apartment outright, he or she is "in partnership" with the other condominium owners in the complex with regard to ownership of the common elements of the structure, such as the exterior walls, and roofs and hallways within the building. Also exterior additions such as swimming pools, tennis courts, and landscaping amenities are considered part of the common elements for this purpose.

Because those common elements need maintenance, and because the housing complex needs workers, doormen, or porters, a monthly homeowners' fee must be paid. Depending on the size of the complex, on how many workers are involved, and on many other costs such as payments to local utilities for lighting common areas and the like, the homeowners' fee will vary from complex to complex. A service group is established from among all the owners to run the complex for everyone. This group usually is known as the homeowners' association.

COOPERATIVES

When you buy a cooperative apartment you are not strictly buying an apartment; you are buying shares in a housing corporation which owns the building. Instead of getting a deed, the cooperative buyer is given what is called a *proprietary lease*. Resales and subletting may be and usually are restricted by the board of directors of the building, who are drawn from building tenant–owners. By law, a cooperative apartment is not considered real property but rather personal property in all states except California, Colorado, Minnesota, and New

Jersey. A cooperative buyer and the board of directors are in a landlord–tenant relationship.

Again, you have monthly fees, called *maintenance*, which are assessed to cover the upkeep of the building or buildings. In addition, maintenance charges are also allocated for payment of real estate taxes, local utility charges, and any mortgage payments on the buildings that might be outstanding.

If large capital improvements are necessary in the cooperative building (such as the installation of a new roof or landscaping), a second mortgage can be obtained to secure the needed funds. This is not permitted in a condominium.

Since each owner of a condominium unit owns the apartment free of control by others in the building, the taking out of a second mortgage on the building is impossible. In theory, a mortgage can be taken out on a condominium building, but it can only be accomplished if there is unanimous consent from all the homeowners; in reality that usually is very difficult, if not impossible, to do. The only realistic way that condo owners can get any major repairs done is by raising the homeowners' fee or by assessing each homeowner a set amount to cover the cost of the repairs.

Renovation and repair of individual apartments is easier in a condominium setup than in a cooperative. The cooperative board usually has strict rules and regulations regarding decorating and repair. Since a condominium buyer owns his apartment in *fee simple* (the legal term for complete and total ownership), he or she has the right to do whatever renovation he deems necessary as long as it doesn't interfere with the ownership of his neighbor's apartment or of the common areas.

Condominium owners can deduct from their taxes mortgage interest and real estate taxes just as any single-family homeowner can. In a cooperative, however, you deduct from taxes that portion of your monthly maintenance payment that is allocated to the payment of real estate taxes, interest on the building's mortgage (if any), and interest on the loan you took out to buy the shares.

Another point: When you seek funds from a lender to buy a condominium, you obtain a mortgage that is a loan secured by real property—the apartment. However, if you wish to buy into a coop you must get a personal loan because you are buying personal property, not real property (in all but the four states mentioned earlier);

the personal loan usually is not secured by anything except your own good credit rating.

It's easy to see that owning a condominium or cooperative apartment can be significantly cheaper than owning a single-family house. If you were to own a single-family dwelling you would have to pay for all capital improvements yourself, such as that new roof or swimming pool. Condominium and cooperative owners share those costs and, therefore, the cost of living in a condo or coop is actually less.

What follows is a comparison between condominiums and cooperatives with regard to: building financing, real estate taxes, monthly costs, allocation of monthly costs, resale, form of government, form of ownership, alterations of individual apartments.

	Condominium	Cooperative*
Building Financing	No underlying mortgage	Mortgage(s)
Real Estate Taxes	Owner of individual apartment pays	Corporation pays
Monthly costs	Homeowners' dues	Maintenance
Allocation of Monthly Costs	Upkeep of building and salaries of building workers	Same as condo, plus real estate taxes and building's mortgage payments
Resale	No outside approval needed	Board of directors' approval normally required
Form of Government	Homeowners' association	Board of directors
Form of Ownership	Deed	Proprietary lease and corporate shares
Alterations of Individual Apartments	No permission needed	Permission must be obtained from board of directors

*Details may vary here because of state laws, but on the whole, these statements apply.

3

Lifestyle Considerations

Before you begin your apartment search you and the members of your family who are going to live in the apartment should sit down and think long and hard about the type, size, and location of the apartment you want. Get a piece of paper and put down the requirements that you absolutely can't live without and those on which you might be able to compromise. For instance, if you absolutely have to have an apartment with a terrace that faces south and that has a dining room big enough for your dining table, those would be absolute musts. But if you can live without a fireplace and a living room that is not 30 feet by 20 feet, then those are your compromise items. Stick to your guns when you begin your search, but be realistic too. The ideal apartment may be unobtainable, so be prepared to compromise a little on your absolutes if you have to. It comes down to knowing your own lifestyle and how you want to live.

For example, in New York City (where I have experience in the sale of apartments), most buyers more than anything want an apartment that has light streaming in the windows. But finding such an apartment in New York is difficult because of the multitude of high-rise buildings that block out the sun from smaller buildings. Some buyers will search for months for an apartment with suitable light, only to discover that everybody else is looking for the same thing. Therefore, they end up compromising on the brightness of an apartment.

Other buyers will compromise on light if they can find an apartment with two bathrooms instead of the traditional one, or a large kitchen with a great deal of counter space, or if they must have a terrace that faces south, or a third bedroom that is larger than a closet. Again, some measure of compromise probably will be necessary; you must realize that before you begin your apartment search.

After you have seen four or five apartments you will have a pretty good feel for the market in the locale in which you are interested. Your choice of apartment should be based on the realities of what is available in that particular area. In certain areas of the country you may get larger kitchens than in others, or room sizes might be essentially uniform; you will have to adjust to these realities. Once you do that, your search will fall into place.

BUILDING TYPES AND THEIR AMENITIES

There are all types of condominium and cooperative apartment complexes, ranging from high-rise buildings to garden-apartment types. Some have swimming pools, horseback riding, and tennis courts. A few cater to older couples with no children, some are "singles only," and others will be a mixture. Also, some will be located in downtown areas close to the business and cultural centers; others will be located on or near golf courses or the ocean. You must decide what kind of building you want and what kind of amenities you want. If you don't decide, your apartment search will drag on and on from complex to complex from locale to locale. If you and your family are not athletically inclined, you certainly don't want to pay for tennis courts and riding stables you won't use. Don't forget that your monthly homeowners' fee goes to maintaining the common elements, and athletic facilities are just that.

On the other hand, if you *are* looking for an apartment with a swimming pool, tennis courts, or other athletic facilities, you must make sure that those facilities are not leased back to the homeowners' association or board of directors by the developer of the property. Typically, 99-year leases are drawn up whereby the homeowners' association will lease the swimming pool or tennis courts and will pay the rent to the developer, who gets a periodic rent increase every few years or so. If in your search you run into one of these arrangements, steer clear. *Don't buy an apartment in a complex where there is a recreational facility lease arrangement.* Leaseback situations such as these have caused a great deal of trouble and gave black eyes to some condo developments in the early 1970s, because they made mandatory homeowners' fee increases every few years. There may still be a few of these around, so be on your guard.

TIME TO CONDUCT THE SEARCH

The key to finding the right apartment is the efficient use of your time. Obviously, if you can look only on weekends you will want to see as many apartments as you can. Map out a plan before you do, so you can maximize your looking time.

One good way of using your time efficiently is by carrying a note-book with you and by taking notes on each and every apartment you see. That way when you go back home you will have a record of what you saw, and you can make decisions in a rational and relaxed manner. If you see 10 apartments in one weekend there is no way you will remember the details of all of them if you don't write those details down. Once you match your notes against your list of absolutes (prepared before you began your search), then you can make reasoned judgments about the apartments you saw. For more about this see Chapter 10.

QUESTIONS CONCERNING LIFESTYLE

1. Is it important that the apartment be located in a complex near my work?
2. Is it vital that it be located near recreational facilities?
3. Is it necessary that it be located near shopping and entertainment?

The Building and Its Surroundings

4. What kind of amenities are important to me?
5. Are the building and the complex clean and well cared for?
6. Does it have the facilities that I want?
7. What are the restrictions with regard to pets and children?
8. Is the general neighborhood a good one or is it declining?
9. Are sewers and water facilities in good working order?
10. Is the area exclusively zoned for residential uses?
11. Is flooding a common problem?
12. How about noise, both from automobiles and airplanes?
13. What kind of people live in the complex?
14. Are utilities metered separately?

The Apartment Itself

15. Are the room sizes sufficient to accommodate my furniture?
16. Do the plumbing and electrical systems work properly?

17. Does the apartment meet most of my needs?
18. Is the layout suitable for the family and for visitors?
19. Do the bathrooms and kitchen have enough space to satisfy all members of the family?

A QUICK APARTMENT SEARCH CHECKLIST

Category	Question	Yes	No
Location	Is the apartment located close to work?		
	Is the apartment near good shopping areas?		
	Is it convenient to recreation?		
	Is the area a vital one?		
Builder's/converter's history	Has the builder or converter erected or converted any other buildings that can be visited?		
	Does my observation of these buildings seem positive?		
	Are the tenants pleased with the building?		
	Has the builder or the converter been operating for more than three years?		
Financing	Is the financing involved workable for me?		
	Do I understand the financing options?		
	Does the development have more than 50% rental tenants? (If so, there might be less concern for the property than if it has all owners.)		

4

Renting versus Buying

If you presently are renting, probably the most difficult problem you will face is should you continue to rent or should you buy. Unfortunately, there are no clear-cut answers to the problem, and in the end it comes down to an individual analysis. You must work out the numbers for yourself. You may find, when you put a pencil to it, that your own situation favors renting. If that is so, you may want to consider the other factors that favor home ownership, such as the possibility of borrowing against the equity buildup in a home or the fact that you are your own landlord. Most financial experts agree that the bottom line is: *Buy if you can afford it*.

Obviously, if you are paying $200 for a two-bedroom apartment or house in a desirable neighborhood and it would cost you $1,000 a month to carry the same apartment if you owned it, renting is the logical alternative. However, unless you are in a rent-controlled situation (where your rent does not rise periodically as you sign new leases), as time goes on the costs of owning versus renting draw closer and closer together. No matter what you are paying in rent, you would be wise to at least investigate what it would actually cost to buy an apartment of the size and in the location you would like. Local real estate brokers should be able to provide you with most of the details you need.

Of course, you have many expenses associated with owning that you don't have with renting. Those include paying your own maintenance and repair bills, as well as real estate taxes and utility charges. You do get tax deductions for real estate taxes, mortgage interest payments, and some repairs, but overall you probably will find that it will cost you more on a month-to-month basis to buy than to rent.

THE CASE FOR RENTING

Some individuals prefer to rent rather than to own for a number of good reasons. It should be emphasized that the rent-versus-buy decision is an individual one, and you may fall into the class of people who prefer to rent. But as we soon will see, buying seems to be the preferred alternative for most people.

Advantages of renting:

The renter is freed from maintenance and upkeep chores.

The renter can move at will without having to sell a residence and without all of the hassle involved in that.

The renter may get some recreational amenities such as tennis courts or swimming pools that the buyer may not get. Normally, these amenities might cost the renter extra money over and above the rent.

The final advantage may be the most important to most renters. That is, the renter can keep his or her savings invested as he or she sees fit. Buying a residence is very expensive and requires a large initial outlay of money, which some may feel is better invested in something other than a house or cooperative or condominium apartment.

THE CASE FOR BUYING

If renting is so favorable, then why would anyone want to buy. One word can answer that question—appreciation. A home is an asset that will continue to increase in value to some degree over the years you own it. Historically, the value of a home has increased over the years, and although there has been a softening of real estate prices recently and many more homes and apartments are vacant, in no way can it be said that the real estate bubble has burst. Even though prices and values have moderated, there should be some growth—albeit modest—over the next few years. When you take inflation into account, the cost (which after all is a reflection of market value) of housing will be higher in the near term as well as the long term.

TAX DEDUCTIONS

As you are probably aware, you get some tax deductions as a result of owning a house or apartment that you don't get with renting. For example, if you want to make improvements in a rental apartment you cannot deduct any of the costs associated with making those improvements. In addition, you may have to leave the improvements in the apartment when you move. If you owned the apartment, not only would you get a hefty tax deduction but you could add the cost of the improvements on to your selling price when it comes time to sell.

Let's consider another item—real estate taxes. Obviously, you are not responsible for the payment of real estate taxes if you rent, but don't for a moment think that you are not paying for some of the land-lord's real estate taxes. You do that when your rent is increased. In determining the rent that you are to pay, the landlord allocates real estate tax payments among all his tenants as part of his expenses. If you live in a rental property with fewer than, say, five units, a large portion of your rent will go toward paying the landlord's real estate tax bill, and you are not getting any tax break. Real estate taxes are fully tax deductible to condominium and cooperative apartment owners.

EQUITY BUILDUP

Besides being a place to live, a home is an asset. As an asset, a lender will allow you to borrow against the equity or value you have accrued during your period of ownership. For people with few other assets that is an important feature. There may come a time when you may need to borrow against your apartment for some reason or another, such as a child's education. Of course, you can't borrow against a rental unit because you have not built up any equity in it. As a matter of fact, all of your rental payments have just gone down the drain during the period you have rented.

OTHER ADVANTAGES TO OWNING

Financial experts point out two other advantages of home ownership that you should consider in making your rent-or-buy decision. The first advantage is purely psychological. It is the sense of security or pride of ownership that you will have. Even though it is purely a mental thing, it is nevertheless important to the well-being of many individuals.

The second advantage is much more tangible, that is the improvement in your credit standing. Owning a home will do wonders for an otherwise lackluster credit rating. This will enable you, if you wish, to take advantage of borrowing privileges you might not otherwise have.

Also, many housing and financial professionals predict that rents will continue to rise over the next few years. If that is so, it may actually become cheaper to own than to rent. If you obtain financing, you will probably know what your mortgage or loan payment will be five years from now. With rent, unless you have a long-term lease (which is highly unlikely), you can't be sure how much rent you will have to pay for the same apartment or house five years from today.

RENT-OR-BUY ANALYSIS

Conducting a rent-or-buy analysis requires the same kind of discipline that is needed in evaluating an investment of any type. If you were to contemplate the purchase of stocks or bonds or investing in a money market fund, you would sit down and logically think through all the alternatives and the advantages of one type of investment over another.

Here are some questions you should consider when thinking about renting or buying. First, does buying an apartment (or house, for that matter) really make sense for me as an investment, or would the money I have to lay out be put to better use elsewhere? Also, do I have the money to put down for a down payment as well as the cash flow to cover all the necessary payments once a purchase is made? And, most fundamentally, is the cost of the investment I am making in line with the expected return I might receive when it comes time to sell? Needless to say, each individual's situation is different, and your answer may be different from your neighbor's. To get a handle on the problem you must go through the exercises outlined below.

The following excerpt is from a booklet issued by the Department of Labor entitled *Rent or Buy? Evaluating Alternatives in the Shelter Market*. "The amount you can spend for rent and be as well off from the viewpoint of investments as if you owned the home, over a specified number of years, depends on a number of factors. These include (1) the terms of purchase for shelter that meets your needs; (2) the monthly outlays required to retain and maintain your home; (3) the tax savings you experience as a homeowner; (4) your estimate of net proceeds from the sale of your home after a given number of

years; and (5) the plans you make for alternative use of your money." I
will call these five factors *decision factors*.

We will look at each of these decision factors individually, just as
you should and, by evaluating each of these factors in the ways suggested, you should be able to come to a reasoned decison on whether
you should rent or buy.

The first decision factor mentioned was the terms of purchase. That
factor involves five considerations that must be dealt with. They are
the downpayment; the cost of settlement (or closing); the terms of the
mortgage (or the deed of trust, as it is called in some states); the interest rate applicable to the mortgage; and the effect of terms on the cost
of financing.

Downpayment—Decision Factor 1

Let's consider the downpayment. Most downpayments in the country
are a function of local real estate practices. In some areas (most notably the Southwest) you may be able to put down as little as 5%. However, if you want to buy an apartment in New York City, you will
probably have to put down 25–33% of the entire purchase price. Obviously, if you don't have enough for a downpayment in the area in
which you are looking, you won't be able to buy. Lenders are very
willing to allow you to put down a larger amount than is standard for
the area, but they won't allow you to put down less.

The money for a downpayment should come out of savings or from
the proceeds of the sale of unneeded assets. If you have to borrow to
get the downpayment (as will be mentioned later), you will probably
put yourself too heavily in debt to carry the apartment you want.
Therefore, you should have the downpayment available from readily
reachable funds.

The next consideration that must be evaluated is the cost of settlement. Any time real property is transferred from one owner to another, closing or settlement costs are incurred. These costs can range
anywhere from several hundred to a few thousand dollars. Closing
costs will be discussed in detail in Chapter 18.

The considerations of the term of the mortgage and interest rate
applicable to the mortgage are interrelated, and must be discussed
together as they are in Chapter 7 of this volume. Suffice it to say that
you should have a complete and accurate picture of the exact costs

involved before you proceed with any further sales-versus-rental analysis. This means that you should have discussed with a bank or other lender how much you can afford to spend on shelter. This includes your monthly mortgage payment as well as the monthly carrying charge, be it homeowners' dues or maintenance.

The final consideration is the effect of terms on the cost of financing. The terms you get for paying off the mortgage of course will determine whether you pay more or less each month. The longer the term of the mortgage, the less your monthly payment will be. But if you can only obtain a short-term mortgage with a balloon payment, at the end of five years your monthly payout may be much larger.

Monthly Outlays—Decision Factor 2

Of course, the largest monthly outlays for apartment owners, besides the mortgage or loan payment, will be the homeowners' fee or maintenance charge. Also, there are utility costs that must be paid monthly, as well as property insurance and other payments, such as repairs, that should be budgeted for on a monthly basis. The seller or the real estate agent you deal with should be able to give you reasonable estimates of these charges. As a matter of fact, you should ask to see, if possible, the seller's cancelled checks for the past year for the payment of insurance, utilities, and other monthly payouts made on a regular basis.

You should be aware, however, that homeowners' fees and maintenance charges can be raised quickly, and in many complexes are raised almost annually, so you must factor that into your calculations as well. If you can just barely afford to buy an apartment that you want this year, you probably will not be able to afford it next year unless your income keeps up with monthly operating cost increases.

Tax Savings—Decision Factor 3

As you will see in Chapter 6, there are some large tax savings available to homeowners that are not given to renters. The effect of tax savings is to lower the gross monthly outlays of the apartment owner. The amount of such savings obviously depends on the total amount of income that would be taxed if the deductions were not taken and on your specific tax bracket. Here is where you may want to seek the advice of a first-rate tax attorney or accountant who can sit down with you and intelligently discuss your financial and tax needs based on your individual situation.

Estimate of Net Proceeds After Sale—Decision Factor 4

This is the most difficult of all the factors to evaluate. Who really knows what the real estate market will look like one, two, five, or twenty years from now? All you can do is rely on the historical record. For the sake of our analysis, let's figure that the worth of any piece of real property increases at least about 3% per year. In many areas it may increase more than that, but for the purposes of this evaluation figuring on the low side is better than figuring on the high side. There are so many other factors at work here, such as improvement or decline of the neighborhood that you buy in and the economic situation when you sell, that coming up with a figure to work with here is pure guesswork. However, you can also figure that rents will go up rather than down no matter what, so you can't be off by far if you figure 3% per year as indicated above.

Alternative Investments—Decision Factor 5

If you now rent, what you can do is figure the difference between your rent payment and an amount that you would pay if you buy. The difference is what you could invest in alternatives other than a home. The big problem with an apartment, a house, or any other real estate investment is that it is an illiquid investment. That is, you cannot sell the asset quickly to take advantage of rapidly changing economic conditions. If you have stocks or bonds they can be sold hurriedly and, of course, with a savings account you need only go to the bank to deposit or withdraw funds.

Besides the monthly payout, an amount that you would put out for the downpayment and settlement costs can also be invested alternatively by the individual who prefers to rent. In order to figure exactly how much you could earn alternatively, study Tables 1 and 2 that follow. By looking at Table 1 you see that $5,000 invested at 6% earns $300 in interest for the full year. To gain this same amount in one year, the purchaser who used the same $5,000 to purchase a $42,000 apartment would have to sell it for enough to recover the $5,000 in-

Table 1. Value of $5,000 Compounded Annually at Selected Rates of Return

Period	5%	6%	7%
1 year	$ 5,250	$ 5,300	$ 5,350
5 years	6,381	6,691	7,013
10 years	8,144	8,954	9,836
20 years	13,266	16,036	19,348
30 years	21,610	28,717	38,061

Table 2. Value of $50 per Month at Selected Rates of Return

Period	5%	6%	7%
5 years	$ 3,400	$ 3,450	$ 3,550
10 years	7,700	8,100	8,550
20 years	20,300	22,650	25,400
30 years	40,750	48,750	58,450

vestment plus the $300 that could have been earned by investing the money at 6%.

By studying Table 2 you can easily ascertain that you can earn $3,000 a year by saving as little as $50 a month. This, of course, requires a regular commitment on the part of the renter to save this extra amount each month.

Now, by combining the value of the $5,000 investment (Table 1) and of the savings of $50 a month (Table 2) over a 10-year period at 6% interest, the result is $17,054 ($8,954 plus $8,100). This is what the renter would get after the 10-year period, and might be equal to the amount that the owner would get over the same period of time through tax deductions and other quantifiable benefits. If, as a renter, you were able to save $165 a month at the same 6% figure, the investment amount would total $35,684 after 10 years ($26,730 plus $8,954).

Although the analysis presented may not satisfy everyone, it is valid and the kind of simplified analysis that is most understandable. You may wish to engage in a similar exercise on your own or have someone familiar with such analyses perform it for you. In any case, it is a good guide for those who can't decide whether to buy or rent.

5

Financial Considerations:
Where Do You Stand?

W hen you come right down to it, purchase of a residence usually depends almost exclusively on two things. First, whether or not you have enough money to make the required downpayment and, second, whether or not you can generate enough of a monthly cash flow to carry the apartment once you move in.

DOWNPAYMENTS

Downpayments on condominium and cooperative apartments are by no means uniform throughout the country. For example, condominiums in the Washington, D.C., and Dallas-Fort Worth areas can be purchased for as little as 5% down. This is true whether you finance the purchase through a bank or through a private lending institution. In New York City, though, lenders normally require one fourth to one third of the total purchase price down before a sale can be made.

Obviously, part of your initial search preparations should include inquiries as to the customary downpayment required in the locale in which you are interested. Real estate brokers and lenders working in the area should be able to answer all questions about downpayments and other financing practices in the area.

A note of caution: Bankers are all of the opinion that if you have to borrow money to make the downpayment then you shouldn't buy. You would undoubtedly be spreading yourself very thin, and if you have to pay off a loan for the downpayment as well as for a mortgage, you might get into deep trouble. So you must be sure that you can cover the downpayment with presently available funds.

If you are one of the fortunate ones who has the option of putting down a large downpayment or a small one because you have the funds available, you may want to consider the advantages of both.

Advantages of a Large Downpayment

The obvious first advantage is that you have to borrow less from the bank; therefore, your monthly outlay will be less if you are granted a mortgage.

Because your mortgage is lower, the total amount paid in interest to the lender will be lower. This can be a disadvantage, however, if you are looking to maximize your tax deductions. See Chapter 6.

You may be able to negotiate for a mortgage with more favorable terms if you give a large downpayment.

Most important, equity in your apartment will build faster and you can use that equity to finance other investments if you wish.

Advantages of a Small Downpayment

If you don't use all of your savings on a downpayment, you can invest the remainder in high-yielding securities or for other personal uses such as starting a new business.

You get a tax deduction for interest payments made on an annual basis; the lower your downpayment, the higher the interest deduction you can take.

Inflation reduces the costs of future payments made, because the dollar of tomorrow will purchase less than it does today.

Calculating the downpayment and your monthly payments, which are a function of your own personal cash flow, should determine whether in fact you can afford the apartment or not.

CARRYING THE APARTMENT

The other important financial judgment you will have to make is whether or not your own cash flow will allow you to carry the apartment once you buy it. Remember, in a condominium or cooperative apartment you will be making two payments each and every month; one payment will cover your mortgage (or personal loan in the case of a coop) and the second will be the monthly maintenance or homeowners' fee, which goes toward the upkeep of the common areas. The charts and other information that follow this chapter will aid you in calculating your cash flow.

A lender will probably not give you the mortgage or personal loan if an analyst at the lending institution decides that your cash flow is insufficient to carry the apartment. How do they make that judgment? Each lender is different to some degree, but generally the old rule that an individual's salary or income for one week should cover *all* monthly housing costs is still used almost universally. In other words, when you add up the monthly mortgage payment and the monthly carrying charge, it should not add up to roughly more than

25% of your gross income for the month. However, lenders may give you a little leeway on this. For a full discussion, see Chapter 7.

INCOME AND OUTGO

To get a completely balanced picture of what you have to spend on housing, some fairly simple calculations should be made. Determining how much money comes in on a monthly basis and how much goes out to pay bills is called *cash flow*. You should be familiar with your own cash flow patterns, you should know at what times of the month money comes in and at what points it goes out.

Right now you should sit down with a pencil and paper and work out your income and fixed nonhousing expenses for the month. You can get these expense figures by looking at checkbook stubs, and receipts, and bills that you may have received.

Income

What actually constitutes income? For this purpose we are talking about take-home pay, that is *net income*. Net income is defined as all your income minus taxes and other items that are withheld from you on a regular basis. If you are self-employed and you do not have taxes withheld, you should arrive at net income by deducting estimated tax payments that you make on a quarterly basis.

All other sources of *regular* income, such as royalties, interest, dividends, and rents, should also be added in. The key here is that the items must be received regularly. If you regularly receive bonuses or commissions they should be added in as well.

Fixed Nonhousing Expenses

So that you can properly figure your potential housing expenses, you must calculate what your fixed nonhousing monthly expenses are. These include taxes; regular monthly loan payments such as auto and credit cards; life, health, and auto insurance payments; medical outlays; telephone; auto expenses; commuter fares; parking fees; and any regular contributions to savings accounts or investment plans. Some expenses (such as medical expenses) may have to be converted to monthly expenses by dividing the yearly outgo by 12. When you have gathered all your expenses, simply total them and you will have your monthly, fixed nonhousing related expenses.

In addition to fixed expenses, you have discretionary or variable expenses. These include food, clothing, toiletries, dry cleaning, entertainment, contributions, club dues, and a myriad of other expenses. When you total these items you will come up with a figure that is your total monthly nonhousing expense.

What you have just done, whether you know it or not, is created a personal revenue and expense statement minus all housing costs.

Personal Balance Sheet

Since you have drawn up your own revenue and expense statement, you have one more chore ahead of you—a personal balance sheet. A balance sheet is nothing more than a snapshot of an individual's or company's financial condition at one point in time.

Here's how you do a balance sheet on yourself. List all your present assets such as savings and checking account balances; securities holdings; real estate; cars; cash value (also called whole life) life insurance; retirement plan balances including Individual Retirement Accounts (IRAs), Keogh plan accounts, company profit-sharing and savings plans; marketable personal assets such as antiques, paintings, and jewelry; any outstanding debts owed to you; and other personal assets such as television sets and stereo equipment. These constitute your total assets.

Since a balance sheet has two sides to it, you must offset your assets with your liabilities. For the purpose of a balance sheet, remember that you have to list liabilities for the same period in time that you have listed your assets. Liabilities are nothing more than debts that you owe. These include outstanding mortgage balances, current bills, all installment balances, insurance premiums, car loan and furniture loan balances, taxes owed, and all other outstanding debts. Once you add up your total liabilities you can subtract that figure from your total assets and you will come up with a figure known as your *current net worth*.

By now you have all the tools you need to begin drawing up a housing budget. This should give you a pretty good idea of how much you can spend on housing if you want to buy. Monthly variable expenses were mentioned briefly; they are important because by cutting down on those expenses you will be able to add to your housing availability figure. Monthly mortgage tables are shown below. These give specifics on what your mortgage loan will cost you and how large a mortgage you can afford.

Remember, when you calculate housing costs you must include a monthly mortgage (condominium) or personal loan (cooperative) payment, a real estate tax payment in the case of a condominium, utility expenses, repair and maintenance costs, and insurance expenses. Of course, you can't overlook your other major monthly outlay—that is your homeowners' dues or maintenance payment. By adjusting these numbers a bit you should be able to come up with an approximate monthly housing allowance based on your monthly income. Bankers usually figure that two thirds of your monthly housing costs should be allocated towards paying off your mortgage or personal loan. The remaining third should be spread among your other housing payments.

Amount of Loan	Years	Interest Rate									
		10%	11%	12%	13%	14%	15%	16%	17%	18%	19%
$45,000	25	$409	$441	$474	$508	$542	$576	$612	$647	$683	$719
	30	395	429	463	498	533	569	605	642	678	715
	35	387	422	457	493	529	566	602	639	676	713
$50,000	25	454	490	527	564	602	640	679	719	759	799
	30	439	476	514	553	592	632	672	713	754	794
	35	430	468	508	548	588	628	669	710	751	793
$55,000	25	500	539	579	620	662	704	747	791	835	879
	30	483	524	566	608	652	695	740	784	829	874
	35	473	515	559	602	647	691	736	781	827	872
$60,000	25	545	588	632	677	722	769	815	863	910	959
	30	527	571	617	664	711	759	807	855	904	953
	35	516	562	609	657	705	754	803	852	902	951
$65,000	25	591	637	685	733	782	833	883	935	986	1039
	30	570	619	669	719	770	822	874	927	980	1033
	35	559	609	660	712	764	817	870	923	977	1031
$70,000	25	636	686	737	789	843	897	951	1006	1062	1118
	30	614	667	720	774	829	885	941	998	1055	1112
	35	602	656	711	767	823	880	937	994	1052	1110
$75,000	25	682	735	790	846	903	961	1019	1078	1138	1198
	30	658	714	771	830	889	948	1009	1069	1130	1192
	35	645	703	762	821	882	943	1004	1065	1127	1189
$80,000	25	727	784	843	902	963	1025	1087	1150	1214	1278
	30	702	762	823	885	948	1012	1076	1141	1206	1271
	35	688	750	812	876	941	1005	1071	1136	1202	1268
$85,000	25	772	833	895	959	1023	1089	1155	1222	1290	1358
	30	746	809	874	940	1007	1075	1143	1212	1281	1351
	35	731	796	863	931	999	1068	1138	1207	1277	1348
$90,000	25	818	882	948	1015	1083	1153	1223	1294	1366	1438
	30	790	857	926	996	1066	1138	1210	1283	1356	1430
	35	774	843	914	986	1058	1131	1205	1278	1353	1427

Mortgage Table: Monthly Interest Plus Principle

Congratulations! You have now finished the rent-or-buy analysis. If, after performing all the calculations, it appears that you can afford to buy, you still have to decide if you want to buy or continue to rent. That is where the discussion in the first part of this chapter comes in; study it, talk to any financial advisors you choose, and make up your mind.

6

Tax Considerations

The owner of a condominium or cooperative apartment is entitled to certain tax breaks that a renter does not get. There are tax deductions that a buyer gets at the time of purchase and there are deductions that the owner gets while residing in the apartment.

TIME OF PURCHASE

As you probably know, you are allowed to deduct real estate taxes paid to local taxing authorities on your federal tax return. Condominium and single-family-home owners are eligible in the same way for the entire deduction. When it comes to time of purchase, the important date for tax purposes is the date of acquisition of the apartment, or the *closing date,* as it is sometimes called.

The seller of the apartment pays the taxes and therefore gets the deduction up until the day prior to the closing date. The buyer pays taxes and gets the deduction beginning on the closing date and from then on. All of this normally is spelled out and detailed in the closing statement that the buyer gets at the closing. Prior to purchase, you should have an accurate idea of exactly what taxes you will have to pay and what deductions you will be entitled to.

Another deductible item is interest paid on a mortgage or personal loan, in the case of a cooperative. Of course, after you acquire the apartment you will be paying mortgage or loan interest, but in some cases you may also have to pay some interest prior to the closing. If so, that is all fully deductible.

A frequently overlooked deduction is the one you get for *points* you may have had to pay to buy the property. Many lenders impose a processing fee of up to 3% of the total loan for the paperwork involved in granting a mortgage. If you have to pay such points, then the amount is fully deductible. However, to take the deduction properly, the condominium or cooperative apartment must be your *principal* residence (not a vacation home), and furthermore the charging of points by the lending institution must be a common practice in the locale. Don't forget to take this deduction—as much as $500–600 or more can be involved.

TAX DEDUCTIONS YOU CAN TAKE ONCE YOU OWN THE APARTMENT

As a condominium or cooperative apartment owner you probably should itemize your deductions. That's because when you add up all your housing deductions together with other deductions for which you are undoubtedly eligible, the amount of deductions should be much greater than the standard deduction or, as it is now called, the *zero bracket amount*. Each taxpayer, of course, should do his or her own calculations to verify this, but in most cases if you own a house or apartment you will want to itemize. You itemize your deductions by completing Schedule A on your tax return (that Schedule is reproduced at the end of this chapter).

If you own a condominium you are entitled to deduct real estate taxes assessed against your apartment, as discussed. Additionally, however, you are also permitted to deduct any taxes paid on the land and common elements. In a condominium complex, the taxes assessed on the land and common areas are divided among all the condominium owners and you can only deduct your portion.

Also, as mentioned earlier, you can deduct the interest you pay on your mortgage. Your lending institution should provide you with an end-of-year statement that shows the amount of interest paid and hence the amount deductible.

Deductions Available for Cooperative Apartment Owners

If you plan on buying a cooperative apartment instead of a condominium, you of course are allowed to deduct the interest paid on the personal loan that you obtained to purchase the apartment. But, and here it differs from a condominium, you can also deduct your share of the corporation's deductible mortgage interest and real estate taxes. When a sales agent tells you that this cooperative apartment is 40% tax deductible, in effect what he or she is saying is that 40% of your yearly maintenance goes for the payment or mortgage interest and real estate taxes on the building; therefore, that percentage of your yearly maintenance can be taken as a deduction. For example, if your annual maintenance cost comes to $4,800 ($400 a month) and 40% is tax deductible, you will be able to claim $1,920 as a tax deduction in addition to your personal loan interest. Again, you will be informed by the apartment corporation of the exact amount of your deduction in time for you to file your tax return.

Other Deductions for which All Apartment Owners Might Be Eligible

If you use one or more rooms in your apartment exclusively and regularly for business purposes, you may be entitled to take the home-office deduction. However, according to tax regulations, the room or rooms have to be (1) your main place of business, (or where you conduct a second business), or (2) a place where your clients or customers can meet with you in the normal course of doing business. Normally, certain business-related expenses can be deducted, such as electrical and heating costs. To see if you qualify, check with a tax accountant or an attorney.

People who buy and then rent out condominium or cooperative apartments purely for investment purposes can take a depreciation deduction for the property. The rules for depreciation deductions are quite complicated and as such are beyond the scope of this book. However, if you rent out a condominium or cooperative apartment for profit you should see Publication #588 in Appendix A of this volume. That publication will tell you all you need to know about the depreciation deduction.

An additional note for sellers of apartments: If you are over 55 years of age and you sell your apartment or home, the first $125,000 of profit you make on the sale is totally excluded from federal taxation. However, if your profit is less than $125,000—say, for instance, $30,000—then that is the amount that you can exclude. You can never again exclude any portion of the remaining $125,000 (or any other amount) if you sell another apartment later. This exclusion can only be used once and is limited to the total gain, up to $125,000.

Tax Credits

As an owner of a cooperative or condominium apartment you are entitled also to a share of the Residential Energy Credit if your complex installs certain energy-saving devices, such as a solar hot water heater or solar collectors. Windmills and geothermal devices also qualify. The amount of the credit is based on your share of the total cost of the installed device. To take this credit properly you must report it on line 45 of your 1040 form, after calculating it on Form 5695, a copy of which follows this chapter.

Special Tax Break for Homeowners Who Trade Down to a Cooperative Apartment

As mentioned earlier, cooperative apartments in most cases are cheaper than are single-family detached homes. As a result, individuals who have sold a house that is more expensive than the cooperative they are planning to buy, normally would expect to pay ordinary income tax on the difference between the selling price of the house and the purchase price of the apartment. However, there is one little-known gimmick that you can use that will allow you to defer the paying of the tax until you sell the cooperative apartment.

This strategy works because each owner in a cooperative building or complex is allowed a tax deduction for the *prorata* portion of the interest paid on the building's mortgage. If you sell your principal residence and buy a new one within two years, you can postpone paying the tax if the new one costs more than the old one.

However, if a cooperative apartment costs less, it seems you can't avoid paying the tax. But you can. Here's how: Let's say you sell your old home for $100,000 and you buy a cooperative apartment for $75,000. Based on what you have learned so far you would expect to pay tax on the $25,000 difference, but as you will see presently, you need not. Further assume that the cooperative building (or buildings, as the case may be) has a mortgage with a present balance of $2,500,000, and that the cooperative building has 100 apartments of equal size in it. The tax laws allow you to add 1/100 of the total mortgage to the cost of your apartment. Therefore, by using these figures, $25,000 can be added to your purchase price which brings you up to $100,000, the same amount you sold your house for. As a result, you are not subject to any tax payment.

Remember though, tax is deferred here, not eliminated entirely. You will have to square up with Uncle Sam when you sell the cooperative, unless you are over 55—if the over-55 rule is still applicable you may be able to avoid the tax altogether.

Schedules A&B
(Form 1040)
Department of the Treasury
Internal Revenue Service   (0)

Schedule A—Itemized Deductions
(Schedule B is on back)
▶ Attach to Form 1040. ▶ See Instructions for Schedules A and B (Form 1040).

OMB No. 1545-0074

1981
07

Name(s) as shown on Form 1040

Your social security number

Medical and Dental Expenses (Do not include expenses reimbursed or paid by others.) *(See page 17 of Instructions.)*

1 **One-half (but not more than $150) of insurance premiums you paid for medical care. (Be sure to include in line 10 below.)** . ▶

2 Medicine and drugs .

3 Enter 1% of Form 1040, line 31 . . .

4 Subtract line 3 from line 2. If line 3 is more than line 2, enter zero . .

5 Balance of insurance premiums for medical care not entered on line 1 . . . .

6 Other medical and dental expenses:

  a Doctors, dentists, nurses, etc. . . .

  b Hospitals . . . .

  c Transportation . . . .

  d Other (itemize—include hearing aids, dentures, eyeglasses, etc.) ▶

7 Total (add lines 4 through 6d) . . .

8 Enter 3% of Form 1040, line 31 . . .

9 Subtract line 8 from line 7. If line 8 is more than line 7, enter zero . . .

10 **Total medical and dental expenses (add lines 1 and 9). Enter here and on line 33 .** ▶

Taxes *(See page 18 of Instructions.)*

11 State and local income . . . . . .

12 Real estate . . . .

13 a General sales (see sales tax tables) .

  b General sales on motor vehicles . .

14 Personal property . . . .

15 Other (itemize) ▶

16 **Total taxes (add lines 11 through 15). Enter here and on line 34 . . .** ▶

Interest Expense *(See page 18 of Instructions.)*

17 Home mortgage . . . .

18 Credit and charge cards . . . . . .

19 Other (itemize) ▶

20 **Total interest expense (add lines 17 through 19). Enter here and on line 35** ▶

Contributions *(See page 19 of Instructions.)*

21 a Cash contributions (If you gave $3,000 or more to any one organization, report those contributions on line 21b) .

  b Cash contributions totaling $3,000 or more to any one organization (show to whom you gave and how much you gave) ▶

22 Other than cash (see page 19 of Instructions for required statement) . . . .

23 Carryover from prior years . . . . .

24 **Total contributions (add lines 21a through 23). Enter here and on line 36** ▶

Casualty or Theft Loss(es) *(You must attach Form 4684 if line 29 is $1,000 or more, OR if certain other situations apply.) (See page 19 of Instructions.)*

25 Loss before reimbursement . . . .

26 Insurance or other reimbursement you received or expect to receive . . . .

27 Subtract line 26 from line 25. If line 26 is more than line 25, enter zero . . .

28 Enter $100 or amount from line 27, whichever is smaller . . . .

29 **Total casualty or theft loss(es) (subtract line 28 from line 27). Enter here and on line 37** ▶

Miscellaneous Deductions *(See page 19 of Instructions.)*

30 a Union dues . . . .

  b Tax return preparation fee . . . .

31 Other (itemize) ▶

32 **Total miscellaneous deductions (add lines 30a through 31). Enter here and on line 38 . . . .** ▶

Summary of Itemized Deductions *(See page 20 of Instructions.)* **A**

33 Total medical and dental—from line 10 .

34 Total taxes—from line 16 . . . . .

35 Total interest—from line 20 . . . .

36 Total contributions—from line 24 . . .

37 Total casualty or theft loss(es)—from line 29 .

38 Total miscellaneous—from line 32 . . .

39 Add lines 33 through 38 . . . . .

40 If you checked Form 1040, Filing Status box:
  2 or 5, enter $3,400 . . . . .
  1 or 4, enter $2,300 . . . . .
  3, enter $1,700 . . . . . .

41 **Subtract line 40 from line 39. Enter here and on Form 1040, line 32b. (If line 40 is more than line 39, see the Instructions for line 41 on page 20.) . . . . .** ▶

For Paperwork Reduction Act Notice, see Form 1040 Instructions.

Schedule A

40

QUESTIONS CONCERNING TAXES

1. What is the total amount of all tax deductions I can take if I buy this particular apartment?
2. If I am financing part of the cost, what portion of my monthly mortgage or loan payment is tax deductible?
3. Are any points involved in the purchase of the apartment?
4. Has the building installed energy-saving devices that will allow me to qualify for a Residential Energy Credit?

Form 5695
Department of the Treasury
Internal Revenue Service (O)

Residential Energy Credit

▶ Attach to Form 1040. ▶ See Instructions on back.

OMB No. 1545-0214

1981

33

Name(s) as shown on Form 1040	Your social security number

Enter in the space below the address of your principal residence on which the credit is claimed if it is different from the address shown on Form 1040.

If you have an energy credit carryover from a previous tax year and no energy savings costs this year, skip to Part III, line 24.

Part I Fill in your energy conservation costs (but do not include repair or maintenance costs).

1 Was your principal residence substantially completed before April 20, 1977? . . . . ▶ ☐ Yes ☐ No

Note: You MUST answer this question. Failure to do so will delay the processing of your return. If you checked the "No" box, you CANNOT claim an energy credit under Part I and you should not fill in lines 2 through 12 of this form.

2 a Insulation	2a	
b Storm (or thermal) windows or doors	2b	
c Caulking or weatherstripping	2c	
d A replacement burner for your existing furnace that reduces fuel use	2d	
e A device for modifying flue openings to make a heating system more efficient	2e	
f An electrical or mechanical furnace ignition system that replaces a gas pilot light	2f	
g A thermostat with an automatic setback	2g	
h A meter that shows the cost of energy used	2h	
3 Total (add lines 2a through 2h)	3	
4 Enter the part of expenditures made from nontaxable government grants and subsidized financing . .	4	
5 Subtract line 4 from line 3	5	
6 Maximum amount of cost on which credit can be figured	6	$2,000 00
7 Enter the total energy conservation costs for this residence from your 1978, 1979, and 1980 Form 5695, line 2	7	
8 Subtract line 7 from line 6	8	
9 Enter the amount of nontaxable government grants and subsidized financing entered on line 4 . . .	9	
10 Subtract line 9 from line 8. If zero or less, do not complete the rest of this part	10	
11 Enter the amount on line 5 or line 10, whichever is less	11	
12 Enter 15% of line 11 here and include in amount on line 23 below	12	

Part II Fill in your renewable energy source costs (but do not include repair or maintenance costs).

13 a Solar _____ ⎪ 13 b Geothermal _____ ⎪ 13 c Wind _____ ⎪ Total ▶	13d	
14 Enter the part of expenditures made from nontaxable government grants and subsidized financing . .	14	
15 Subtract line 14 from line 13	15	
16 Maximum amount of cost on which credit can be figured	16	$10,000 00
17 Enter the total renewable energy source cost for this residence from your 1978 Form 5695, line 5 and your 1979 and 1980 Forms 5695, line 9	17	
18 Subtract line 17 from line 16	18	
19 Enter the amount of nontaxable government grants and subsidized financing entered on line 14 . . .	19	
20 Subtract line 19 from line 18. If zero or less, do not complete the rest of this part	20	
21 Enter the amount on line 15 or line 20, whichever is less	21	
22 Enter 40% of line 21 here and include in amount on line 23 below	22	

Part III Fill in this part to figure the limitation

23 Add lines 12 and 22. If less than $10, enter zero	23	
24 Enter your energy credit carryover from a previous tax year. **Caution**—Do not make an entry on this line if your 1980 Form 1040, line 47, showed an amount of more than zero	24	
25 Add lines 23 and 24	25	
26 Enter the amount of tax shown on Form 1040, line 37	26	
27 Add lines 38 through 44 from Form 1040 and enter the total	27	
28 Subtract line 27 from line 26. If zero or less, enter zero	28	
29 Residential energy credit. Enter the amount on line 25 or line 28, whichever is less. Also, enter this amount on Form 1040, line 45. Complete Part IV below if this line is less than line 25	29	

Part IV Fill in this part to figure your carryover to 1982 (Complete only if line 29 is less than line 25)

30 Enter amount from Part III, line 25	30	
31 Enter amount from Part III, line 29	31	
32 Credit carryover to 1982 (subtract line 31 from line 30)	32	

For Paperwork Reduction Act Notice, see instructions on back.

Form 5695

Paperwork Reduction Act Notice

The Paperwork Reduction Act of 1980 says we must tell you why we are collecting this information, how we will use it, and whether you have to give it to us. We ask for the information to carry out the Internal Revenue laws of the United States. We need it to ensure that you are complying with these laws and to allow us to figure and collect the right amount of tax. You are required to give us this information.

General Instructions

Two energy credits make up the residential energy credit, each with its own conditions and limits. These credits are based on: (1) Costs for home energy conservation, and (2) Costs for renewable energy source property.

The credit is based on the cost of items installed in your principal residence after April 19, 1977, and before January 1, 1986.

Purpose.—Use this form to figure your residential energy credit if you had qualified energy saving items installed in your principal residence. The instructions below list conditions you must meet to take the credit. If you have an energy credit carryover from the previous tax year and no energy saving costs this year, skip to Part III of the form. Attach Form 5695 to your tax return. For more information, please get Publication 903, Energy Credits for Individuals.

What is your principal residence?—To qualify as your principal residence, your residence must be the home in the United States where you live (you may own it or rent it from another person).

A summer or vacation home does not qualify.

For energy conservation items to qualify, your principal residence must have been substantially completed before April 20, 1977. A dwelling unit is considered substantially completed when it can be used as a personal residence even though minor items remain unfinished.

Special Rules.—If you live in a condominium, occupy a dwelling unit jointly, or share the cost of energy property, see Publication 903 for more details.

What are energy saving items?—You can take the credit for energy conservation and renewable energy source items.

Energy conservation items are limited to:
- insulation (fiberglass, cellulose, etc.) for ceilings, walls, floors, roofs, water heaters, etc.
- storm (or thermal) windows or doors for the outside of your residence.
- caulking or weatherstripping for windows or doors for the outside of your residence.
- a replacement burner for your existing furnace that reduces fuel use. The burner must replace an existing burner. It does not qualify if it is acquired as a component of, or for use in, a new furnace or boiler.
- a device for modifying flue openings to make a heating system more efficient.
- an electrical or mechanical furnace ignition system that replaces a gas pilot light.
- a thermostat with an automatic setback.
- a meter that shows the cost of energy used.

To take the credit for an energy conservation item, you must:

- install the item in your principal residence which was substantially completed before April 20, 1977,
- be the first one to use the item, and
- expect it to last at least 3 years.

The maximum credit for energy conservation items cannot be more than $300 ($2,000 × 15%) for each principal residence.

Renewable energy source items include solar, wind, and geothermal energy items that heat or cool your principal residence or provide hot water or electricity for it. Examples of solar energy items that may qualify include:
- collectors,
- rockbeds,
- heat exchangers, and
- solar panels installed on roofs (including those installed as a roof or part of a roof).

An example of an item that uses wind energy is a windmill that produces energy in any form (usually electricity) for your residence.

To take the credit for a renewable energy source item, you must:
- be the first one to use the item, and
- expect it to last at least 5 years.

The maximum credit for renewable energy source items cannot be more than $4,000 ($10,000 × 40%) for each principal residence.

What items are NOT eligible for the energy credit?—Do not take credit for:
- carpeting;
- drapes;
- wood paneling;
- wood or peat-burning stoves;
- hydrogen fueled residential equipment;
- siding for the outside of your residence;
- heat pump (both air and water);
- fluorescent replacement lighting system;
- replacement boilers and furnaces; and
- swimming pools used to store energy.

Federal, State, or local government nontaxable grants and subsidized financing.—Qualified expenditures financed with nontaxable Federal, State, or local government grants cannot be used to figure the energy credit. Also, if Federal, State, or local government programs provide subsidized financing for any part of qualified expenditures, that part cannot be used to figure the energy credit. You must reduce the expenditure limits on energy conservation and renewable energy source property by the part of expenditures financed by Federal, State, or local government subsidized energy financing, as well as by the amount of nontaxable Federal, State, or local government grants used to purchase conservation or renewable energy source property.

Figuring the credit for more than one principal residence.—You can take the maximum credit for each principal residence you live in. If you use all of your credit for one residence and then move, you may take the maximum credit amount on your next residence.

To figure your 1981 energy credit for more than one principal residence:

(1) Fill out Part I or II on a separate Form 5695 for each principal residence.

(2) Enter the total of all parts on line 23 of one of the forms.

(3) In the space above line 23, write "More than one principal residence."

(4) Attach all forms to your return.

Caution: You should keep a copy of each Form 5695 that you file for your records. For example, if you sell your principal residence, you will need to know the amount of the credit claimed in prior tax years. If the items for which you took the credit increased the basis of your principal residence, you must reduce the basis by the credit you took.

If the credit is more than your tax.—If your energy credit for this year is more than your tax minus certain other credits, you can carry over the excess energy credit to the following tax year.

Specific Instructions

Part I, lines 2a through 2h.—Enter your energy conservation costs (including expenditures made with nontaxable government grants and subsidized financing) only for this tax year. Count the cost of the item and its installation in or on your principal residence. Do not include the cost of repairs or maintenance for energy conservation items.

Part I, line 4.—Enter the amount of nontaxable government grants and subsidized financing used to purchase the energy items. If you do not know the amount, check with the government agency that gave you the grant or subsidized financing.

Part I, line 7.—Enter your total energy conservation costs from 1978, 1979, and 1980 for this principal residence. If you had energy conservation costs in the previous tax year but could not take a credit because it was less than $10, enter zero.

Part I, line 9.—Enter the part of nontaxable government grants and subsidized financing received under Federal, State, or local programs to purchase energy items. You must use the amounts received under these programs to reduce the maximum amount of cost used to figure the credit. If you do not know the amount of the nontaxable grant, check with the government agency which gave you the grant or subsidized financing.

Part II, lines 13a through 13d.—Enter your renewable energy source costs (including expenditures made with nontaxable government grants and subsidized financing) only for this tax year. Do not include the cost of repairs or maintenance for renewable energy source items.

Part II, line 14.—See Part I, line 4 for explanation.

Part II, line 17.—Enter your total renewable energy source costs from 1978, 1979, and 1980 for this principal residence. If you had renewable energy source costs in the previous tax year but could not take a credit because it was less than $10, enter zero.

Part II, line 19.—See Part I, line 9 for explanation.

Part III, line 24.—If line 47 of your 1980 Form 1040 is zero or less and on your 1980 Form 5695, line 20 is less than line 17, enter the difference between line 20 and line 17 on line 24 of this year's form. Exception—If the alternative minimum tax applied, see Publication 909, Minimum Tax and Maximum Tax.

Part IV.—Complete this part only if line 29 is less than line 25. You can carryover the amount entered on line 32 to your next tax year. Exception—If the alternative minimum tax applies, see Publication 909.

Form 5695 (*Continued*)

7

Obtaining Financing

M ost people cannot buy their condominium or cooperative apartment for cash, so they must obtain financing in the form of a mortgage (in the case of a condominium) or personal loan (for a cooperative apartment).

WHERE TO LOOK FOR FINANCING— CONDO AND COOP BUYERS

When you obtain financing you are, in effect, "buying" money. And as with anything else you buy, you should shop around for the best financing deal. This means being aware of all the sources that are available and having a knowledge of the new creative financing techniques that are being employed these days to sell slow-moving units.

As far as lending institutions are concerned, just because you have dealt with one particular bank or savings and loan for a number of years and for all sorts of banking transactions, doesn't necessarily mean that you will get the best deal there. It's up to you to get the best deal you can. There are a number of alternatives you have. The first that comes to mind is your local commercial (full-service) bank. Some of the biggest and best known include the Bank of America, Citibank, and Chase Manhattan. But few of these institutions are in the condominium or cooperative lending business. Call them anyway and ask.

Then there are mutual savings banks. These institutions are prevalent in the eastern part of the United States and include such institutions as New York's Bowery Savings Bank. Many of these institutions are in the residential loans business and you may do well to check all the banks in your area for their rates.

In most parts of the country, savings and loan associations constitute a large part of the lending market. Most Midwestern cities and California and Texas locales are served by savings and loans.

If you are a member of a labor union or if you work for a large corporation you may have access to a credit union. Credit unions are now allowed to give mortgages, so check on their rates if you qualify. Credit unions can often give mortgages at rates below those of traditional lenders.

Privately owned and operated mortgage companies are another source of funds for prospective buyers. Not only do they buy and sell mortgages on the mortgage market, they also give them to individual purchasers as well. Your real estate broker should be able to recommend one or two local mortgage companies for you.

If you are looking at newly built condominiums that have not been occupied before, your best source of financing and the cheapest may well be the builder of the condominium project. The builder usually has arranged with a lender to provide what are called *end loans* to fully qualified purchasers of apartments in the new building. Because the lender has faith in the builder and in the project, the builder can usually get loans for his buyers as much as three percentage points below the prevailing mortgage loan rate for that particular area.

Another financing technique that can be used is that of the *purchase money mortgage* (PM). Although new builders sometimes use it, generally it is employed by individual owners who are having trouble selling their apartments because of high prices or skyrocketing mortgage rates. A purchase money mortgage is no different from a regular mortgage in form, but it is quite different in substance. Just as with a conventional mortgage you make monthly payments, but you make them to the *seller*, not to a bank or mortgage company. The interest rate and payback schedule are arranged with the seller prior to the sale. Normally, purchase money mortgages run for fairly short periods of time, such as 5 or 10 years. The monthly payments give a steady source of income that sellers might need, especially if they are retired and are looking for a source of constant cash other than a pension or Social Security. You should always ask your real estate agent if the seller is willing to "take back" (that is, give you) a PM on any previously owned apartment. It may be the best deal you can get anywhere.

Besides the purchase money mortgage, you may be able to assume an old low-interest mortgage of the seller, if you are lucky. Some recent developments, however, have restricted this option, but in some cases you still may be able to find a terrific deal through mortgage assumption.

As its name suggests, you actually "assume" the mortgage that the previous owner had. However, and here is the kicker, *the seller's bank must consent to the assumption*. Most mortgages contain a clause known as the "Due on Sale" clause, which requires sellers to pay off any outstanding mortgage balance out of the proceeds of the sale. But for a variety of reasons the seller's bank couldn't or wouldn't enforce these clauses. However, because many savings and loan associations and savings banks have been stuck with many low-interest mortgages on their books, the Supreme Court came partially to the rescue in mid-1982.

The court rendered a decision that allowed *federally chartered* savings and loans to enforce these due-on-sale clauses. This effectively did away with mortgage assumptions in a good number of cases. However, and this is important, in some states you can still assume a mortgage from a state-chartered savings institution. Of course, state law could change that at any time, but you will have to make inquiries about it yourself.

This is not a totally gloomy situation for buyers, however. Because assuming mortgages is now much more difficult, some sellers may lower the prices of their apartments to compensate, and that is certainly good news if you are struggling to put enough together to buy a condominium or cooperative apartment.

Who Gets Financing and Who Doesn't

Credit is the name of the game when it comes to financing. If you have a credit history studded with lawsuits and bankruptcies, your chances of getting a loan from any financial source are nil. But if you have an untarnished credit report, lenders will be more than happy to lend you money; that is, after all, what they are in business for. The importance of a clean credit rating cannot be overemphasized. It is your best and most important tool in obtaining financing. If you are unaware of how good or bad your own credit rating is you can obtain a credit report on yourself by contacting a local credit reporting agency. Getting a copy may cost you two or three dollars, but it is a small price to pay for assurances about your credit standing.

VA and FHA Loan Guarantees

It is possible, however, that even though you have a sound credit rating and you meet most of the qualifications as a good risk, the lender may still refuse to give you a mortgage. If that should happen, you might qualify for a Veteran's Administration (VA) or Federal Housing Administration (FHA) guarantee. Most prospective condominium purchasers don't realize that VA and FHA guaranteed mortgages are just as available to them as they are to single-family-house buyers.

To get a VA guarantee you must have served in the United States Armed Forces during certain designated periods. If you are turned down by a lender for a mortgage, ask the lender if he or she will accept you if the mortgage is guaranteed by the VA or FHA. You should be aware, however, that if your credit rating and repayment records on debts are poor, the FHA and VA may turn you down as well. Remember, you are not getting a mortgage from the VA or FHA, the lender is getting a guarantee of repayment from a government-backed organization if you should default. One good thing: If you do obtain a VA or FHA backed mortgage you may be able to get it at a lower rate than a conventional mortgage.

What the Lender Looks for—Condominium Purchasers

You have a fine credit rating, your downpayment is sufficient, and you walk into the lender's office fully expecting to get your loan or mortgage. What criteria does the lender use in deciding to give you the money you need? Fortunately, most lenders use the same general outlines with some regional or local variations. The reason for the universality of the guidelines is based on simple fact. Whoever holds your mortgage may wish at some later time to sell that instrument to another financing or lending institution or investor. Therefore, the mortgage that they grant you must fall within certain specified guidelines.

One of the largest purchasers of home mortgages is the Federal Home Loan Mortgage Corporation (FHLMC, more popularly known as Freddie Mac). Another buyer of mortgages is the Federal National Mortgage Association or Fannie Mae. These two federally affiliated agencies have issued a series of underwriting guidelines for purchasing mortgages, and if a lender wants to sell his mortgage to FHLMC or Fannie Mae he must adhere to those established guidelines. Therefore, most lenders throughout the nation follow those guidelines in granting mortgages to consumers. For details on the guidelines see Appendix B. Here are the guidelines:

All housing expenses should not exceed 25–28% of the "stable monthly income of the borrower." Housing expenses that are included in this definition are monthly principal and interest payments on the mortgage, homeowners' dues or maintenance payments, monthly real estate tax payments, and homeowners' insurance premiums that are paid on a monthly basis. However, *regularly* received bonuses, commissions, or income from part-time work also can be included for purposes of this computation.

The borrower must be creditworthy, as evidenced by an acceptable credit report.

Employment stability is another important guideline. If the borrower has shown a tendency to jump from job to job every year or so, that would be looked on with disfavor by most lenders and by the FHLMC and FNMA.

Finally, the total of *all* monthly debt payments (including credit card charges, charge accounts, car payments, etc.) *plus* housing expenses that have more than 10 months to run cannot exceed a range of 33–36% of that same stable monthly income defined earlier.

It must be pointed out that these guidelines are not set in stone; there is a good deal of flexibility allowed. For example, if you were able to come up with a larger downpayment than is customary, some of the income and debt guidelines might be stretched. And if you have demonstrated a past history of being able to maintain a good credit rating and have maintained a debt-free financial position, along with an ability to accumulate savings, then some leeway will almost certainly be given. For more on these guidelines see Appendix B.

Senior citizens note: A federal law prohibits discrimination in the granting of loans to seniors. Of course, you must otherwise qualify for the loan before the law would apply.

If you are not dealing with a lender of exceptional credentials (such as a bank), it is vital that you find out whether or not your mortgage is to be sold to FHLMC or FNMA. If it is, you can be reasonably sure that the lender with whom you are dealing has complied with all the requirements of those organizations, such as strict financial disclosure and proper preparation of the budget for homeowners' dues. In other words, if your lender is going to sell your mortgage (or can sell it if they wish) to Freddie Mac or Fannie Mae, you have assurance of reliability and expertise. This is especially important when you are buying an apartment in a newly built complex and you are one of the first purchasers. The rule of thumb is then, *steer clear of projects that are not Freddie Mac or Fannie Mae approved.*

What the Lender Looks for—Cooperative Buyers

Since a cooperative apartment loan is not a mortgage, in which the apartment itself stands as collateral, but is rather a simple personal loan, you have to comply with the personal loan requirements of the lender involved. Again, however, credit rating and credit history play the key role in granting a loan. Remember that when you buy a cooperative apartment you are not buying an apartment per se, you are purchasing shares in an apartment house corporation and the lender is loaning you the money to buy the shares.

Caveat for cooperative apartment buyers: If you are trying to purchase an apartment in a small building with six units or less, you may have difficulty in obtaining financing. Banks and other lenders are often reluctant to give loans to buyers in small buildings. They fear that if one person in the building defaults, the other owners will have to make up for the lost income to the corporation by a significant increase in their own maintenance charge. That increase in the maintenance could be so large that it could be too much of a burden for the remaining owners and therefore they might default as well.

REQUIRED PAPERWORK—CONDOMINIUM AND COOPERATIVE BUYERS

Whether you get your financing from a bank, a savings and loan, or from a mortgage company, you will undoubtedly have to follow a procedure very similar to the following.

The lender will ask you to fill out a rather detailed application form (a sample of which appears at the end of this chapter as an example). If the application does not contain all the information needed for a credit check, you may be asked to fill out additional documents detailing your credit history.

You will probably be asked to bring a letter from your employer stating how long you have worked there, what your salary is, and information concerning bonuses, overtime, and other pay you may be entitled to.

If you are self-employed the lender will normally ask for copies of your federal tax returns for the last two (sometimes three) years. Also, if you have a regular part-time job or business that contributes sub-stantially to your income, the lender may still require copies of tax returns even if you work full-time elsewhere.

Verifications of bank accounts, real estate holdings, and securities accounts are also a common requirement of lenders.

You may also be asked by the lender to purchase a life and/or disa-bility insurance policy, so that the lender will be protected and the loan will be paid off should you die or become totally disabled. If ob-taining such a policy is a requirement for getting the financing, ask the lender to recommend two or more policies to you that you can investigate. Normally, the lenders will have at least one insurer that they will recommend for this purpose.

Undoubtedly, the policy will cost a rather modest sum and it shouldn't make much of a difference in your overall financial outlay under any circumstances.

While you are getting all this material together, the lender will normally send an appraiser around to look at the apartment you're buying. It is the appraiser's job to make sure that the apartment you are asking for the loan or mortgage on actually exists and to assess its condition. The appraiser normally does not make a determination as to whether you are paying too much or too little for the apartment; rather his or her job is to see if it is worth enough for the lender to get its money back, should you default. The appraiser normally does his or her job by looking at comparable sales of similar apartments in the same neighborhood over the last few months. Your loan is based on the purchase price or appraisal value of the apartment, whichever is lower. That means that if you are buying the apartment for more than its appraisal price, you will have to make up the difference with either more cash or a higher downpayment.

TYPES OF MORTGAGES

Lenders want to make loans and give mortgages but, with interest rates at such high levels recently, it has been difficult to attract buyers who can afford a home these days. To solve this difficult problem, lenders have become very creative and have designed all sorts of new kinds of mortgages. A discussion of the various types of mortgages fol-lows.

Conventional Mortgages

Most of us are familiar with the conventional mortgage, which requires the borrower to pay the same amount every month for the entire term of the mortgage be it 20, 25, or 30 years. For many years, all mortgages were conventional mortgages. In a conventional mortgage, interest and principal are combined and, during the early years of payment, most of your monthly payments go to the paying off of the interest accrued on the mortgage. As you steadily pay the mortgage off year by year, more and more of the payment goes to the payment of principal. But the monthly payment always remains the same. Since there is no change in the interest rate over the term of the mortgage, buyers have been reluctant to go for conventional mortgages when interest rates are in the 14–16% range.

Creative Mortgages

In order to alleviate this problem some new forms of mortgages have evolved including:

The Variable Rate Mortgage
Under this type of financing, the interest rate the borrower pays rises and falls in conjunction with a designated index, such as Treasury Bill rates. This means that the rate could be adjusted monthly and you would have to make a different mortgage payment every few months or so, if the rates on Treasury Bills fluctuated frequently. However, it is just this uncertainty over the monthly payment that makes such mortgages unattractive to borrowers who are looking for some stability in their budgets.

Renegotiable Rate Mortgage
This type is similar to the variable rate with one large difference. Instead of adjusting rates on a monthly basis, they would be changed at agreed-upon intervals, such as every three or five years. During the entire term of the mortgage, however, the interest rate cannot fluctuate more than a maximum amount, typically 5%. So, for example, if you were to get a renegotiable rate mortgage and you were to begin by paying an interest rate of 15%, that rate could not rise above 20% or fall below 10%.

Graduated Payment Mortgage

This is an excellent mortgage for the individual or the young couple just beginning a career. The way this mortgage is structured keeps monthly payments low when you start paying off the mortgage. Then, as your earnings rise, the mortgage payments rise gradually over a set number of years, normally five years. After the five-year period, the payments level off and remain steady for the rest of the term of the mortgage.

Shared Appreciation Mortgage

This increasingly popular type allows the borrower to get the mortgage at a lower interest rate (possibly two or three points less) in exchange for giving the lender a share of the profit when the apartment is sold. The amount of that profit is determined at the beginning, but usually cannot exceed 40% of the net appreciation. Most financial experts advise consumers to avoid shared appreciation mortgages, because this mortgage (as with most types) only finances a portion of the total purchase price, yet the lender shares in all of the appreciation including improvements made by the borrower. However, it may be your only alternative in some situations.

For the more affluent buyer there are shorter term mortgages such as the balloon and the rollover, usually written for no longer than 5 years and requiring a large unpaid balance to be paid at the end of the period. The major difference between a balloon and a rollover is that in a balloon the lender does not have to renew the loan; with a rollover he does.

Some lenders may offer one, some, or all of these mortgage options, and it will definitely pay for you to shop around for a lender who offers the type of mortgage most suited to your particular circumstances. Don't forget that you have two other options as well: the purchase money mortgage if you are buying a previously owned apartment, and there is the good possibility that the builder or developer of a new property may have arranged some kind of mortgage financing as well.

In any case, since each borrower's circumstances are different, you would be wise to get together with an accountant or attorney and figure out which type of mortgage is truly right for you. The important thing to know, however, is that you do have a choice and the rules of the game have changed.

INFORMATION YOU MUST GET IF YOU ARE APPLYING FOR ANY KIND OF FINANCING OTHER THAN A CONVENTIONAL MORTGAGE

You know that if you are applying for a conventional mortgage you will be paying the same amount every month for the entire period of the mortgage. If you get a 25-year conventional mortgage you know, for instance, that your mortgage payment will be exactly the same the first month of the first year as it will be the last month of the twenty-fifth year. However, the very nature of the variable type of mortgage is that the payment you make this month may not be the same as you make three years from now. Because these rates change in such a fundamental way, you must know all you can about the variable mortgages before you get one. There is certain information that you must get from the lender before you sign on the dotted line for the mortgage. For instance, you must find out:

Exactly what kind of mortgage am I applying for?

What kind of index makes the interest rate change?

What kind of fluctuation has that index experienced over the past three years?

What are the prospects for that index over the next year?

Are there any limits as to how high or how low my payment will be over the term of the mortgage?

Will the interest rate be renegotiated after a certain period of time?

If so, what will the index be and what will be the limitations applicable at that time?

Can I choose another kind of mortgage that might suit my needs better?

In other words, when you walk out of the lender's office you must have a clear idea of exactly what you are getting yourself into. With the conventional mortgage you know exactly what you have to pay every month, but with the new mortgages being offered you must get as much information as you can before you make a commitment.

What follows are some typical loan application forms. If you did the exercises in Chapter 5 where you prepared a personal balance sheet and revenue statement, you will have no difficulty inserting your own appropriate numbers.

Note the following important items on the forms:

1. If you are self-employed, you must include a copy of the prior year's tax return and a financial statement on the condition of your business before the bank will consider your application.
2. You must include a complete listing of all outstanding debts.
3. There are a number of questions asked about the applicant's credit history with particular emphasis on any bankruptcies that may have occurred recently.

Although the application forms you fill out may not look exactly like these, most of the information sought will undoubtedly be identical. Therefore, you should prepare all relevant information prior to filling out the forms; that way you will save time. Some people have had trouble getting all the relevant information together quickly because their records are scattered about or are inaccessible for one reason or another.

For example, you should have all credit information at hand, such as bank account numbers, credit card numbers, and other relevant data. The quicker you get the loan forms filled out and back to the lender, the faster you will receive a yes or no decision on your application.

Go through the sample application and other forms carefully now, so that you can see what kind of information you can expect to be asked and to gather when you fill out your loan papers.

QUESTIONS CONCERNING FINANCING ALTERNATIVES

1. As a potential borrower do I have a good credit rating?
2. Have my income and my employment been stable for three years?

3. How much debt am I already carrying?

4. Have I thoroughly investigated downpayment rates in the neighborhood in which I want to live?

5. Do I have enough for that downpayment?

6. Am I getting a mortgage from a lender that follows Fannie Mae and Freddie Mac guidelines?

7. What kind of mortgage options does the lender offer?

8. Is the lender experienced in condominium and cooperative lending?

9. If it is a new unit, has the owner arranged financing?

10. If an older, previously owned unit, is a purchase money mortgage available?

11. If the mortgage is a renegotiable rate mortgage, what index determines the rate at the end of the initial three- or five-year period?

12. How much has that index rate changed over the past few years?

13. If an adjustable rate mortgage, how often does the rate change? How much can it rise? How far down can it go?

14. Will I have to pay a late charge if I am tardy in making a payment? If so, how much is it?

15. Can I pay off the mortgage early and not incur a prepayment penalty?

Citibank, N.A.
APPLICATION FOR ☐ Residential ☐ Co-op Loan

LOAN APPLIED FOR ▶ ☐ 6 Month Adjustable ☐ Other
☐ 30 Month Adjustable _____

Application No.

Copy of Contract of Sale must Accompany this Application Together with a Non-Refundable Check for $ _____ Payable to the Bank, to be Applied Toward Cost of Appraisal.

Customer Initial _____

Subject Property

Property Street Address | Amount $ | Apt. No. | City | County | State | Zip

Legal Description (Attach description if necessary)

For Co-ops Only

No. of Rooms | No. of Apartments | No. of Shares for Apt. | Monthly mainten-ance | Name of Cooperative Corporation | New Building ☐ Resale ☐ Conversion ☐ | Census Tract No.

Managing Agent Name & Address | Seller's Name & Address | Broker Name & Address

Purpose of Loan: ☐ Purchase ☐ Construction-Permanent ☐ Construction ☐ Refinance ☐ Other (Explain)

Complete this line if Construction-Permanent or Construction Loan ▶ | Lot Value Date | Year Acquired | Original Cost $ | Present Value (a) $ | Cost of Imps. (b) | Total (a + b) $

Complete this line if a Refinance Loan | Purpose of Refinance | Describe Improvements [ ] made [ ] to be made

Year Acquired | Original Cost $ | Amt. Existing Liens $

Title Will Be Held In What Name(s) | Manner In Which Title Will Be Held | Cost: $

Source of Down Payment and Settlement Charges

No. of Mos. | Monthly Payment Principal & Interest $ | Escrow/Impounds (to be collected monthly) ☐ Taxes ☐ Hazard Ins. ☐ Mtge Ins. ☐

Enter Total As Purchase Price In Details Of Purchase. ↓

This application is designed to be completed by the borrower(s) with the lender's assistance. The Co-Borrower Section and all other Co-Borrower questions must be completed and the appropriate box(es) checked if ☐ another person will be jointly obligated with the Borrower on the loan, or ☐ the Borrower is relying on income from alimony, child support or separate maintenance or on the income or assets of another person as a basis for repayment of the loan, or ☐ the Borrower is married and resides, or the property is located, in a community property state.

Borrower

Name | Age | School Yrs ____

Present Address | No. Years ____ | ☐ Own ☐ Rent
Street _____
City/State/Zip _____
Former address if less than 2 years at present address
Street _____
City/State/Zip _____
Years at former address | ☐ Own ☐ Rent
Marital Status ☐ Married ☐ Separated ☐ Unmarried (incl. single, div-orced, widowed)
Dependents other than listed by Borrower | No. | Ages

Co-Borrower

Name | Age | School Yrs ____

Present Address | No. Years ____ | ☐ Own ☐ Rent
Street _____
City/State/Zip _____
Former address if less than 2 years at present address
Street _____
City/State/Zip _____
Years at former address | ☐ Own ☐ Rent
Marital Status ☐ Married ☐ Separated ☐ Unmarried (incl. single, div-orced, widowed)
Dependents other than listed by Borrower | No. | Ages

58

Cooperative Loan Application Form

Name and Address of Employer			Name and Address of Employer	
	Year: employed in this line of work or profession?			Years employed in this line of work or profession?
	_____ years			_____ years
	Years on this job			Years on this job
	☐ Self Employed*			☐ Self Employed*
Position/Title	Type of Business		Position/Title	Type of Business
Social Security Number***	Home Phone	Business Phone	Social Security Number***	Home Phone	Business Phone

Gross Monthly Income

Item	Borrower	Co-Borrower	Total
Base Empl. Income	$	$	$
Overtime			
Bonuses			
Commissions			
Dividends/Interest			
Net Rental Income			
Other (Before completing, see notice under Describe Other Income Below.)			
Total	$	$	$

Monthly Housing Expense**

Rent	Present $	Proposed $
First Mortgage (P&I)		$
Other Financing (P&I)		
Hazard Insurance		
Real Estate Taxes		
Mortgage Insurance		
Homeowner Assn.		
Other:		
Total Monthly Pmt.	$	$
Utilities		
Total	$	$

Details of Purchase

Do Not Complete If Refinance

a. Purchase Price	$
b. Total Closing Costs (Est.)	
c. Prepaid Escrows (Est.)	
d. Total (a + b + c)	$
e. Amount This Mortgage	( )
f. Other Financing	( )
g. Other Equity	( )
h. Amount of Cash Deposit	$
i. Closing Costs Paid by Seller	( )
j. Cash Reqd. For Closing (Est.)	$

Describe Other Income

☞ B—Borrower   C—Co-Borrower   NOTICE:† Alimony, child support, or separate maintenance income need not be revealed if the Borrow-er or Co-Borrower does not choose to have it considered as a basis for repaying this loan.

	Monthly Amt.
	$

If Employed In Current Position For Less Than Two Years Complete The Following

B/C	Previous Employer/School	City/State	Type of Business	Position/Title	Dates From/To	Monthly Income
						$

These Questions Apply To Both Borrower And Co-Borrower

If a "yes" answer is given to a question in this column, explain on an attached sheet.	Borrower Yes or No	Co-Borrower Yes or No	If applicable, explain Other Financing or Other Equity (provide addendum if more space is needed).
Have you any outstanding judgments? In the last 7 years, have you been declared bankrupt?			
Have you had property foreclosed upon or given title or deed in lieu thereof?			
Are you a co-maker or endorser on a note?			
Are you a party in a law suit?			
Are you obligated to pay alimony, child support, or separate maintenance?			
Is any part of the down payment borrowed?			

*FHLMC/FNMA require business credit report, signed Federal Income Tax returns for last two years, and, if available, audited Profit and Loss Statements plus balance sheet for same period.
**All Present Monthly Housing Expenses of Borrower and Co-Borrower should be listed on a combined basis.
***Neither FHLMC nor FNMA requires this information.

FHLMC 65

ITEM 356659 (MRE 731 REV. 7-82) PAD 100
CITIBANK REVISED FNMA 1003   7-82

59

STATEMENT OF ASSETS AND LIABILITIES

This Statement and any applicable supporting schedules may be completed jointly be both married and unmarried co-borrowers if their assets and liabilities are sufficiently joined so that the Statement can be meaningfully and fairly presented on a combined basis; otherwise separate Statements and Schedules are required (FHLMC 65A/FNMA 1003A). If the co-borrower section was completed about a spouse, this statement and supporting schedules must be completed about their spouse also. □ Completed Jointly □ Not Completed Jointly

ASSETS		LIABILITIES AND PLEDGED ASSETS			
Description	Cash or Market Value	Indicate by (*) those liabilities or pledged assets which will be satisfied upon sale of real estate owned or upon refinancing of subject property			
		Creditors' Name, Address and Account Number	Acct. Name if Not Borrower's	Mo. Pmt. and Mos. left to pay	Unpaid Balance
Cash Deposit Toward Purchase Held By	$	Installment Debts (include "revolving" charge accts)		$ Pmt./Mos.	$
Checking and Savings Accounts (Show Names of Institutions/Acct. Nos.)					
Stocks and Bonds (No./Description)					
Life Insurance Net Cash Value Face Amount ($)		Other Debts Including Stock Pledges			
SUBTOTAL LIQUID ASSETS	$				
Real Estate Owned (Enter Market Value from Schedule of Real Estate Owned)		Real Estate Loans			
Vested Interest in Retirement Fund					
Net Worth of Business Owned (ATTACH FINANCIAL STATEMENT)					
Automobiles (Make and Year)		Automobile Loans			
Furniture and Personal Property		Alimony, Child Support and Separate Maintenance Payments Owed To			
Other Assets (Itemize)					
		TOTAL MONTHLY PAYMENTS		$	
TOTAL ASSETS	A $	NET WORTH (A minus B) $		TOTAL LIABILITIES	B $

60

SCHEDULE OF REAL ESTATE OWNED (If Additional Properties Owned Attach Separate Schedule)

Address of Property (Indicate S if Sold, PS if Pending Sale or R if Rental being held for income)	Type of Property	Present Market Value	Amount of Mortgages & Liens	Gross Rental Income	Mortgage Payments	Taxes, Ins. Maintenance and Misc.	Net Rental Income
		$	$	$	$	$	$
TOTALS →		$	$	$	$	$	$

LIST PREVIOUS CREDIT REFERENCES

	Creditor's Name and Address	Account Number	Purpose	Highest Balance	Date Paid
B - Borrower C - Co-Borrower				$	

List any additional names under which credit has previously been received _____

AGREEMENT   The undersigned applies for the loan indicated in this application to be secured by a first mortgage or deed of trust on the property described herein, and represents that the property will not be used for any illegal or restricted purpose, and that all statements made in this application are true and are made for the purpose of obtaining the loan. Verification may be obtained from any source named in this application. The original or a copy of this application will be retained by the lender, even if the loan is not granted. The undersigned ☐ intend or ☐ do not intend to occupy the property as their primary residence.

I/we fully understand that it is a federal crime punishable by fine or imprisonment, or both, to knowingly make any false statements concerning any of the above facts as applicable under the provisions of Title 18, United States Code, Section 1014.

Borrower's Signature _____ Date _____   Co-Borrower's Signature _____ Date _____

INFORMATION FOR GOVERNMENT MONITORING PURPOSES

The following information is requested by the Federal Government if this loan is related to a dwelling, in order to monitor the lender's compliance with equal credit opportunity and fair housing laws. You are not required to furnish this information, but are encouraged to do so. The law provides that a lender may neither discriminate on the basis of this information, nor on whether you choose to furnish it. However, if you choose not to furnish it, under Federal regulations this lender is required to note race and sex on the basis of visual observation or surname. If you do not wish to furnish the above information, please initial below.

BORROWER: I do not wish to furnish this information (Initials) _____
RACE/ ☐ American Indian, Alaskan Native ☐ Asian, Pacific Islander
NATIONAL ☐ Black ☐ Hispanic ☐ White
ORIGIN ☐ Other (specify) _____
SEX ☐ Female ☐ Male

CO-BORROWER: I do not wish to furnish this information (Initials) _____
RACE/ ☐ American Indian, Alaskan Native ☐ Asian, Pacific Islander
NATIONAL ☐ Black, ☐ Hispanic ☐ White
ORIGIN ☐ Other (specify) _____
SEX ☐ Female ☐ Male

FOR LENDER'S USE ONLY

(FNMA REQUIREMENT ONLY) This application was taken by ☐ face to face interview ☐ by mail ☐ by telephone

_____ (Interviewer)   Name of Employer of Interviewer _____

FHLMC 65   FNMA 1003

Cooperative Loan Application Form (*Continued*)

61

RESIDENTIAL LOAN SUPPLEMENT

CITIBANK●

MORTGAGE LOAN

APP. NO.

BRANCH / DISTRICT (NAME &EXP. CODE)

TO BE COMPLETED FOR HOME MORTGAGE LOAN

PURCHASE PRICE $	ADDRESS (INCLUDE ZIP CODE)		NEAREST CROSS STREET
COUNTY	PLOT SIZE	NO. STORIES	TYPE OF CONSTRUCTION

NO. BEDROOMS	NO. BATHS	TOTAL ROOMS	TYPE HEATING	TYPE FUEL	DOES CITIBANK HOLD PRESENT MORTGAGE?

NAME OF PROPERTY OWNER - IF OTHER THAN APPLICANT

ADDRESS	TELEPHONE NO.

PROPERTY CAN BE INSPECTED BY CONTACTING - NAME

ADDRESS	TELEPHONE NO.

SIGNATURE OF BORROWER	SIGNATURE OF CO-BORROWER

MORTGAGE #

DATE

Citibank normally obtains Credit Reports for all loan applications, and for updates, renewals, or extensions of any credit granted. Upon request, Citibank will inform you if a report has been obtained and will give you the name and address of the agency furnishing the report.

FOR BANK USE ONLY

TYPING INSTRUCTIONS:

1 SUBJECT TO INSPECTION UPON FULL COMPLETION.

2 SUBJECT TO ISSUANCE OF CERTIFICATE OF OCCUPANCY.

3 SUBJECT TO CERTIFICATE OF OCCUPANCY AS A TWO FAMILY DWELLING.

4 THIS LETTER SUPERSEDES OUR COMMITMENT LETTER DATED _____.

5 REFER TO CITIBANK FILE NO. _____.

6 YOU WILL PRESENT TO US, AT CLOSING, A POLICY OF FLOOD INSURANCE IN THE MAXIMUM AMOUNT AVAILABLE BUT NOT GREATER THAN THE AMOUNT OF THE MORTGAGE.

7 SUBJECT TO A SATISFACTORY ENGINEER'S REPORT REGARDING CONDITION OF HOUSE.

8 FURNISH A CERTIFICATE FROM A LICENSED AND BONDED TERMITE CONTROL OPERATOR THAT THE HOUSE IS FREE OF TERMITES. IF ANY INFESTATION IS LOCATED, IT MUST BE ERADICATED AND ALL UNSOUND INFECTED MATERIAL MUST BE REPLACED.

9 FURNISH CERTIFICATE FROM HEALTH INSPECTOR THAT WATER SUPPLY IS POTABLE.

10 OTHER

☐ NEW LOAN	☐ ASSUMPTION		☐ REFINANCE
AMOUNT APPROVED $	YEARS	RATE %	MONTHLY PAYMENT $
FIRE INSURANCE REQUIRED $		FLOOD INSURANCE REQUIRED	
LEGAL FEE $	APPRAISAL FEE $		ORIGINATION FEE $

CONDITIONS:

BRANCH /DISTRICT APPROVAL

BY	BY	BY

REAL ESTATE APPROVAL

BY

CSG 1374

Cooperative Loan Application Form (*Continued*)

8

Resale Potential
of an Apartment

According to real estate professionals, too many individuals worry about the resale potential of an apartment even before they buy it. That is not to say that resale potential is not an important factor in purchasing an apartment, but it should not be the most important, unless you are buying it purely for speculative reasons.

Most people buy an apartment because they v. ant to live in it, and that should be the most important consideration. Obviously, though, you don't want to buy an apartment whose value will decrease over the years you live there. However, unless you buy in a slum area or are just plain unlucky, the chances are small that the worth of the apartment will decrease significantly.

RESALE FACTORS

What are the factors that determine the price of an apartment after a certain period of time? There is an old saying in the real estate business that the three most important factors in determining the worth of a piece of real estate are location, location, and location. That little joke still proves itself as the determining factor in most real estate transactions, whether they be a condominium or cooperative apartment or a multimillion-dollar office building.

But part of the problem with location is that your timing has to be good. Sections of town will change over time; what was desirable 10 years ago may not be so desirable today, and areas that look pretty awful today may soon be undergoing revitalization and renewal which will make a purchase now very rewarding when it comes time to sell.

Like clothing, real estate is subject to fashions and fads. The important thing in making your search for your apartment is that you feel good about the area now. If the apartment is a good one and the location is not terrible when you sell, you will probably make some kind of profit on the sale unless the economy falls through the floor between the time of your purchase and its ultimate sale.

Making a profit on the apartment when you sell is not only a function of location but of initial cost and any improvements that you have made since purchase. None of this is a guarantee, of course. However, in most parts of the country over the past 30 years, homes— whether single-family detached dwellings or condominium or cooperative apartments—have kept up with or in some cases exceeded inflation rates, so that sellers have received a nice return on their investments.

However, there is a school of thought that says that housing is a necessity and that you shouldn't expect to get rich on the sale of a necessity when you decide to sell. Real estate investors and speculators do it, but that is their business and they should be entitled to a profit for the risk that they take. There is probably a kernel of truth in this idea also. What can be said is that you as a prospective buyer should not expect to make a huge profit when you sell your apartment. Be content with a small profit or at least no loss; that way you won't expect too much when you buy.

RESTRICTIONS ON RESALE

There are two problems of immediate significance concerning resale that must be considered and investigated before you make the purchase decision. The first is, does the homeowners' association or cooperative board have the right of first refusal when it comes time for you to sell? In other words, do you have to offer your apartment to the governing board first before you can sell to an outsider? Obviously, having to offer your apartment to the board will restrict your right to sell (at least for some period of time) and of course you may not get as much for the apartment as you might if you sold it to an outside buyer.

If the board has the right of first refusal, that provision will most probably be found in the rules, regulations, or bylaws of the homeowners' association or cooperative corporation. If you find such a clause, you must realize what it means and that your right of resale is somewhat restricted.

A newer variation of the right of first refusal and the second resale problem is the so-called *profit turnback* that some operating boards have recently instituted (it usually only comes into play in conversion situations). What happens here is that when you sell your apartment (and you are free to sell to whomever you wish, providing you have received board approval), you must turn back to the operating board a certain percentage of your profit on the sale—typically 8–10%.

This is how it works: As you may know, when a building converts from rental ownership to coop or condo, the tenants already living in the building are allowed to buy their units at as much as one third to one fourth off of the going market price of the unit. As a result, the buyer starts off with a built-in equity in the apartment. Assume that the buyer purchases the unit for $50,000 and sells it five years later for $75,000. The governing board would then ask for 10% of the profit, less any brokerage commissions. So, if the unit is sold for $75,000 and the typical brokerage commission is 6%, the seller would net $70,500 ($75,000 minus 6%, or $4,500, equals 70,500). Therefore out of the $20,500 profit (assuming again a 10% turnback), $2,050 would have to be turned back to the building. Between brokerage commissions and turnbacks, a hefty amount is cut away from your profit. And when you take into consideration the fact that you may have to pay capital gains tax on the profit as well, the amount that is actually netted on the sale is diminished even further.

Another term for profit turnback that is coming into popular usage is *flip tax*. The word *flip* is real estate parlance for the turnover of an apartment quickly. For example, someone in a conversion situation buys an apartment with the express purpose of selling it as soon as possible, that is, flipping an apartment over.

Commenting on the flip tax one prominent New York attorney wrote in the *Real Estate Review*:

> Although authority to impose such fees must usually be contained in the offering plan or approved by a vote of the holders of at least two thirds of the shares of a cooperative, some boards have imposed flip taxes without shareholder approval. These taxes will stand unless they are challenged by shareholders, and if not challenged, they may be justified under broad authority in the offering plan for the corporation to collect service fees upon the transfer of cooperative apartments.
>
> Even when a purchaser knows from the offering plan that a flip-tax exists, he may be surprised by the method of implementing the flip-tax that the board of directors has imposed. In one newly converted building, the flip-tax was specified to be a percentage of the difference between the selling price and the seller's original cost for the apartment. The board was determined to avoid any evasion in the payment of the tax. It therefore resolved that if the "selling price" of an apartment were less than the fair market value, the board would not approve a transfer unless either the seller or the purchaser voluntarily agreed to pay the flip-tax based upon the difference between the fair market

the board would establish by examining the selling prices of comparable apartments) and the seller's cost.*

Right of first refusal and profit turnback procedures are perfectly legal and are proliferating, so it is incumbent on the knowledgeable buyer to be aware of any of these restrictions on resale before the purchase is made. These could influence your decision greatly.

If the resale potential is of great concern to you, you should carefully read all of the second section of this volume, entitled Selling.

*Richard Siegler, "Apartment Purchasers Can Buy Unexpected Problems," *Real Estate Review*, Vol. 12, No. 1, p. 78.

9

Rights and Responsibilities of Condominium and Cooperative Apartment Owners

As mentioned in Chapter 2, one of the big differences between a condominium and a cooperative is that in the usual condo situation, owners can buy and sell their apartments without the approval of anyone else in the complex. However, in the case of a cooperative, the managing board can withhold approval of a sale of your apartment to a prospective buyer for any number of reasons.*

Therefore, if you buy into a condominium you cannot be sure who your neighbors are going to be. If the neighbors are noisy or dirty or use offensive language or disturb your peace and quiet, getting rid of them may be difficult, if not downright impossible. If, however, you have bought into a cooperative, an offending tenant-owner can be evicted without too much difficulty.

Hence it is very important for any prospective purchaser of a condominium apartment to study the bylaws and any other rules and regulations of the condominium association that deal with the handling of problem purchasers. Some condominium projects will have stricter rules and regulations than others, and you may wish to buy into a project that has more rigid regulations. In any case, become familiar with the operating procedures of the complex *before* you purchase an apartment, not after.

The vital thing here is to know what you are getting into before you buy. Know those rules well before your next-door neighbor starts practicing his drum playing at 2 A.M. or your upstairs neighbor has nonstop weekend parties.

The one thing you must remember is that whether you are living in a cooperative or condominium, you are living with and sharing facilities with other people who are, in most cases, strangers when you move in, and that relations between owners may be strained for one reason or another. One of the facts of condo and coop living is: *You must be prepared to live with other people and to deal with all the political problems that entails.*

If you and your family are the type of people who like your privacy and prefer being away from the world while you are at home, you should consider very carefully whether or not a group living situation is your cup of tea. It may not be; therefore you might be better off buying a single-family house in a secluded area rather than buying an apartment where, inevitably, you will encounter neighbors who may have a different lifestyle from your own.

*Some states may vary in their approach to these matters because of differences in local laws, but on the whole these statements apply.

In cooperative buildings the boards are usually very strict about whom they allow to buy into the building. In New York City, for example, there are numerous cases of cooperative boards that have refused the sale of an apartment to prominent show business personalities for no other reason than the fear of loud parties and obnoxious behavior. As indicated earlier, it is perfectly within the rights of cooperative boards of directors to refuse a sale to anyone they deem undesirable.

Every once in a while, however, a rotten apple slips through in a cooperative building too. Since cooperative boards are responsible for the collection of maintenances from each owner-tenant, habitual late payers can be a problem. From time to time certain board members have been known to harass late payers. So, if you are looking to buy a coop you should know the policies of the building with regard to this and other problems once an owner is in possession of an apartment.

Operating boards constitute the government of the condominium or cooperative building and, as with any kind of governmental body, political problems arise and passions can run high. All this usually results in bitter election battles and highly charged owners' meetings. It is difficult for an owner or tenant to stay above the fray, so be prepared for political action when you buy into a cooperative or condominium complex. The battles usually revolve around raising the monthly fee or maintenance charge, but ancillary problems often cause wrangling as well. To repeat, if this sort of thing is what you want to stay away from, don't buy a cooperative or condominium apartment. You can't really avoid politics when your neighbors are so close.

APARTMENT IMPROVEMENTS

Most buyers of condominium or cooperative apartments want to make improvements or structural changes in the apartment at one time or another during the period of their ownership. Unfortunately, in some cases they are not as free to make those improvements as they would be if they owned a single-family residence. The by-laws of the complex usually spell out in detail the kinds of improvements that can and cannot be made. It is important that you examine closely those clauses in the by-laws and rules and regulations if you anticipate doing work on the apartment at some future time.

Many governing boards of cooperatives require that all proposed work in an apartment be submitted to them for their approval prior to starting the construction. It is imperative that you find out about this and understand it before you buy. If the rules and regulations concerning improvements are not set out in the bylaws, house rules, or other documents that you should acquire before making your final purchase decision, ask the real estate agent or go to the governing board itself and find out what the policy is as it relates to improving the unit you wish to buy. If part of your decision to buy (especially if it's a formerly occupied apartment) hinges on improvements you foresee making, then it is foolhardy not to find out what the policies are with regard to improvements.

If you read and understand nothing else in the documents that you get from the seller, read and fully understand by-laws and rules and regulations governing the conduct of owners once they occupy units in the complex. All of your rights, responsibilities, and duties are spelled out in those papers, and therefore your entire lifestyle while you are in residence will undoubtedly be affected by those rules and regulations. Know them well.

Immediately following this chapter is a set of by-laws and house rules for an actual New York City cooperative. By-laws and rules for other locales may differ in content, but these are representative examples.

SOME TYPICAL BY-LAWS

Prospective buyers should seriously examine the bylaws, rules, and regulations of the cooperative or condominium apartment complex that they are interested in buying. Here are the most important items and some comments about the bylaws that follow this chapter. You should look for similar clauses and others that may have a dramatic effect on how you live while in residence in the apartment.

1.   In Section 7 of these bylaws is a paragraph titled Annual Cash Requirements. The wording indicates that the power to determine maintenance charges is exclusively vested in the Board of Directors. You should look for any limiting or nonlimiting language concerning maintenance charges or homeowners' fees. The wording in the example is such that the board has "discretionary power" to make any determination it wishes as to raising or lowering maintenance charges.

This is a rather standard clause, but some clauses may allow or specifically disallow the unit apartment owners to vote on a proposed increase in monthly charges.

These types of clauses give you a good clue as to the kind of power that the board of directors or homeowners' association has. Some are granted almost unlimited power; others are given less authority. The significance of all this is that it has a direct impact on how you will live once you move into the complex.

2. Article 5 Section 5 contains a fascinating clause. It allows the board to assess a charge against any owner who wants to sublet his or her apartment. Obviously this was put in to discourage subletting. If you had some notions about subletting your apartment, this clause should raise a red flag to you before you move in.

If the bylaws of the complex you are considering have a similar requirement, find out what constitutes a "reasonable fee" for subletting and who determines what kind of a fee is reasonable or not.

These are the kinds of things you should look for and the kinds of questions you should ask if confronted by similar language.

3. Article 5 Section 7 details exactly how apartments may be subdivided or combined. If you plan to do any construction work in your apartment, make sure you understand fully any similar provisions that may appear in the bylaws of the building you are interested in.

4. Also examine closely the House Rules section. The rules and regulations that all owners must live by while in residence are found in this section. Be on the lookout for clauses such as Item 28, which prohibits the placing of any "plantings" on any terrace, balcony, or roof without first obtaining the consent of the board of directors. Such prohibitions may interfere with your way of life, and you may find them onerous. Make sure you know about such rules before, not after, you move in.

All limitations placed on your occupancy should be noted carefully by you and a record kept, so that when you make your final decision on which apartment you wish to buy, these limitations can be properly factored into your decision.

BY-LAWS

of

TWO CHARLTON OWNERS CORP.

ARTICLE I

Principal Office and Place of Business

Section 1. *Location of Office:* The principal office and place of business of the Corporation shall be in the County of New York or at such other place as may be designated by the Board of Directors.

ARTICLE II

Meetings of Shareholders

Section 1. *Annual Meeting:* The annual meeting of the shareholders of the Corporation, for the election of directors and for such other business as may properly come before such meeting, shall be held in the Borough of Manhattan, City of New York, at such time and place before the 31st day of May each year as may be designated by the Board. The notice of the meeting shall be in writing and signed by the president or a vice president or the secretary or an assistant secretary. Such notice shall state the time when and the place within the state where it is to be held, and the secretary shall cause a copy thereof to be delivered personally or mailed to each shareholder of record of the Corporation entitled to vote at such meeting not less than ten nor more than forty days before the meeting. If mailed, it shall be directed to each such shareholder at his or her address as it appears on the share book, unless he or she shall have filed with the secretary of the Corporation a written request that notices intended for him or her be mailed to some other address, in which case it shall be mailed to the address designated in such request. The first annual meeting shall be held within 30 business days after closing of title to premises (in connection with the first offering by Offering Plan of shares and proprietary leases), and subsequent annual meetings shall be held as provided above commencing with the year following the year in which the first annual meeting is held.

Section 2. *Special Meetings:* Special meetings of shareholders, other than those the calling of which is regulated by statute, may be called at any time by the president or secretary or by a majority of the Board of Directors. It shall also be the duty of the secretary to call such meetings whenever requested in writing so to do by shareholders owning at least twenty-five per cent of the outstanding shares of the Corporation. The secretary shall cause a notice of such special meeting stating the time, place and object thereof and the officer or other person or persons by whom the meeting is called, to be delivered personally or mailed as provided in Section 1 of this Article to each shareholder of record of the Corporation entitled to vote at such meeting not less than ten nor more than forty days before such meeting. No business other than that stated in such notice shall be transacted at such special meeting unless the holders of all the outstanding shares of the Corporation be present thereat in person or by proxy.

Section 3. *Waiver of Notices:* The notice provided for in the two foregoing sections is not indispensable but any shareholders' meeting whatever shall be valid for all purposes if all the outstanding shares of the Corporation are represented thereat in person or by proxy, or if a quorum is present, as provided in the next succeeding section, and waiver of notice of the time, place and objects of such

By-Laws of a Cooperative Building

meeting shall be duly executed in writing either before or after said meeting by such shareholders as are not so represented and were not given such notice.

Section 4. *Quorum:* At each meeting of shareholders, except where otherwise provided by law, shareholders representing, in person or by proxy, a majority of the shares then issued and outstanding shall constitute a quorum; in case a quorum shall not be present at any meeting, the holders of a majority of the shares represented may adjourn the meeting to some future time and place. No notice of the time and place of the adjourned meeting need be given other than by announcement at the meeting. Only those shareholders who, if present at the original meeting, would have been entitled to vote thereat, shall be entitled to vote at any such adjourned meeting.

Section 5. *Voting:* At each meeting of shareholders each shareholder present in person or by proxy shall be entitled to one vote for each share registered in his name at the time of service of notice of such meeting or at such prior date, not more than forty days before such meeting, as may be prescribed by the Board of Directors for the closing of the corporate share transfer books or fixed by the Board of Directors as the date for determining which shareholders of records are entitled to notice of and to vote at such meeting. The proxies shall be in writing duly signed by the shareholder but need not be acknowledged or witnessed, and the person named as proxy by any shareholder need not himself be a shareholder of the Corporation. Voting by shareholders shall be viva voce unless any shareholder present at the meeting, in person or by proxy, demands a vote by written ballot, in which case the voting shall be by ballot, and each ballot shall state the name of the shareholder voting and the number of shares owned by him, and in addition, the name of the proxy of such ballot if cast by a proxy.

All elections shall be determined by a plurality vote and unless otherwise specified in these By-Laws or the Certificate of Incorporation, the affirmative vote of a majority represented cast at any meeting of shareholders shall be necessary for the transaction of any item of business and shall constitute the act of the shareholders.

Section 6. *Inspectors of Election:* Inspectors of election shall not be required to be appointed at any meeting of shareholders unless requested by a shareholder present (in person or by proxy) and entitled to vote at such meeting and upon the making of such request inspectors shall be appointed or elected as provided in Section 610 of the Business Corporation Law.

Section 7. *Order of Business:* So far as consistent with the purpose of the meeting, the order of business of each meeting of shareholders shall be as follows:

1. Call to order.

2. Presentation of proofs of due calling of the meeting.

3. Roll call and presentation and examination of proxies.

4. Reading of minutes of previous meeting or meetings, unless waived.

5. Reports of officers and committees.

6. Appointment or election of inspectors of election, if requested.

7. If the annual meeting or a special meeting called for that purpose, the election of directors.

8. Unfinished business.

9. New business.

10. Adjournment.

By-Laws of a Cooperative Building (*Continued*)

ARTICLE III

Directors

Section 1. *Number:* The number of the Directors of the Corporation shall be not less than three nor more than seven, as may from time to time be herein provided and, in the absence of such provision shall be three (3). Commencing with the first election of Directors by tenant-shareholders of the Corporation, and until changed by amendment of this By-law provision, as hereinafter provided, the number of Directors shall be three (3). The number of Directors shall not be decreased to a number less than the number of Directors then in office except at an annual meeting of shareholders.

Section 2. *Election:* The Directors shall be elected at the annual meeting of shareholders or at a special meeting called for that purpose as provided by law, by a plurality of votes cast at such meeting. Their term of office shall be until the date herein fixed for the next annual meeting, and thereafter until their respective successors are elected and qualify. It shall not be necessary for a director of this Corporation to be a shareholder.

Section 3. *Quorum:* A majority of the Directors then authorized by these By-laws shall constitute a quorum.

Section 4. *Vacancies:* Vacancies in the Board of Directors resulting from death, resignation or otherwise may be filled without notice to any of the shareholders by a vote of a majority of the remaining directors present at the meeting at which such election is held even though no quorum is present, which may be at any regular meeting of the Board of Directors or any special meeting thereof called for such purpose. In the event of the failure to hold any election of directors at the time designated for the annual election of directors or in the event that the Board of Directors shall not have filled any such vacancy, a special meeting of shareholders to elect a new Board of Directors or to fill such vacancy or vacancies may be called in the manner generally provided for the calling of special meetings of shareholders. Vacancies in the Board of Directors resulting from an increase of the Board of Directors by amendment of these By-laws shall be filled in the manner provided in the resolution adopting such amendment. In case of a reduction of the authorized number of directors by amendment of these By-laws, the directors, if any, whose term of office shall cease, shall be determined in the manner provided in the resolution adopting such amendment.

Section 5. *Meetings:* The Board of Directors shall meet immediately after the annual meeting of shareholders without notice and also whenever called together by any officer of the Corporation or upon the written request of any two directors then holding office, upon notice given to each director, by delivering personally, mailing or telegraphing the same to him at least two days prior to such meeting at the last address furnished by him to the Corporation. Regular meetings may be held without notice at such times and places as the Board of Directors may determine. Any meeting of the Board at which all the members shall be present, or of which notice shall be duly waived by all absentees, either before or after the holding of such meeting, shall be valid for all purposes provided a quorum be present. Meetings of directors may be held either at the principal office of the Corporation or elsewhere within the State of New York as provided in the notice calling the meeting, unless the Board of Directors by resolution adopt some further limitation in regard thereto. At all meetings of the Board of Directors, each director shall be entitled to one vote. The vote of a majority of the Board of Directors present at the time of a vote of a duly constituted meeting shall be the act of the Board of Directors.

Section 6. *Resignation and Removal:* Any director may resign at any time by written notice delivered in person or sent by certified registered mail to the President or Secretary of the Corporation. Such resignation shall take effect at the time specified therein, and unless specifically requested acceptance of such resignation shall not be necessary to make it effective.

By-Laws of a Cooperative Building (*Continued*)

Any director may be removed from office for cause by the shareholders of the Corporation at a meeting duly called for that purpose. Any director may be removed without cause at any time by a vote of the shareholders (other than holders of Unsold Shares) at a meeting duly called for that purpose, after the passage of two full years from the date of the first annual meeting.

Section 7. *Annual Cash Requirements:* The Board of Directors shall, except as may be otherwise restricted by the Proprietary Lease of the Corporation, from time to time, determine the cash requirements as defined in the Corporation's proprietary leases, and fix the terms and manner of payment of rent under the Corporation's proprietary leases. The Board of Directors shall have discretionary power to prescribe the manner of maintaining and operating the apartment house of the Corporation and to determine the cash requirements of the Corporation to be paid as aforesaid by the shareholder-tenants under their respective proprietary leases. Every such determination by the Board of Directors shall be final and conclusive as to all shareholder-tenants and any expenditures made by the Corporation's officers or its agent under the direction or with the approval of the Board of Directors of the Corporation shall, as against the shareholder-tenants, be deemed necessarily and properly made for such purpose.

Section 8. *House Rules:* The Board of Directors may from time to time, adopt and amend such house rules as it may deem necessary in respect to the apartment building of the corporation for the health, safety and convenience of the shareholder-tenants. Copies thereof and of changes therein shall be furnished to each shareholder-tenant.

Section 9. *Executive Committee and Other Committees:* The Board of Directors may by resolution appoint an Executive Committee, and such other committees as it may deem appropriate, each to consist of three or more directors of the Corporation. Such committees shall have and may exercise such of the powers of the Board in the management of the business and affairs of the Corporation during the intervals between the meetings of the Board as may be determined by the authorizing resolution of the Board of Directors and so far as may be permitted by law, except that no committee shall have power to determine the cash requirements defined in the proprietary leases, or to fix the rent to be paid under the proprietary leases, or to vary the terms of payment thereof as fixed by the Board.

Section 10. *Distributions:* The shareholder-tenants shall not be entitled, either conditionally or unconditionally, except upon a complete or partial liquidation of the Corporation, to receive any distribution not out of earnings and profits of the Corporation.

ARTICLE IV

Officers

Section 1. *Election and Removal:* The officers of the Corporation shall be a president, one or more vice presidents, a secretary and a treasurer. Such officers shall be elected at the first meeting of the Board of Directors after these By-laws become effective, and thereafter at the regular meeting in each year following the annual meeting of shareholders, and shall serve until removed or until their successors shall have been elected. The Board of Directors may at any time or from time to time appoint one or more assistant secretaries and one or more assistant treasurers to hold office at the pleasure of the Board and may accord to such officers such power as the Board deems proper. Any officer may be removed at any time, with or without cause, by the affirmative vote of a majority of the then authorized total number of directors. The president shall be a member of the Board of Directors, and shall be a shareholder or the spouse of a shareholder, but none of the other officers need be a member of the Board of Directors or a shareholder or the spouse of a shareholder. One person may hold not more than two offices at the same time, except that the president and the secretary may not be the same person.

By-Laws of a Cooperative Building (*Continued*)

Vacancies occurring in the office of any officer may be filled by the Board of Directors at any time.

Section 2. *Duties of President and Vice Presidents:* The president shall preside at all meetings of the stockholders and of the Board of Directors. The president or any vice president shall sign in the name of the Corporation all contracts, leases and other instruments which are authorized from time to time by the Board of Directors. The president, subject to the control of the Board of Directors, shall have general management of the affairs of the Corporation and perform all the duties incidental to the office. In the absence from the City of New York or inability of the president to act, any vice president shall have the powers and perform the duties of the president.

Section 3. *Duties of Treasurer:* The treasurer shall have the care and custody of all funds and securities of the Corporation, and shall deposit such funds in the name of the Corporation in such bank or trust companies as the directors may determine, and he shall perform all other duties incidental to his office. If so required by the Board of Directors, he shall, before receiving any such funds, furnish to the Corporation a bond with a surety company as surety, in such form and amount as said Board from time to time shall determine. The premium upon such bond shall be paid by the Corporation. By the next March 15th after the close of each calendar year, the treasurer shall cause to be furnished to each shareholder-tenant whose proprietary lease is then in effect, a statement of the Certified Public Accountant of the Corporation of any deductions available for income tax purposes on a per share basis and indicating thereon on a per share basis any such other information as may be necessary or useful to permit him to compute his income tax returns in respect thereof. Such statement shall not relate to professional use or operations, unless authorized by Lessor upon conditions required, including the imposition of a special fee for additional accounting or record-keeping services required, in cases where the shareholder-tenant uses the apartment for such purposes.

Within four months after the end of each fiscal year, the treasurer shall cause to be transmitted to each shareholder-tenant whose proprietary lease is then in effect, an annual report of operations and balance sheet of the Corporation which shall be certified by a licensed independent Public Accountant.

In the absence or inability of the treasurer, the assistant treasurer, if any, shall have all the powers and perform all the duties of the treasurer.

Section 4. *Duties of Secretary:* The secretary shall keep the minutes of the meetings of the Board of Directors and of the meetings of shareholders; he shall attend to the giving and serving of all notices of the Corporation and shall be empowered to affix the corporate seal to all written instruments authorized by the Board of Directors or these By-laws. He shall also perform all other duties incidental to his office. He shall cause to be kept a book containing the names, alphabetically arranged, of all persons who are shareholders of the Corporation, showing their places of residence, the number of shares held by them, respectively, the time when they respectively became the owners thereof, and the amount paid thereon, and the denomination and the amount of all share issuance or transfer stamps affixed thereto, and such book shall be open for inspection as provided by law. In the absence or inability of the secretary, the assistant secretary, if any, shall have all the powers and perform all the duties of the secretary.

ARTICLE V

Proprietary Leases

Section 1. *Form of Lease:* The Board of Directors shall adopt a form of proprietary lease to be used by the Corporation for the leasing of all apartments and

By-Laws of a Cooperative Building (*Continued*)

other space in the apartment building of the Corporation to be leased to shareholder-tenants under proprietary leases. Such proprietary leases shall be for such terms, with or without provisions for renewals, and shall contain such restrictions, limitations and provisions in respect to the assignment thereof, the subletting of the premises demised thereby and the sale and/or transfer of the shares of the Corporation appurtenant thereto, and such other terms, provisions, conditions and covenants as the Board of Directors may determine.

After a proprietary lease in the form so adopted by the Board of Directors shall have been executed and delivered by the Corporation, all proprietary leases (as distinct from the house rules) subsequently executed and delivered shall be in the same form, except with respect to the statement as to the number of shares owned by the lessee, the use of the premises and the date of the commencement of the term, unless varied in accordance with the terms thereof.

Section 2. *Assignment:* Proprietary leases shall be assigned or transferred only in compliance with, and shall never be assigned or transferred in violation of, the terms, conditions or provisions of such proprietary leases. A duplicate original of each proprietary lease shall always be kept on file in the principal office of the Corporation or with the managing agent of the apartment building.

Section 3. *Allocation of Shares:* The Board of Directors shall allocate to each apartment or other space in the apartment building of the Corporation to be leased to shareholder-tenants under proprietary leases the number of shares of the Corporation which must be owned by the proprietary lessee of such apartment or other space.

Section 4. *Assignment of Lease and Transfer of Shares:* No assignment of any lease or transfer of the shares of the Corporation shall take effect as against the Corporation for any purpose until a proper assignment has been delivered to the Corporation; the assignee has assumed and agreed to perform and comply with all the covenants and conditions of the assigned lease or has entered into a new lease for the remainder of the term; all shares of the Corporation appurtenant to the lease have been transferred to the assignee; all sums due have been paid to the Corporation; and all necessary consents have been properly obtained. The action of the Board of Directors with respect to the written application for consent of a proposed assignment or subletting must be made within 30 days after receipt of said written application.

Where the Sponsor named in the Plan of Cooperative Organization or a designee of the Sponsor is a lessee (holder of "Unsold Shares") consent to an assignment or transfer of his lease and the shares appurtenant thereto or a subletting or occupancy of the demised premises will be required only from the Managing Agent of the building (or in lieu thereof at the option of such holder of "Unsold Shares" from the Board of Directors) who shall consent to such assignment, subletting or transfer only when the assignee or transferee or subtenant or occupant is a reputable person, which consent shall not be unreasonably withheld or delayed.

No person to whom the interest of a lessee or shareholder shall pass by law, shall be entitled to assign any lease, transfer any share, or to sublet or occupy any apartment, except upon compliance with the requirements of the lease and these By-laws.

Section 5. *Fees on Assignment:* The Board of Directors shall have authority before an assignment or sublet of a proprietary lease or reallocation of shares takes effect as against the Corporation as lessor, to fix a reasonable fee to cover actual expenses and attorneys' fees of the Corporation, a service fee of the Corporation and such other conditions as it may determine, in connection with each such proposed assignment including, without limitation, a credit or title search of the apartment or parties. The Board may provide that attorneys' fees be paid directly to its attorneys.

By-Laws of a Cooperative Building (*Continued*)

Nothing herein shall restrict any tenant-shareholder or assignee or sublessee from employing an attorney, title company, broker or other firm or person of their own free choice to service or advise them personally, or to freely negotiate fees therewith; and no part of such latter fees shall be payable to the Corporation, directly or indirectly.

Section 6. *Lost Proprietary Leases:* In the event that any proprietary lease in full force and effect is lost, stolen, destroyed or mutilated, the Board of Directors may authorize the issuance of a new proprietary lease in lieu thereof, in the same form and with the same terms, provisions, conditions and limitations. The Board may, in its discretion, before the issuance of any such new proprietary lease, require the owner thereof, or the legal representative of the owner, to make an affidavit or affirmation setting forth such facts as to the loss, destruction or mutilation as it deems necessary, and to give the Corporation a bond in such reasonable sum as it directs, to indemnify the Corporation.

Section 7. *Regrouping of Space:* The Board of Directors, upon the written request of the owner or owners of one or more proprietary leases covering one or more apartments in the apartment building and of the shares issued to accompany the same, may in its discretion, at any time, permit such owner or owners, at his or their own expense, A: (1) to subdivide any apartment into any desired number of apartments; (2) to combine all or any portions of any such apartments into one or any desired number of apartments; and (3) to reallocate the shares issued to accompany the proprietary lease or leases, but the total number of the shares so reallocated shall not be less than the number of shares previously allocated to the apartment or apartments involved, and, in connection with any such regrouping, the Board of Directors may require that the number of shares allocated to the resulting apartment or apartments be greater than the number of shares allocated to the original apartment or apartments, and may authorize the issuance of shares from its treasury for such purpose; or B: to incorporate one or more servant's rooms, if any, or other space in the building not covered by a proprietary lease, into one or more apartments covered by a proprietary lease, whether in connection with any regrouping of space pursuant to subparagraph A of this Section 7 or otherwise, and in allocating shares to any such resulting apartment or apartments, shall determine the number of shares from its treasury to be issued and allocated in connection with the appropriation of such additional space.

Upon any regrouping of space in the building, the proprietary leases so affected, and the accompanying share certificates shall be surrendered, and there shall be executed and delivered in place thereof, respectively, a new proprietary lease for each separate apartment involved, and a new certificate for the number of shares so reallocated to each new proprietary lease.

ARTICLE VI

Capital Shares

Section 1. No shares hereafter issued or acquired by the Corporation shall be issued or reissued except in connection with the execution by the purchaser and delivery by the Corporation of a proprietary lease of an apartment in the building owned by the Corporation. The ownership of shares shall entitle the holder thereof to occupy the apartment for the purposes specified in the proprietary lease to which the shares are appurtenant, subject to the provisions, covenants and agreements contained in such proprietary lease.

Section 2. *Form and Share Register:* Certificates of the shares of the Corporation shall be in the form adopted by the Board of Directors, and shall be signed by the president or a vice president and the secretary or an assistant secretary or the treasurer or an assistant treasurer, and sealed with the seal of the Corporation, and shall be numbered in the order in which issued. Such signatures and seal may be

By-Laws of a Cooperative Building (*Continued*)

facsimiles when and to the extent permitted by applicable statutory provisions. Certificates shall be issued in consecutive order and there shall be recorded the name of the person holding the shares, the number of shares and the date of issue. Each certificate exchanged or returned to the Corporation shall be cancelled, and the date of cancellation shall be indicated thereon and such certificate shall be retained in the Corporate records.

Section 3. *Issuance of Certificates:* Shares appurtenant to each proprietary lease shall be issued in the amount allocated by the Board of Directors to the apartment or other space described in such proprietary lease and shall be represented by a single certificate.

Section 4. *Transfers:* Transfers of shares shall be made upon the books of the Corporation only by the holder in person or by power of attorney, duly executed and filed with the secretary of the Corporation and on the surrender of the certificate for such shares, except that shares sold by the Corporation to satisfy any lien which it holds thereon may be transferred without the surrender of the certificate representing such shares.

Section 5. *Units of Issuance:* Except as otherwise provided in Article V, Section 7, unless and until all proprietary leases which shall have been executed by the Corporation, shall have been terminated, the shares appurtenant to each proprietary lease shall not be sold or assigned except as an entirety to the Corporation or an assignee of such proprietary lease, after complying with and satisfying the requirements of such proprietary lease in respect to the assignment thereof.

Section 6. *Corporation's Lien:* The Corporation shall at all times have a first lien upon the shares owned by each shareholder for all indebtedness and obligations owing and to be owing by such shareholder to the Corporation, arising under the provisions of any proprietary lease issued by the Corporation and at any time held by such shareholder or otherwise arising. Unless and until such shareholder as lessee shall make default in the payment of any of the rental or in the performance of any of the covenants or conditions of such proprietary lease, and/or unless and until such shareholder shall make default in the payment of any indebtedness or obligation owing by such shareholder to the Corporation otherwise arising, such shares shall continue to stand in the name of the shareholder upon the books of the Corporation, and the shareholder shall be entitled to exercise the right to vote thereon as though said lien did not exist. The Corporation shall have the right to issue to any purchaser of such shares upon the enforcement by the Corporation of such lien, or to the nominee of such purchaser, a certificate of the shares so purchased substantially of the tenor of the certificate issued to such defaulting shareholder, and thereupon the certificate for such shares theretofore issued to such defaulting shareholder shall become void and such defaulting shareholder agrees to surrender such last mentioned certificate to the Corporation upon the latter's demand, but the failure of such defaulting shareholder so to surrender such certificate shall not affect the validity of the certificate issued in replacement thereof. The Corporation may refuse to consent to the transfer of shares of any shareholder indebted to the Corporation unless and until such indebtedness is paid.

Section 7. *Lost Certificates:* In the event that any share certificate is lost, stolen, destroyed or mutilated, the Board of Directors may authorize the issuance of a new certificate of the same tenor and for the same number of shares in lieu thereof. The Board may, in its discretion, before the issuance of such new certificate, require the owner of the lost, stolen, destroyed or mutilated certificate, or the legal representative of the owner, to make an affidavit or affirmation setting forth such facts as to the loss, destruction or mutilation as it deems necessary, and to give the Corporation a bond in such reasonable sum as it directs to indemnify the Corporation.

Section 8. *Legend on Share Certificates:* Certificates representing shares of the Corporation shall bear a legend reading as follows:

By-Laws of a Cooperative Building (*Continued*)

"The rights of any holder hereof are subject to the provisions of the By-laws of TWO CHARLTON OWNERS CORP. and to all the terms, covenants, conditions and provisions of a certain proprietary lease made between the person in whose name this certificate is issued, as Lessee, and TWO CHARLTON OWNERS CORP. as Lessor, for an Apartment in the premises known as 2 Charlton Street, New York, N.Y., which lease limits and restricts the title and rights of any transferee hereof. The shares represented by this certificate are transferable only as an entirety and only to an approved assignee of such proprietary lease. Copies of the proprietary lease and the By-laws are on file and available for inspection at the office of the Managing Agent of this Corporation.

The directors of this Corporation may refuse to consent to the transfer of the shares represented by this certificate until any indebtedness of the shareholder to the Corporation is paid. The Corporation, by the terms of said By-laws and proprietary lease, has a first lien on the shares represented by this certificate for all sums due and to become due under said proprietary lease."

Section 9. *Distributions:* The tenant-shareholders shall not be entitled (either conditionally or unconditionally) to receive any distribution not out of earnings and profits of the Corporation, except upon a complete or partial liquidation of the Corporation.

ARTICLE VII

Indemnification

Section 1. To the extent allowed by law, the Corporation shall indemnify any person, made a party to an action by or in the right of the Corporation to procure a judgment in its favor by reason of the fact that he, his testator or, intestate, is or was a director or officer of the Corporation, against the reasonable expenses, including attorneys' fees, actually and necessarily incurred by him in connection with the defense of such action, or in connection with an appeal therein, except in relation to matters as to which such director or officer is adjudged to have breached his duty to the Corporation, as such duty is defined in Section 717 of the Business Corporation Law. To the extent allowed by law, the Corporation shall also indemnify any person, made, or threatened to be made, a party to an action or proceeding other than one by or in the right of the Corporation to procure a judgment in its favor, whether civil or criminal, including an action by or in the right of any other corporation, domestic or foreign, which he served in any capacity at the request of the Corporation by reason of the fact, that he, his testator or, intestate was a director or officer of the Corporation or served it in any capacity against judgments, fines, amounts paid in settlement, and reasonable expenses, including attorneys' fees actually and necessarily incurred as a result of such action or proceeding, or any appeal therein, if such director or officer acted, in good faith, for a purpose which he reasonably believed to be in the best interests of the Corporation and, in criminal actions or proceedings, in addition, had no reasonable cause to believe that his conduct was unlawful.

Nothing contained in this provision shall limit any right to indemnification to which any director or any officer may be entitled by contract or under any law now or hereinafter enacted.

ARTICLE VIII

Seal

Section 1. The seal of the Corporation shall be circular in form and have inscribed thereon the name of the Corporation, the year of its organization and the words "Corporate Seal" and "New York".

By-Laws of a Cooperative Building (*Continued*)

ARTICLE IX

Negotiable Instruments

Section 1. All checks, drafts, orders for payment of money and negotiable instruments shall be signed by such officer or officers or employee or employees as the Board of Directors may from time to time, by standing resolution or special order, prescribe.

Section 2. Endorsements or transfers of shares, bonds, or other securities shall be signed by the president or any vice president and by the treasurer or an assistant treasurer or the secretary or an assistant secretary unless the Board of Directors, by special resolution in one or more instances, prescribe otherwise.

Section 3. *Safe Deposit Boxes:* Such officer or officers as from time to time shall be designated by the Board of Directors, shall have access to any safe of the Corporation in the vault of any safe deposit company.

Section 4. *Securities:* Such officer or officers as from time to time shall be designated by the Board of Directors shall have power to control and direct the disposition of any bonds or other securities or property of the Corporation deposited in the custody of any trust company, bank or other custodian.

ARTICLE X

Fiscal Year

Section 1. The fiscal year of the Corporation shall be the calendar year unless otherwise determined by resolution of the Board of Directors.

ARTICLE XI

Miscellaneous

Section 1. *Salaries:* No salary or other compensation for services shall be paid to any director or officer of the Corporation for services rendered as such officer unless and until the same shall have been authorized in writing or by affirmative vote taken at a duly held meeting of shareholders, by shareholders owning at least a majority of the then outstanding shares of the Corporation.

ARTICLE XII

Amendments

Section 1. These By-laws may be amended, enlarged or diminished either (a) at any shareholders' meeting by vote of shareholders owning two-thirds of the amount of the outstanding shares, represented in person or by proxy, provided that the proposed amendment or the substance thereof shall have been inserted in the notice of meeting or that all of the shareholders be present in person or by proxy, or (b) at any meeting of the Board of Directors by a majority vote, provided that the proposed amendment or the substance thereof shall have been inserted in the notice of meeting or that all of the Directors are present in person, except that the Directors may not repeal a By-law amendment adopted by the shareholders as provided above.

By-Laws of a Cooperative Building (*Continued*)

ARTICLE XIII

Additional Clauses

Section 1. Anything hereinabove contained to the contrary notwithstanding, the holders of Unsold Shares shall have the absolute right, without payment of any fee or charge of whatsoever nature, to change the size and layout of any apartment owned by them, into two or more apartments or to combine all or any portion of any such apartments into one or any desired number of apartments, subject only to obtaining the prior consent of the then managing agent of the building with respect to any reallocation of shares issued and accompanying proprietary lease or leases so affected by such subdivision or combination (as the case may be). The reallocation of shares shall be based upon the fair market value of the equity in the property (including the building(s)) attributable to the subdivided or combined apartment, but in any event, the total number of shares so reallocated shall remain the same. Upon the surrender of the share certificate or certificates and proprietary lease or leases affected by such subdivision or combination, the board of directors shall issue a new share certificate or certificates and accompanying proprietary lease or leases covering the subdivided or combined apartments (as the case may be) in accordance with the foregoing.

Section 2. *Allocation of Shares to Additional Space.* The Board of Directors may, in its discretion, authorize the conversion of space in the building(s) not covered by a proprietary lease into space suitable for the primary purposes of the corporation, as set forth in the certificate of incorporation, allocate theretofore unissued shares to such space, and authorize the execution of a proprietary lease or leases covering such space.

. . .

(10) Messengers and tradespeople shall use such means of ingress and egress as shall be designated by the Lessor.

(11) Kitchen supplies, market goods and packages of every kind are to be delivered only at the service entrance of the building and through the service elevator to the apartments when such elevator is in operation.

(12) Trunks and heavy baggage shall be taken in or out of the building through the service entrance.

(13) Garbage and refuse from the apartments shall be disposed of only at such times and in such manner as the superintendent or the managing agent of the building may direct.

(14) Water closets and other water apparatus in the building shall not be used for any purposes other than those for which they were constructed, nor shall any sweepings, rubbish, rags or any other article be thrown into the water closets. The cost of repairing any damage resulting from misuse of any water closets or other apparatus shall be paid for by the Lessee in whose apartment it shall have been caused.

(15) No Lessee shall send any employee of the Lessor out of the building on any private business of a Lessee.

(16) No bird or animal shall be kept or harbored in the building unless the same in each instance be expressly permitted in writing by the Lessor; such permission shall be revocable by the Lessor. In no event shall dogs be permitted on elevators or in any of the public portions of the building unless carried or on leash. No pigeons or other birds or animals shall be fed from the window sills, terraces, balconies or in the yard, court spaces or other public portions of the building, or on the sidewalks or street adjacent to the building.

By-Laws of a Cooperative Building *(Continued)*

(17) No radio or television aerial shall be attached to or hung from the exterior of the building without the prior written approval of the Lessor or the managing agent.

(18) No vehicle belonging to a Lessee or to a member of the family or guest, subtenant or employee of a Lessee shall be parked in such manner as to impede or prevent ready access to any entrance of the building by another vehicle.

(19) The Lessee shall use the available laundry facilities only upon such days and during such hours as may be designated by the Lessor or the managing agent.

(20) The Lessor shall have the right from time to time to curtail or relocate any space devoted to storage or laundry purposes.

(21) Unless expressly authorized by the Board of Directors in each case, the floors of each apartment must be covered with rugs or carpeting or equally effective noise-reducing material, to the extent of at least 80% of the floor area of each room excepting only kitchens, pantries, bathrooms, maid's rooms, closets, and foyer.

(22) No group tour or exhibition of any apartment or its contents shall be conducted, nor shall any auction sale be held in any apartment without the consent of the Lessor or its managing agent.

(23) The Lessee shall keep the windows of the apartment clean. In case of refusal or neglect of the Lessee during 10 days after notice in writing from the Lessor or the managing agent to clean the windows, such cleaning may be done by the Lessor, which shall have the right, by its officers or authorized agents, to enter the apartment for the purpose and to charge the cost of such cleaning to the Lessee.

(24) The passenger and service elevators, unless of automatic type and intended for operation by a passenger, shall be operated only by employees of the Lessor, and there shall be no interference whatever with the same by Lessees or members of their families or their guests, employees or subtenants.

(25) Complaints regarding the service of the building shall be made in writing to the managing agent of the Lessor.

(26) Any consent or approval given under these House Rules by the Lessor shall be revocable at any time.

(27) If there be a garage in the building, the Lessee will abide by all arrangements made by the Lessor with the garage operator with regard to the garage and the driveways thereto.

(28) No Lessee shall install any plantings on the terrace, balcony or roof without the prior written approval of the Lessor. Plantings shall be contained in boxes of wood lined with metal or other material impervious to dampness and standing on supports at least two inches from the terrace, balcony or roof surface, and if adjoining a wall, at least three inches from such wall. Suitable weep holes shall be provided in the boxes to draw off water. In special locations, such as a corner abutting a parapet wall, plantings may be contained in masonry or hollow tile walls which shall be at least three inches from the parapet and flashing, with the floor of drainage tiles and suitable weep holes at the sides to draw off water. It shall be the responsibility of the Lessee to maintain the containers in good condition, and the drainage tiles and weep holes in operating condition. Any damage caused to the building or any portion thereof as a result of the placement of plantings on terraces or patios shall be repaired at the sole cost and expense of the Lessee.

(29) The agents of the Lessor, and any contractor or workman authorized by the Lessor, may enter any apartment at any reasonable hour of the day for the

By-Laws of a Cooperative Building (*Continued*)

purpose of inspecting such apartment to ascertain whether measures are necessary or desirable to control or exterminate any vermin, insects or other pests and for the purpose of taking such measures as may be necessary to control or exterminate any such vermin, insects or other pests. If the Lessor takes measures to control or exterminate carpet beetles, the cost thereof shall be payable by the Lessee, as additional rent.

(30) These House Rules may be added to, amended or repealed at any time by resolution of the Board of Directors of the Lessor.

By-Laws of a Cooperative Building (*Continued*)

10

Locating the Proper Apartment

Locating an apartment involves two main elements, knowing your own lifestyle and the type of apartment that fits that style (Chapter 3), and knowing what you can afford (Chapter 5).

Finding the right apartment requires asking a lot of questions and making judgments based on the answers you get to those questions. It also involves in many cases good old-fashioned legwork and research.

For instance, after you have settled on a location, the obvious first place to look for an apartment is a local newspaper or, rather, all the local newspapers in the area. The ads in those papers, especially the weekend editions, will provide you with two things—actual apartments for sale and the names of real estate brokers who handle condominium or cooperative apartments. However, don't rely exclusively on brokers. Many developers who are building new condo or coop projects don't use outside brokers, but instead use their own sales staff. In addition, many individual owners prefer to sell their own apartments to avoid the brokerage commission.

Not all offerings are advertised, however. If you have friends in the area you have settled on, tell them to keep their eyes and ears open for possible apartments, especially those that may be holding an "open house" in the near future. You must exhaust all possibilities in searching for an apartment.

Once you have started to look at apartments, comparison shopping is the key. Smart buyers keep a notebook and they mark down the pros and cons of every apartment they can see. Few people have good enough memories to remember the important details of 15 or 20 apartments (see Chapter 3).

Remember that you have a set of lifestyle goals that you want to meet as closely as possible so comparison shopping in the appropriate price range is your main aim. But, on the other hand, if you are looking for the "perfect" apartment that will meet all the criteria you have set down, you probably will never find it. Some compromises will undoubtedly have to be made.

ASSESSING THE PHYSICAL CONDITION

When you see an apartment that interests you, the most important consideration should be the condition of the apartment. By the way, don't assume that just because an apartment is newly built it is in perfect condition—that may not be the case.

In your notebook provide yourself with a checklist of things to look at when you are in the apartment. Also, don't forget to take along that most valuable of all potential buyer's tools—the tape measure—so that you can *accurately* record room sizes.

Here are some suggestions for that checklist that you may add to or subtract from as you see fit:

Walls.   Are there cracks? If so, that may be an indication of a leak somewhere within the walls, or it could also be a symptom of shoddy construction.

Bathrooms.   Is the water pressure in the sinks, bathtubs, and showers good? Is the water rusty? If so, that could indicate trouble.

Kitchen.   Shelf, cupboard, and counter space must be adequate for your needs. If you or your family do a lot of cooking, this space is vital and should be double-checked before you leave the apartment.

Heating and Cooling Systems.   Do they function well and can you control them within your own apartment, or is there a central unit? Most people favor the individual systems, especially if they suffer from any type of respiratory trouble.

Electrical Outlets and Wiring.   Count the number of outlets in each room, including the kitchen, and note them. If you use a great number of electrical appliances, that information is vital; adding new outlets later can be expensive. Can the wiring support air conditioning units and large appliances such as a clothes washer and dryer?

Ceilings.   Again look for cracks and areas of leakage. Signs of flaking and discoloration are telltale signs of trouble.

Windows.   Are the frames fitting properly? How well insulated are the windows? Are storm and screen windows provided with the apartment and, if so, what kind of condition are they in? If the apartment is in a high-rise or is the garden type, how is the sound-proofing? Can you hear the people in the apartment above you or next door?

Finally, Room Sizes.   Here is where the tape measure comes in handy. Since your furniture has to fit comfortably into the apartment, know the sizes of your furniture as well as the dimensions of the rooms you want to each piece into.

Your inspection, however, is only half over at this point. Now you should inspect the exterior of the building. Although you will not be totally responsible for the outside areas, in cooperative and condominium buildings something that happens to the outside of the building could cause a great deal of damage in your particular unit. For instance:

Does the roof leak or does it appear to be in poor condition? A leaky roof can be a particular hazard to penthouse apartments.

How about brick or stonework? It may require very expensive pointing.

Are the common areas well lit, heated, and ventilated? A poorly lit hallway, for example, can invite burglaries.

What are the conditions of the elevators? A poorly maintained elevator is a sign of a poorly maintained building.

Last, and very important, are utilities metered separately? If the apartment complex has rental tenants in it, they may not care about running up high energy bills if they don't have to pay. Therefore, separate utility meters are much better.

Exterior and common area problems will probably be set out in an engineer's report and should be included in the documents you ask for when seriously considering a purchase. Make sure you get a copy of that report.

One relatively simple way to get a handle on how good or bad a condominium or cooperative complex is by asking people who presently live there whether or not they would buy an apartment in that same complex again. Although you may get some answers that amount to "sour grapes" probably most of the answers will be candid and forthright.

Ask owners what the problems are as far as construction, management, and other owners are concerned. If you are able, try to talk to three or more owners. If you keep hearing the same thing from each person independently, then you should have a pretty fair idea of what problems and difficulties the complex has.

If a real estate broker, manager, or other sales person who is trying to sell you an apartment tries to keep you from talking to other owners, be suspicious and tread cautiously. They may be trying to hide something.

HOME INSPECTION SPECIALISTS

If you are unsure of your own abilities to judge good construction from bad, or if you simply want to back up your own inspection, you should definitely consider hiring a home inspection specialist to look over the property and apartment before you make a final offer to buy. Such an inspection may cost you several hundred dollars, but it will be money well spent if it allows you peace of mind.

Real estate brokers can often provide you with a list of such inspectors as can your mortgage lender, and additionally there may be a list in the Yellow Pages of the local phone directory.

Once these inspections have been completed, the most difficult of all inspections still lies ahead of you; that is, judging the builder in the case of new construction, the converter in the case of a conversion, and the operating board in an established condominium or cooperative.

NEW CONSTRUCTION

If a building is in the process of construction or has been recently finished and you are looking at a newly completed apartment, and the construction and inspections you have made seem adequate, you can still make a big mistake if the builder goes bankrupt or for some other reason can't finish the building. Therefore, you must make a judgment about the builder. The only proper way of doing that is by checking into his or her reputation. You'll want to know whether or not he has built other condominium or cooperative projects and, if so, how have they fared? Are the builder's financial sources reputable? Are there any lawsuits pending against the builder? And from your point of view the most important question, are there any legal agreements to protect you against his failure to complete the building or against shoddy construction. Don't be afraid to ask these questions of the builder or his representative. A reputable builder with nothing to hide will be more than happy to give you straightforward answers.

If this is the builder's first condo or coop project, be extra wary and check things out very carefully. Don't buy until the entire complex has been completed. As a backup, be sure to get copies of all of the builder's financial statements and copies of the proposed budget for the complex as well.

In the end, though, it all comes back to reputation. Ask questions and keep an open mind. If the builder has built another project nearby, go look at it and ask residents of the building what they think of their apartments and of the construction of the building. Obviously, the more positive things you hear about the builder, the better for you.

CONVERSIONS

Although more will be said about conversions later in Chapter 14, at this point it is vital to again emphasize reputation. The reputation of the converter is probably the most important element in deciding whether or not to buy. If the converter's reputation is a bad one, you can be fairly sure that it is probably well deserved, and unless you are getting a deal you possibly can't turn down, be careful. *Caveat emptor* is the rule to follow in conversions. Here, again, financial statements and engineer's reports should be studied carefully, especially if the building is more than 15 years old.

If the building is an older one it could be that the converter is converting the building to cooperative or condominium ownership because the plumbing or wiring is outdated or because a new roof or boiler is needed and he doesn't want to foot the bill for those large repairs. Some landlords think that they will get around expensive capital improvements by shifting the financial burden for making those repairs onto new owners, namely the condominium or cooperative buyers of his building.

Rehabilitated Buildings

Many times an individual developer will purchase an older building and will rehabilitate it and then sell the units as condominium or cooperative apartments. It is very difficult (unless you are a builder yourself) for you to walk into such a building and ascertain whether or not a good rehab job has been done. You can't see behind the walls and there is no way to be sure.

Sometimes, just a cosmetic job will be done. A lobby or the hallways will be painted and that is all. In such a situation you must be extra careful, and you should get as much professional advice as you can from expert engineers.

Watch out especially for "as-is" apartments. There is a famous case in Washington, D.C., where buyers purchased apartments in a 40-year-old building. The owner of the building sold the apartments "as is." That means that the buyers took the apartments as they saw them. No work was to be done by the developer and all the buyers knew this. These were expensive apartments in a beautiful old high-rise building in a fashionable section of the city. Well, not long after the last owner moved in, the building literally began falling apart. And the tenants, among whom were some very influential people including at least one U.S. Senator, decided to sue the developer. However, he had a very good defense—he sold the units "as is." Everybody knows that "as is" means that the buyer assumes the risk of an as-is product. The moral of this story is that you can't be too careful when you buy rehabilitated apartments.

If you feel uneasy about a rehabilitated apartment, just don't buy. Again, you must depend on the reputation of the developer who has done the job. If you can find out what kind of work the rehabber has done in the past, and if he has a good reputation, that is really all you can go on. Make inquiries of bankers, real estate agents and brokers. Also, if you can visit one of the developer's former rehab jobs and question owners who live there whether they are satisfied or whether some real problems have developed. A professional is usually someone who takes pride in his or her work. If the person doing the rehab job has established a reputation—good or bad—enough people will know about it so that you should be able to find out what you want to know fairly quickly.

OPERATING BOARDS

Properly examining the operating board of an ongoing condominium or cooperative apartment complex is just as important as judging the interior and exterior of the building. More will be said about operating boards in Chapter 16, but while you are searching for an apartment you must be aware of the philosophy and procedures of the board. One thing every prospective buyer should do that few actually do is to *interview the operating board*. You should ask them about their philosophy with regard to raising monthly homeowners' dues or maintenance charges, and when and how they will do it. You should inquire similarly about what they are doing about installing energy-saving devices and if they are adding insulation to the common areas to cut down on heating costs. If the building is a cooperative, how does the board feel about renewing outstanding mortgages or paying off balloon mortgages? You should ask when and under what circumstances assessments are made. Is the building insured adequately? What about parking places and recreational facilities? These and other questions that occur to you should be asked when you interview the board. If you don't like the answers you get, you should consider buying elsewhere.

RESERVE FUNDS

As you know, most cooperative and condominium buildings have a reserve fund that is set aside to take care of capital improvements and emergencies, such as the replacement of a boiler or the sudden destruction of a roof in a hurricane, tornado, or other natural calamity.

When complexes are built initially or when rental buildings are converted to condominium or cooperative ownership, the money for the reserve fund comes from the builder or the converter. An initial sum is paid to start the fund going, and then homeowners' fees and/or maintenance charges are supposed to supplement the fund.

However, there have been problems with landlords and builders putting money into these funds. As Richard Siegler, a New York attorney, recently pointed out:

Unfortunately, sometimes the promised fund is not really there. Consider the following. In a recent cooperative conversion, the sponsor (converter) established a working capital fund of $500,000. The existence of the fund was undoubtedly a material inducement for shareholders to purchase shares in the cooperative housing corporation. However, another provision in the offering plan required the cooperative corporation to reimburse the sponsor, upon the transfer of title, for closing adjustments like real estate taxes.

The total amount of adjustments that the cooperative corporation owed the sponsor at the time of the closing was roughly equivalent to the money in the working capital fund. The plan specified that the cooperative corporation would pay any closing adjustments in excess of $25,000 by executing and delivering to the sponsor promissory notes that would be payable in 12 equal monthly installments commencing a few months after it acquired title. Although the sponsor knew what the size of these adjustments would be, he did not indicate their magnitude in the offering plan.

When the control of the cooperative corporation passed to directors elected by tenant-shareholders, they suddenly became aware that the reserve fund provided by the sponsor would be virtually depleted at the end of the first year because of the payments they had to make against the notes due to the sponsor for the closing adjustments. Thus the reserve fund turned out to have been illusory.*

Obviously, not all buildings will have horror stories similar to that one, but it does illustrate how you must be on your guard and look at all aspects of the deal before you buy.

As a result of prudent management, some buildings will have more money in their reserve funds than others. Most real estate experts agree that the ideal situation is if about 20% of the total annual payments made by the owners is set aside in the reserve account. An amount under 20% is considered dangerous and, if you are looking at an apartment in a building where there is less than 20%, you might consider looking elsewhere or ask why the fund is so low. If some recent work has been performed the fund may have become depleted temporarily; try to find out as much as possible about the reserve fund. You should not, however, choose an apartment solely because the building has a high reserve fund; it should be just one of the many factors that you consider.

THE REAL ESTATE BROKER

Many people underestimate the importance of the real estate broker or salesperson in real estate deals. Even though you are not paying the commission that the broker wants to earn, it is necessary that you feel comfortable with a broker or salesperson. Only deal with brokers and salespeople who are specialists in condominium or cooperative

*Siegler, "Apartment Purchasers Can Buy Unexpected Problems."

apartments. If the brokers try to show you apartments that are above your price range or are outside the geographic area you desire, just don't work with them any longer. Don't let them waste your time. They are supposed to aid your search, not hinder it.

A good broker or agent will know about the board, the builder, and the history of the building. Many agents will introduce a prospective buyer to other people they have placed in the same building, so that the potential buyer can ask any questions he or she feels are necessary. You should encourage this sort of thing if you can.

The bottom line is that you must trust the salesperson with whom you are dealing. A good salesperson can make or break the deal.

BUYER'S BROKERS

If you wish, you can hire a broker on your own who will search for an appropriate apartment for you. These brokers, known as *buyer's brokers*, are a relatively new phenomenon. Buyer's brokers charge one of two ways: by the hour ($50 an hour is common) or a flat fee (say $2,000). Supposedly buyer's brokers will find you more apartments than a broker who is working for sellers will turn up, but you would be wise to check out the buyer's broker's track record before you hire one.

Since a real estate broker is normally hired by the seller, the price you will pay for any piece of property, including an apartment, will normally reflect the 6% standard broker's commission. So, for example, if you buy an apartment for $100,000 through a real estate broker, $6,000 of that goes to the broker. This means that the effective price of the apartment was really $94,000. If a buyer's broker had found you that same apartment and could convince the owner that $94,000 is the proper selling price, and you in fact buy it for that price, you have saved a few thousand dollars, depending on the buyer's broker's fee. That seems to be a good deal for everyone except the traditional real estate broker. You therefore might check in the area in which you want to live about the availability of buyer's brokers and what they can do for you.

A QUICK APARTMENT SEARCH CHECKLIST

Is the apartment located close to work, shopping, and recreation?

Is the area one of vitality? Are there other condos or coops in the area?

Has the builder or converter erected or converted any other buildings and, if so, have you checked them out?

How long has the builder or converter been operating in the area?

What kind of financing is involved?

Do you understand your financing options?

Does the development have more than 50% rental tenants? If so, there might be less concern for the property than if it has all owners.

QUESTIONS CONCERNING LOCATING AN APARTMENT

1. Have I picked the location(s) in which I want to live?

2. Have I checked all local newspapers for apartment ads?

3. Have I contacted at least three real estate brokers who specialize in cooperative or condominium apartments in the area?

4. Do all my friends and relatives in the area know that I am looking for an apartment and will they call me if they run across something?

5. Have I personally checked out all apartment projects in the area?

6. Have I prepared a checklist of items that I want to use when inspecting an apartment?

7. Have I inspected the interior of the apartment and the exterior of the building as well?

8. If necessary, have I hired a home inspection specialist?

9. Have I interviewed the builder and/or the operating board of the building?

10. Does the building have an adequate reserve fund?

11

Do You Really Need
an Attorney When You Buy?

Although some may disagree, almost all professionals will tell you that you should have an attorney by your side when you purchase any piece of real estate, be it a house or a condominium or cooperative apartment. It is true that in some states, most notably California, houses and apartments are sold without the buyer being represented by counsel, but that is not recommended procedure.

There are four good reasons to hire an attorney when purchasing an apartment.

1. A competent, experienced attorney will be able to read and interpret for you the very technical documents such as the prospectus, offering plan, or other important items that more often than not are written in "legalese."

2. A lawyer will aid in the negotiation of the contract for the terms you want. For instance, buyers and sellers often clash over when the buyer is going to move in and when the seller is to move out. If you specify a date to your attorney, he or she will work out the move-in date for you.

3. An often-overlooked point is that an attorney is a neutral intermediary who will not be as emotionally involved in the purchase as you might be if you were negotiating directly with the seller. Snags often develop in deals after a bid has been accepted by the seller, and you could lose your temper and thereby lose the apartment if you are not careful. Lawyers are experienced negotiators; use their expertise.

4. The attorney, if he or she is a good one, will help you work out any financial and tax problems associated with the purchase. In this role alone the services of an attorney prove invaluable.

FEES

The fees that your attorney will charge you should be discussed at your initial meeting. Some lawyers will charge a flat fee, others will charge a percentage of the sales price. The average charge around the country seems to be approximately 1% of the total purchase price of the apartment. Therefore, if the apartment costs $100,000, you should expect to pay close to $1,000 in attorney fees.

FINDING AN ATTORNEY

Again, search for an experienced attorney. Your real estate broker, developer, builder, and lender are all people to ask for referrals. In any case, get more than one name and have a talk with the attorneys that have been recommended to you. You should end up hiring the one with whom you feel most comfortable. Most attorneys practicing in the same area charge similar or identical fees, so don't base your decision solely on how much you will be charged. As with anything else, you get what you pay for.

Questions to Ask the Prospective Attorney at the Initial Interview

Most important, does the attorney have experience with condominium or cooperative apartments? If not, go on to the next attorney.

If so, for how long and with how many clients has he or she dealt? The larger the number the better it is for you.

Does the lawyer have time to handle the deal thoroughly, or is he or she swamped with other work? Time can often be of the essence in buying an apartment, and if your lawyer cannot meet deadlines because of overwork you may as well not have an attorney at all.

Will the lawyer you are interviewing actually be working with you, or will a less-experienced associate be doing the work? You want as much experience on your side as you can get, especially when you realize that the seller may have a highly experienced attorney on his side.

The final question should concern the attorney's fee. A family attorney who mainly specializes in drawing up wills may not have the expertise you need when it comes to buying a condominium or cooperative apartment. So pick an attorney carefully. After all, you are probably making the largest purchase of your life and, if you are not careful, you could be sorry later.

12

Bidding, the Binder, and
Locking Up the Deal

Once you have found the apartment you want to buy, you must, of course, arrive at an agreeable price with the seller. This involves a process of making bids until one is finally accepted. Buyers don't expect to pay the full asking price and, frankly, most sellers don't expect to get their total asking price. It is a fact that most sellers expect to get about 10% less for their apartments than they ask for them. Therefore, you can expect to get the apartment for somewhere close to 10% less than the first price you were quoted.

How many bids you should make and how they should be structured should be worked out between you and the real estate broker or other intermediary representing you. All bidding should be conducted through an intermediary, such as a real estate salesperson or attorney. There is no set rule for bidding, but if you are in competition with another individual you may have to make a series of quick bids in a short period of time.

Most real estate salespeople and attorneys are quite competent at negotiating with owners, so you would be wise to leave the actual negotiating to them. Let your intermediary know exactly how high you are willing to bid and let her do the rest. It is true that the real estate salesperson is being paid by the seller (unless you are using a buyer's broker) and gets a commission based on a percentage of the negotiated sales price, but that doesn't mean that he or she will not try to get you the lowest price possible. The philosophy of good salespersons is that a deal made at a slightly lower commission is better than no deal at all. They usually deal in volume, therefore the more apartments or houses that they sell, the higher their income. It is vital, then, that you have trust in your intermediary. You can be fairly sure that, if the real estate salesperson has been around for a few years, he or she has a lot of experience at this sort of thing. You must be as honest and forthright in your dealings with salespeople as you expect them to be with you and the seller.

The entire bidding process should be conducted as speedily as possible. If you spend more than one week on bidding, you have probably spent too much time on it. This is especially true if you are bidding against another potential buyer. Note that during the negotiating and bidding period you should make yourself as available and accessible to the intermediary as possible. The intermediary may have to get in touch with you quickly as things change, so don't pick that period to take your vacation or to leave the country.

GETTING MORE THAN YOU BARGAINED FOR

Occasionally a seller is so anxious to make a deal that you can get a better deal than you originally thought. For example, some sellers have been known to negotiate with buyers on the sharing of the costs of such items as transfer taxes, title insurance, survey costs, and escrow fees, which the buyer would normally have to pay for out of his or her own pocket. You might even be able to strike a bargain with the seller whereby he or she will help you in paying your attorney's fee. Don't be afraid to ask for some concessions on the part of the seller; that is, after all, what negotiating is all about.

Also, you might want to purchase a seller's wall-to-wall carpeting, chandelier, built-in bookcases, or other personal property as part of the deal. If that is the case, you should definitely instruct the attorneys to draw up a separate personal property agreement of sale that should be signed by you and the seller at the same time that the real property contract is signed. By having a separate personal property contract, neither side can later complain that certain items were or were not to be included as part of the deal. Oftentimes the personal property, such as carpeting, is included in the contract of sale. When it is not, a separate agreement should be signed.

BINDERS

To lock up the deal you may be asked to put down a cash deposit on the apartment. The amount of this *binder* may vary, but it is normally no more than 10% of the total purchase price of the apartment. The binder is usually held by the real estate broker, and is applied toward the downpayment if the deal is consummated. Some buyers are so anxious to write out their binder checks that they forget one extremely important matter: they neglect to write on the back of the check that the binder is returnable or refundable in the event that the expected financing is not obtainable. Many real estate brokers and attorneys have a written form that both the seller and buyer sign, but if you are not given one, be sure that the understanding with regard to the binder is written out somewhere. As with any agreement regarding the sale of real property, this one should be written and should not under any circumstances be just an oral understanding. If something were to happen and you couldn't go through with the deal, you could lose your binder if nothing is in writing and if you have not noted that the binder is refundable. Consult an attorney on this if you feel that you are not being sufficiently protected with regard to binders.

The deposit, or *earnest money* as it is sometimes called, must be placed in an escrow account for safekeeping. This protects you from any hanky-panky on the part of an unscrupulous seller. Make sure that your deposit has been put into a separate escrow account and that it hasn't been mixed in with any other funds. And you should do this whether you give the deposit to an attorney, a real estate broker, or to the seller himself.

13

Special Problems
Associated
with Buying a Newly
Converted
or Newly Constructed
Apartment

All condominium or cooperative apartments are new at one time or another. As far as a converted building is concerned, new has nothing to do with age; it has to do with a new status as a cooperative or condominium. All real estate experts agree that older, more established apartment complexes probably have fewer management problems, but do have more physical problems than the newer ones. It is fairly easy to spot a physical defect, but management difficulties are much harder to get hold of. If you plan on purchasing an apartment in a newly converted or newly built complex, you may face a special group of problems of which you should be aware.

Apartment complexes that convert from rental to condominium or cooperative ownership are especially vulnerable to management problems which may lead to physical problems later. A true case in point: A landlord in Colorado knew that the plumbing system in his high-rise building was falling apart. He also undoubtedly knew that, because of that fact, he wouldn't be able to sell the building to a professional real estate developer, because the faulty plumbing would be spotted quickly. So the landlord conveniently got rid of his problem building by converting it and selling apartments to the tenants who were blithely unaware of the plumbing problem. When all the units were sold, the landlord took his money and ran, and left the new owners with a very expensive problem when the pipes burst soon after.

This kind of story is not at all unusual in the wonderful world of condominiums and cooperatives. So it is incumbent on buyers to be on their guard for such situations. If you are purchasing an apartment that has been newly converted, and if you are buying from the landlord, you have the right to obtain a written warranty against major building defects. Such a warranty should cover all apartment buyers and should be drawn up by an attorney with all the *is* dotted and all the *ts* crossed. If the landlord refuses to give you such a warranty, he or she may be hiding something, so buy elsewhere. Of course, you can cover yourself by getting a competent, independent building engineer to come in and search for defects, but a warranty will be upheld in a court of law if you and your fellow owners decide to sue.

Another common problem that plagues purchasers of newly constructed or newly converted apartment complexes is the unreliability of the figures that the landlord or developer gives to potential buyers concerning probable homeowners' dues or maintenance fees. For instance, the builder of a new group of condominium garden apartments may tell you that your monthly fee for the unit you are looking at will be $300 a month. Unless you get that in writing, don't believe it. It is not at all unusual for salespeople or the builders themselves to quote low fees to get buyers to buy. Then, when the new owners are happily ensconced in the new apartment, they find that the homeowners' fee is actually $500 instead of the $300 they were quoted. The moral of the story: *Get all representations in writing.*

Speaking of garden apartment complexes, there is one other problem that is unique to these types of buildings. This is known as the *last phase* problem. Typically, garden apartment complexes are built in phases; one phase will contain a certain number of units all built at the same time and connected by common walls to other apartments in the same phase. If the construction has been completed for the entire complex, you should be especially careful about buying an apartment in the last phase. Why? Developers have been known to run out of money near the end of construction, and it is not uncommon for buildings constructed in the latter phases to be put together in a more slipshod manner than were those in the earlier phases. In this situation you should also get some kind of written warranty against building or unit defects. If the builder balks, look elsewhere.

Not all problems occur before move-in; some occur soon after. The most common is the incompetent managing agent. Usually it takes a managing agent, especially an inexperienced one, a year or so to settle into the job. During the first year the agent will probably be running the complex the way the former landlord did (in the case of a conversion) or under the direction of the builder (in the case of new construction).

The new apartment owners must assert themselves and take control quickly. This will let the managing agent know that the agent works for the new owners and not for someone who formerly ran the building complex. Things can be rammed through novice boards of directors and homeowners' associations by powerful builders or former landlords that are supported by the managing agent. It is only later that the owners discover that what was done was inimical to their interests.

The solution? Have a written agreement with the managing agent that the owners can terminate his services *without cause* with 60 days' notice. This should stop all conflict-of-interest problems with former landlords or builders and should also insure good performance on the part of the agent.

IF YOU DON'T GET A DEED

Condominium buyers in new projects sometimes face an interesting problem. They buy a unit, move in, and are living there, but they have not yet gotten a deed to their apartment because the developer has to sell a certain number of units before his lender will allow the developer to close on the property. If you find yourself in such a situation, you must use every means at your disposal to get a valid deed for your unit. Otherwise, you will be unable to sell your apartment when you want to. You may have to hire an attorney to get your deed for you. Reputable developers will give you a valid deed to your unit whether you are the first or last buyer in a project, so ask about a deed before you buy. If obtaining a deed is conditioned on a certain percentage of sales, be wary; have the name of a good lawyer if you do buy without getting the deed when you close.

QUESTIONS CONCERNING NEWLY BUILT AND NEWLY CONVERTED APARTMENT BUILDINGS

1. Has the apartment you wish to buy been newly built or converted?
2. If so, has an engineering report been issued as to the soundness of the construction?
3. Was the report issued by an independent engineer?
4. Have you obtained a warranty against major defects from the builder or converter?
5. Has the builder or converter's financial background been investigated?
6. Are you aware of any other projects that the builder or converter has been involved with?
7. Did those jobs turn out successfully?

8. Are the monthly homeowner or maintenance fee figures given you by the builder or converter realistic?

9. If not, have you obtained a warranty from that person that any representations made as to those figures will be accurate to the best of his or her knowledge?

10. Have you bought in a last-phase-of-construction area?

11. If so, have you hired an independent engineer to report on the soundness of the construction?

12. Have the managing agents been running the complex for over a year?

14

Strategies and Responses
to Employ if Your Building
is Converted

When a building is undergoing conversion from a rental building to cooperative or condominium ownership, the tenants often panic and do totally irrational things. The first thing to know is that you should be cool, calm, and collected if it should happen to you.

How does the typical conversion work? The scenario usually runs this way: The landlord of a rental building decides for any number of reasons that he does not want to be a landlord of this particular building anymore. He calculates that by selling the building back to the tenants who are already in residence he can get a higher price for it than if he sells it to another landlord. So, he submits a plan for conversion to the tenants. Normally, the plan is to convert the building to cooperative ownership, but every so often a condominium is done this way. The majority of condominium projects, however, are newly built and start life as condominiums, not as rentals.

Now comes the part where tenants panic. Some tenants have been renters all their lives and now they are faced with the choice of buying their apartments or (and this varies with state law) being forced to leave those apartments. To induce tenants to buy, landlords usually offer them an "insider's price," which is significantly below market value for that particular apartment. Typically, you should be able to get a discount of from 10 to 33% off market price. For example, if the market value of a two-bedroom apartment is $100,000 and the landlord offers it to the tenant at $40,000, the tenant could sell it after the building closes as a cooperative at the $100,000, thus making a profit of $60,000. That is the carrot that landlords hold out to tenants to induce them to buy.

However, and here is the problem, some tenants cannot afford the initial $40,000 they need to buy, so it is possible that they may be forced out of apartments that they have occupied for years. All the persuading in the world about the advantages of buying over renting will have no impact on somebody who can't buy in the first place. When people think that they are going to lose their homes because they may be evicted by a "greedy" landlord who wishes to change the status of their building, huge battles ensue. Sometimes landlords have to give all sorts of financial inducements to nonbuying tenants to get them to move. All of this, besides presenting some moral problems, is fodder for lawsuits and other legal actions.

If you find yourself in a conversion situation, what should you do? Well, as the preceding discussion indicates, you may have only two choices, either buy or move. (If you are a senior citizen or are handicapped, you may be allowed to stay on, but that is often determined by state law.) In any case, your first reaction should be the same whether or not you wish to buy: *get expert advice*. Hire an attorney to fight for your rights whether that means getting you the best price possible—if you want to buy—or keeping you from being evicted from your home—if you can't afford to purchase.

There is a third alternative. You might want to fight the cooperative plan and try to defeat it so that the building may remain a rental. Most buildings are eventually converted, however, but if that is the course of action you wish to pursue, hiring an attorney is again the proper response.

Some buildings hire an attorney as soon as a cooperative plan is announced. However, and this is important, this attorney is usually more interested in negotiating the best deal he can for the tenants who wish to buy than he is in working for the tenants who do not want to. Nonbuying tenants must then hire a different attorney to represent them. Then, if any fighting is to be done during the conversion process it can be restricted to the lawyers. Nevertheless, tenant factions inevitably develop, animosities among tenants and neighbors surface, and the building or buildings involved become battlegrounds.

Whether you wish to buy or not, one thing is certain: you must be positive that the attorney you do hire is a specialist in conversion problems and is fully conversant with the local laws as they apply to buying or nonbuying tenants. Also, make sure that you understand fully what your rights are and the time frames attached to those rights. Make sure that the attorney explains to you clearly all your options and their significances.

Once the attorney has been hired, be sure to attend all the meetings that will be held and become conversant with what the lawyer is doing for you *vis à vis* the landlord and the tenants. Only by knowing what is really going on will you be able to make informed choices.

AREAS OF DISAGREEMENT TO ANTICIPATE PRIOR TO CONVERSION

Buildings are rarely converted from rental to condominium or cooperative status without the tenants and the landlord getting involved in arguments concerning certain aspects of the conversion process. If your building is undergoing conversion, you can anticipate that one or more of the following areas will be the subject of a good deal of controversy before the conversion is complete.

1. *The Price of Individual Apartments.* This is the very heart of the conversion process. No matter how low the sponsor (or landlord) has pegged the apartments, some tenants will argue that the price of their particular apartment is too high.

2. *Reserve Fund.* Again, even if the sponsor has been generous, some tenants may argue that it is too low and they will ask that it be added to before they will buy their apartments.

3. *Physical Condition of the Buildings and Common Areas.* Tenants may require that certain work be done, such as putting on new roofs, fixing up lobbies, or installing fencing around a swimming pool before they will agree to purchase their apartments.

4. *Status of Tenants.* Some of the most heated disagreements occur over whether or not certain tenants will be forced out of their apartments if they don't buy, and what happens to senior citizens living on fixed incomes—must they buy? If not, what happens to them?

5. *Financing Arrangements.* In cooperative conversions, the controversy usually centers around the mortgages that the landlord put on the buildings, and when and under what conditions they will expire. In a condominium conversion the arguments normally concern the rate at which end loans have been arranged.

6. *The Sponsor.* Questions concerning the motives of the sponsor in converting are brought up, as are other related problems such as the sponsor's influence on the governing board after the building has been converted.

AGE AND CONDITION OF THE BUILDING

Whether or not you buy in a conversion should depend to a great extent on the age and condition of the building. After hiring an attorney, you should get your hands on a neutral engineering report which will give you accurate information as to the repairs and maintenance that must be done in the building. If extensive work must be done, the cost will come out of the owner-tenants' pockets. You can't realistically expect the former landlord to do any work on the building during the period of conversion.

FINANCIAL ARRANGEMENTS

Landlords who want to convert their buildings quickly and with as little fuss as possible may arrange financing for the tenants. Just as in the situation where a building is newly constructed and the developer arranges end loans, a converter can do the same. You may have to go out and get your own financing, but that should be determined by you before you make your buy decision. Even though you may be buying your apartment for a bargain price as an insider, you probably will still have to get financing (and because of the tax advantages, you may want to), and if you get it on your own the interest rate will be the prevalent rate at the time you apply for the financing.

PROBLEMS WITH THE LANDLORD

Landlords in conversion situations have been known to pull all sorts of shenanigans. Apartments will be left unrented, family members of the landlord will buy apartments, certain tenants may be acting as spies for the landlord, and other things are not that unusual. One of the reasons you hire a lawyer is to keep those things to a minimum, but be prepared to deal with these kinds of problems as well. You can almost bet that there will be some problem with the landlord before your building becomes totally converted. Normally, state laws or law enforcement officials should be looked to for guidance if the abuses get too flagrant.

Also, you and your fellow tenants may have to make up your minds whether or not you want to have the landlord as the managing agent of the building after conversion. Many landlords ask to remain on as managing agents, especially if they have owned the building for some period of time. You must remember, though, that as managing agents the old landlord may exercise a good deal of control over the building after it has been converted.

REASONS FOR BUYING AN APARTMENT IN A CONVERSION

If your building is being converted to either condominium or cooperative ownership from rental and you can afford to buy, you might want to consider the following reasons for buying.

1. You will probably be purchasing the apartment at below-market price.

2. If you do buy it at a price below market rate, you will have a built-in equity that has already accrued from the date of purchase. For example, if your apartment is sold to you as an insider for $50,000, and if you could sell it the day after you bought it for $75,000 (the market rate), you have accrued $25,000 worth of equity before you have made your first mortgage payment.

3. You can then use that built-up equity to obtain refinancing or a second mortgage, if you so desire.

4. The tax advantages outlined in Chapter 6.

5. Appreciation.

6. You don't have to go out on an apartment search, because you already live there. Therefore you are saving time and money.

7. You don't have to learn the ins and outs of a new location. Since you have probably been in residence for some period of time, you already know where all the stores, recreation facilities, and other amenities are.

QUESTIONS CONCERNING CONVERSION

1. Is the apartment being offered to you at 10–33% of its current market price?

2. Have you gotten together with your fellow tenants to hire an attorney?

3. Will a great deal of work have to be done to the building in terms of maintenance and rehabilitation?

4. Does the converter have a good reputation?

5. How is financing to be handled for those who want to buy?

6. Are a majority of the tenants buying?

15

Operating Fees:
What Are You Actually
Paying For?

Whether you intend to buy a condominium or a cooperative you will have a monthly charge that you will have to pay in addition to your mortgage or loan payments. This charge, called a homeowners' fee (in the case of a condominium) or maintenance (for a cooperative), goes toward paying all the expenses of the building or buildings that constitute the building complex. In the case of a condominium, expenses for all of the common elements would be included such as water, electricity, pool and lawn care, porters, doormen, security guards, and management fees.

As a general rule, homeowners' dues for a condominium apartment are less than they would be for a cooperative apartment. There is one very good reason for this: in a cooperative, real estate taxes and other local assessments (such as water and sewer charges) become part of the operating budget of the coop and must be paid out on a regular basis; therefore, they are included in the maintenance charge. In a condominium, on the other hand, real estate, water, and other utility taxes are paid individually by each homeowner.

Obviously, if you are buying a condominium apartment, you must add your taxes to your homeowners' fees to get your total cash outlay. When this is done, the costs of living in a condo and coop probably come much closer together on a monthly basis.

In cooperatives and condominiums, everyone shares expenses for the common areas on a percentage basis usually depending on the size of the particular apartment. That means that the five-room apartment owner will pay a higher monthly fee than will the owner of a three-room apartment.

All buildings—whether they are rental, condominium, or cooperative—must be run under a budget. One of the main duties of the operating board is to establish the budget for the building. The budget is normally drawn up at the beginning of the building's fiscal year, and monthly charges are raised during the year if budgetary constraints are not adhered to. However, many established condominium and cooperative buildings prefer to make singular assessments for large, one-time repair or maintenance jobs rather than to permanently increase the monthly fee. As mentioned in an earlier chapter, whether the monthly charge is raised or whether a one-time assessment is made depends on the management philosophy of the homeowners' association or board of directors.

If, for example, the building has had $50,000 worth of new wiring done and the bill is due, the people who run the building (your neighbors) may decide to assess everyone $200 (assuming 250 apartments) over and above their regular monthly charge, or they may decide to raise everyone's monthly charge $16.66, which would also bring in the $50,000 that they need. The difference here is that the $16.66 once added will probably never come off, and your monthly charge will have an additional $16.66 every month from now on. You can be pretty sure that once a raise in the monthly fee is established, it will not be rescinded.

As mentioned above, budgets and plans for the future are the chief responsibility of operating boards. If you plan to have a say in these matters, you will have to participate in the decision-making process by attending meetings and voting for elected representatives. If you would prefer to have an assessment rather than a permanent increase in your monthly charge, you must make sure that your voice and opinion are heard. Why would anyone choose an assessment over a maintenance increase?

One very good reason may be the salability of the apartment a few years hence. If the maintenance or homeowners' dues are comparatively low in relation to other similar apartments at that time, then an apartment in your complex may be much easier to sell than in one where the monthly charges are higher.

All condominium or cooperative projects will have established some kind of reserve for contingencies account. This is an account that they will dip into when large, unexpected expenses must be paid immediately. If, for instance, the roof of one of the buildings flies off in a tornado, the managers of the building are not going to wait for an insurance settlement to replace the roof; it will have to be done and paid for immediately. This is an example of an instance where the prudent use of the reserve fund is made. You would be wise to know how the operating board manages the reserve fund before you make your final buy decision. Some far-seeing boards are investing unused reserves in liquid securities, such as Treasury Bills or Certificates of Deposit, so that some profit may be made on what might otherwise be idle funds. Liquidity (or fast access to the money) is vital here. The money has to be readily accessible in an emergency, so boards of directors or managers should not get carried away with profit-making opportunities at the expense of safety and liquidity of the funds.

16

Dealing with the Operating Board

Unless you are moving into a new building where the operating board has not yet been formed, working with the board of directors (cooperative) or homeowner association (condominium) is very important. As was indicated in an earlier chapter, before you make your final decision about buying you should interview the board. Since the function of the board is to manage the property and thus to protect your investment, questions should be asked about how the property is maintained, what security is provided, and, most vitally, how budgets are established and whether or not they are adhered to strictly.

Operating boards are mini-businesses. They are running a building or a set of buildings for the owners or tenants, and unless the business is run well, the tenants and owners will be in big trouble.

In a cooperative, the board has broader powers than a condominium board does. A cooperative board can approve or disapprove a potential buyer while a condominium board has no such power.* Cooperative boards subject prospective owner-tenants to an inteview so that the individual or individuals buying the apartment can be "looked over." If you are to be interviewed by a cooperative board, ask them questions about their management philosophy. Good realtors and attorneys should know something about already formed boards and they should guide you through the interview process.

Often a professional management firm will be hired to run the buildings. However, if the board is conscientious they will not abdicate all of their responsibilities to the professional managers. The board hires the management firm and the management pros must report to the board periodically so the board can keep track of all that is going on.

THE COOPERATIVE BOARD INTERVIEW OF YOU AS A PROSPECTIVE TENANT-OWNER

If you are applying to purchase a cooperative apartment, your interview with the board can make or break the sale. Before you go in, get all the help you can from the real estate broker with whom you have

---

*Some states may vary in their approach to these matters because of differences in local laws, but on the whole, these statements apply.

been dealing. He or she should be able to tell you what to expect at the interview. Make sure you come armed with all the necessary paperwork that you will need, such as personal financial statements, letters of recommendation, and whatever else is required.

Dress conservatively and be on your best behavior during the interview. Make sure that you evidence a great interest in moving into the building and your chances of being accepted are therefore greater. Don't be afraid; only a very small percentage of people who meet all the financial qualifications for buying into a cooperative are turned down. If you have gotten this far in the process, it is doubtful that you will be rejected—unless you haven't bathed for six months.

What to Expect During an Interview

As just mentioned, if you are applying to buy a cooperative apartment, you will undoubtedly be subjected to an interview by the cooperative board of directors (or more likely, a committee of the board) before you are approved for purchase. You can expect to be asked questions in the following general areas.

1. *Your Lifestyle.*   For example, do you consistently throw loud parties? Do you expect a good number of visitors, especially at night? How large is your family? Will children visit frequently? Do you have pets? If so, what kind are they?

2. *Your Motives for Wanting to Buy.*   Questions such as: Who will actually be living in the apartment? Are you buying the apartment with the intention of selling it again very soon (known as "flipping")? I know from personal experience that some cooperative boards in New York City will turn down prospective owners who are purchasing the apartment for college-age children or, similarly, they will reject an individual who intends to flip his apartment.

3. *Your Finances and Your Profession.*   What is your income? Do you expect to receive regular raises? How long have you worked for your present employer? How is your credit rating? Does your work require you to travel a good deal?

4. *Your General Philosophy about Group Living.*   Do you think that you can fit in with others in this particular apartment complex? Can we expect you to participate in business meetings and elections?

The purpose of all this questioning, of course, is to see if you can afford to live in the apartment comfortably and whether or not you or your behavior or that of your friends might be a source of trouble within the complex as far as your neighbors are concerned.

You must realize that boards of directors of cooperative buildings see themselves as trendsetters and taste-makers for the complex. Since they have the power to accept or reject who their neighbors will be, they may well go overboard and if they don't like the "cut of your jib"—that is really all they need to reject you.

An excellent example of this is the famous case of former President Nixon, who wanted to purchase an apartment in New York City. Soon after his resignation, Mr. Nixon decided to move into a luxury cooperative apartment so he could be near his children and grandchildren. However, the board of directors of the building turned him down, ostensibly because of alleged concern about the number of journalists that would constantly be in and out of the building and because a special booth would have to be constructed in the lobby to house the former chief executive's Secret Service protection. Whether these were the true reasons for his turndown or not, only the board members of the building know, and they aren't talking. Some people speculate that his rejection may have been purely political. The important thing here is that the decision of the board stuck and President Nixon had to go elsewhere to find suitable lodgings.

Similarly, there are many documented cases of show business personalities, especially rock musicians of great wealth, being rejected because of the fear of loud parties, the kind of friends they might bring into the area, and drug problems. These are all very legitimate concerns to the tenant-owners of cooperative apartments, and so rejections in these situations are not uncommon.

In most states, a reason need not be given for rejection by the board of directors of a cooperative building. Lawsuits have been brought and the boards have won in *all* cases. But unless you are a former U.S. President or are a rock-and-roll star, you can be fairly sure that you will not be turned down by a cooperative board of directors; so relax and answer all their questions as fully as you know how.

17

The Contract of Sale

A contract is a legal instrument that embodies the written agreement between two or more people on any matter. The sales contract on a piece of real estate—including an apartment—is usually drawn up by the seller's attorney, who consults with the buyer's attorney. Most contracts of sale are fairly straightforward and contain the following clauses.

The understanding between the buyer and seller with regard to the final sales price, downpayment, and closing date.

The understanding between the parties as to the inclusion or exclusion of appliances and/or furnishings to remain in the apartment, if any.

Other items such as certain funds to be put into escrow pending the sale, and so on.

A specific spelling out of who is responsible for the payment of real estate taxes, at what time, and whether prior to or after the closing. This applies only to a condominium.

Never, under any circumstances, agree to any of the items mentioned above unless you get a written contract. All contracts for the sale of real estate must be in writing; no oral agreements between parties are binding.

Once the contract has been signed by the buyer and the seller, then the attorneys go ahead with preparing the rest of the paperwork that is needed and the closing is scheduled.

TIME IS OF THE ESSENCE CLAUSES

More and more contracts are being written with *time is of the essence* clauses in them. Such a clause binds the buyer to obtaining his or her financing and to closing the entire deal as of a certain date, therefore making the passage of time very important. Normally, a buyer will be given from 60 to 90 days to line up financing and to prepare for the closing.

Since a copy of the contract usually accompanies an application for financing, a time is of the essence clause forces the lender to make a quick decision and to speed up the paperwork process with regard to your application. If a time is of the essence clause is not included, some lenders have a tendency to drag their feet, therefore delaying the entire buying process.

There is nothing wrong with such a clause from the buyer's point of view, unless financing is just impossible to get. If that is not the case you might want to ask to have such a clause included in your contract, because you probably will be able to get your apartment that much sooner.

It should go without saying that you should read the contract very carefully before you sign it. Does it include the correct agreed upon price and down payment? Are all oral agreements made between you and the seller and between the two attorneys stated accurately in the contract? Obviously your attorney is responsible for the accuracy of the contract. However, if there has been a misunderstanding on something, you had better catch it before you sign the contract, otherwise you will be bound by the terms of the contract.

As mentioned earlier, a copy of the contract is to be included in the loan application paperwork. Therefore, the contract should be drawn as quickly as possible after an oral agreement to buy and sell has been reached.

Immediately following this chapter are two sample contracts of sale that have been approved by the Colorado Real Estate Commission for use in condominium sales in that state.

(RESIDENTIAL CONDOMINIUM)*
RESIDENTIAL CONTRACT TO BUY AND SELL REAL ESTATE
(Sellers Remedy Limited to Liquidated Damages)

The printed portions of this form approved by the Colorado Real Estate Commission. SC28-8-81 THIS IS A LEGAL INSTRUMENT. IF NOT UNDERSTOOD, LEGAL, TAX OR OTHER COUNSEL SHOULD BE CONSULTED BEFORE SIGNING.

_____ , 19 _____

1. The undersigned agent hereby acknowledges having received from _____

the sum of $ _____ , in the form of _____ , to be held by _____ ,

broker, in broker's escrow or trustee account, as earnest money and part payment for the following described real estate in the

County of _____ , Colorado, to-wit: Unit _____ ; Building _____ ;

_____ ;

according to the Map or Plat and Declaration thereof recorded in said county records, together with the interests, easements, rights and benefits appurtenant to the ownership of such Unit and together with all improvements thereon and all fixtures of a permanent nature currently on the premises except as hereinafter provided, in their present condition, ordinary wear and tear excepted, known as No. _____ , and hereinafter called the Property.

_____
(Street Address, City, Zip)

2. Subject to the provisions of pargraph 17, the undersigned person(s) _____

_____ (as joint tenants/tenants in common), hereinafter called Purchaser, hereby agree(s) to buy the Property, and the undersigned owner(s), hereinafter called Seller, hereby agree(s) to sell the Property upon the terms and conditions stated herein.

3. The purchase price shall be U.S. $ _____ , payable as follows: $ _____ hereby receipted for;

4. Price to include any of the following items currently in said Unit: lighting, heating, plumbing, ventilating, and central air conditioning fixtures; attached TV antennas and/or water softener (if owned by Seller); window and porch shades, venetian blinds, storm windows, storm doors, screens, curtain rods, drapery rods, attached mirrors, linoleum, floor tile, awnings, fireplace screen and grate, built-in kitchen appliances, wall-to-wall carpeting _____ ;

all in their present condition, conveyed free and clear of all taxes, liens and encumbrances except as provided in paragraph 11. Price shall also include use of the following parking facility(s): _____ ; and the following storage facility(s): _____

The following fixtures of a permanent nature within said Unit are excluded from this sale: _____ . Personal property shall be conveyed by bill of sale.

5. If a new loan is to be obtained by Purchaser from a third party, Purchaser agrees to promptly and diligently (a) apply for such loan, (b) execute all documents and furnish all information and documents required by the lender, and (c) pay the customary costs of obtaining such loan. Then if such loan is not approved on or before _____, 19 _____, or if so approved but is not available at time of closing, this contract shall be null and void and all payments and things of value received hereunder shall be returned to Purchaser.

6. If a note and trust deed or mortgage is to be assumed, Purchaser agrees to apply for a loan assumption if required and agrees to pay (1) a loan transfer fee not to exceed $ _____ and (2) an interest rate not to exceed _____ % per annum. If the loan to be assumed has provisions for a shared equity or variable interest rates or variable payments, this contract is conditioned upon the Purchaser reviewing and consenting to such provisions within _____ days after receipt of a copy of the loan documents containing such provisions. If the lender's consent to a loan assumption is required, this contract is expressly conditioned upon obtaining such consent without change in the terms and conditions of such loan except as herein provided.

7. If a note is to be made payable to Seller as partial or full payment of the purchase price, this contract shall not be assignable by Purchaser without written consent of Seller.

8. Cost of any appraisal for loan purposes to be obtained after this date shall be paid by _____ .

9. An abstract of title to the Property, certified to date, or a current commitment for title insurance policy in an amount equal to the purchase price, at Seller's option and expense, shall be furnished to Purchaser on or before _____, 19 _____ . If Seller elects to furnish said title insurance commitment, Seller will deliver the title insurance policy to Purchaser after closing and pay the premium thereon.

10. The date of closing shall be the date for delivery of deed as provided in paragraph 11. The hour and place of closing shall be as designated by _____

11. Title shall be merchantable in Seller, except as stated in this paragraph and in paragraph 12. Subject to payment or tender as above provided and compliance by Purchaser with the other terms and provisions hereof, Seller shall execute and deliver a good and sufficient _____ warranty deed to Purchaser on _____, 19 _____, or, by mutual agreement, at an earlier date, conveying the Property free and clear of all taxes, except the general taxes for the year of closing, and except _____ ; free and clear of all liens for special improvements installed as of the date of Purchaser's signature hereon, whether assessed or not; free and clear of all liens and encumbrances except

Contracts of Sale

131

except recorded and/or apparent easements for telephone, electricity, water, sanitary sewer, and easements for _____; and subject to the benefits and burdens of any Declaration of Covenants (hereinafter "Declaration"), Articles of Incorporation of the Owners' Association (hereinafter "Articles"), Bylaws of the Owners' Association (hereinafter "Bylaws"), and party wall agreements, except the following restrictive covenants which do not contain a forfeiture or reverter clause: _____ and subject to building and zoning regulations.

12. Except as stated in paragraph 11, if title is not merchantable and written notice of defect(s) is given by Purchaser or Purchaser's agent to Seller or Seller's agent on or before date of closing, Seller shall use reasonable effort to correct said defect(s) prior to date of closing. If Seller is unable to correct said defect(s) on or before date of closing, at Seller's option and upon written notice to Purchaser or Purchaser's agent on or before date of closing, the date of closing shall be extended thirty days for the purpose of correcting said defect(s). If title is not rendered merchantable as provided in this paragraph, at Purchaser's option, this contract shall be void and of no effect and each party hereto shall be released from all obligations hereunder and all payments and things of value received hereunder shall be returned to Purchaser.

13. Any encumbrance required to be paid may be paid at the time of settlement from the proceeds of this transaction or from any other source.

14. General taxes for the year of closing, based on the most recent levy and the most recent assessment, prepaid rents, water rents, sewer rents, FHA mortgage insurance premiums, interest on encumbrances, and current regular Condominium or Owners' Association assessments, if any; and _____ shall be apportioned to date of delivery of deed. Regular Condominium or Owners' Association assessments paid in advance shall be credited to Seller at the time of closing. Cash reserves held out of the regular Condominium or Owners' Association assessments for deferred maintenance by the Condominium or Owners' Association (hereinafter "Owners' Association") shall not be credited to Seller except as may be otherwise provided by the Declaration, Articles, or Bylaws. Any special assessment by the Owners' Association for improvements that have been installed as of the date of Purchaser's signature hereon shall be the obligation of Seller. Any other special assessment assessed prior to date of closing by the Owners' Association shall be the obligation of _____.

15. Possession of the Property shall be delivered to Purchaser on _____ subject to the following leases or tenancies: _____

If Seller fails to deliver possession on the date herein specified, Seller shall be subject to eviction and shall be liable for a daily rental of $ _____ until possession is delivered.

16. In the event the Property shall be damaged by fire or other casualty prior to time of closing, in an amount of not more than ten percent of the total purchase price, and in the event such damage is not or cannot be repaired within said time or if the damages exceed such sum, this contract may be terminated at the option of Purchaser, and all payments and things of value received hereunder shall be returned to Purchaser. Purchaser may elect to carry out this contract despite such damage. In that event, Purchaser shall be entitled to all the credit for the insurance proceeds resulting from damage to the Unit, not exceeding, however, the total purchase price. Should any fixtures or services fail between the date of this contract and the date of possession or the date of delivery of deed, whichever shall be earlier, then Seller shall be liable for the repair or replacement of such fixtures or services with a unit of similar size, age and quality, or an equivalent credit, but only to the extent that the maintenance or replacement of such fixtures or services is not the responsibility of the Owners' Association.

132

17. Time is of the essence hereof. If any note or check received as earnest money hereunder or any other payment due hereunder is not paid, honored or tendered when due, or if any other obligation hereunder is not performed as herein provided, there shall be the following remedies:

(a) IF SELLER IS IN DEFAULT, (1) Purchaser may elect to treat this contract as terminated, in which case all payments and things of value received hereunder shall be returned to Purchaser and Purchaser may recover such damages as may be proper, or (2) Purchaser may elect to treat this contract as being in full force and effect and Purchaser shall have the right to action for specific performance or damages, or both.

(b) IF PURCHASER IS IN DEFAULT, then all payments and things of value received hereunder shall be forfeited by Purchaser and retained on behalf of Seller and both parties shall thereafter be released from all obligations hereunder. It is agreed that such payments and things of value are LIQUIDATED DAMAGES and (except as provided in subparagraph (c)) are the SELLER'S SOLE AND ONLY REMEDY for the Purchaser's failure to perform the obligations of this contract. Seller expressly waives the remedies of specific performance and additional damages.

(c) Anything to the contrary herein notwithstanding, in the event of any litigation arising out of this contract, the court may award to the prevailing party all reasonable costs and expense, including attorneys' fees.

18. Purchaser and Seller agree that, in the event of any controversy regarding the earnest money held by broker, unless mutual written instruction is received by broker, broker shall not be required to take any action, but may await any proceeding, or at broker's option and discretion, may interplead any moneys or things of value into the court and may recover court costs and reasonable attorneys' fees.

19. Within five calendar days of the date this instrument becomes a contract between the parties, Seller agrees to deliver to Purchaser or Purchaser's agent a current copy of the Declaration, Articles, Bylaws and rules and regulations, if any. If Purchaser shall give written notice of disapproval of any of these documents to Seller or to Seller's agent within _____ calendar days (not less than 5) after receipt of such documents, this contract shall be terminated and all payments and things of value received hereunder shall be returned to Purchaser. If no such timely written notice of disapproval is given, Purchaser shall be deemed to have accepted and approved the terms of said documents, and Purchaser's right to terminate this contract pursuant to this paragraph 19 shall be waived.

20. Seller represents that the amount of the regular Owners' Association assessment is currently $ _____ per _____ and that there are no unpaid regular or special assessments against the Property except the current regular assessments and except _____ _____.

Such assessments are subject to change as provided in the Declaration, Articles, or By-Laws. Seller agrees to request, promptly and diligently, a statement of assessments against the Property, prepared and certified by the Board of Directors of the Owners' Association or its designated agent, and deliver said statement to Purchaser on or before time of closing unless not obtainable after due diligence. Any fees incident to the issuance of such statement of assessment shall be paid by _____.

21. If the Declaration, Articles, or By-Laws require written approval of the sale contemplated by this contract or waiver of right of first refusal, Seller shall, within seven calendar days of the date this instrument becomes a contract, request such approval and/or waiver as may be required and shall deliver it to Purchaser on or before time of closing. If Seller shall be unable to obtain such approval and/or waiver on or before _____, 19 ____, this contract shall be terminated and all payments and things of value received hereunder shall be returned to Purchaser. Purchaser agrees to cooperate with Seller in obtaining the approval and/or waiver and shall make available such information as the Owner's Association may reasonably require.

22. Additional provisions:

Contracts of Sale (*Continued*)

23. If this proposal is accepted by Seller in writing and Purchaser receives notice of such acceptance on or before _____, 19 ____, this instrument shall become a contract between Seller and Purchaser and shall inure to the benefit of the heirs, successors and assigns of such parties, except as stated in paragraph 7.

Purchaser _____   Date _____

Broker _____

By: _____

Purchaser _____   Date _____

Purchaser's Address _____

(The following section to be completed by Seller and Listing Agent)

24. Seller accepts the above proposal this ____ day of _____, 19 ____, and agrees to pay a commission of ____ % of the purchase price for services in this transaction, and agrees that, in the event of forfeiture of payments and things of value received hereunder, such payments and things of value shall be divided between listing broker and Seller, one-half thereof to said broker, but not to exceed the commission, and the balance to Seller.

_____   _____

Seller _____

Seller's Address _____

Listing Broker's name and address _____

* This form may also be used for the sale of Townhouses, Planned Unit Developments and other residential building groups involving ownership of common elements.

(RESIDENTIAL CONDOMINIUM)*
CONTRACT TO BUY AND SELL REAL ESTATE

(Remedies Include Specific Performance)

The printed portions of this form approved by the Colorado Real Estate Commission. SC 29-9-81

THIS IS A LEGAL INSTRUMENT. IF NOT UNDERSTOOD, LEGAL, TAX OR OTHER COUNSEL SHOULD BE CONSULTED BEFORE SIGNING.

_____ , 19 _____

1. The undersigned agent hereby acknowledges having received from _____

_____ the sum of $ _____ ;

in the form of _____ , to be held by _____

_____ , broker, in broker's escrow or trustee account, as earnest money and part payment for the following described real estate in the

County of _____ , Colorado, to-wit: Unit _____ ; Building _____ ;

according to the Map or Plat and Declaration thereof recorded in said county records, together with the interests, easements, rights and benefits appurtenant to the ownership of such Unit and together with all appurtenant improvements and fixtures of a permanent nature, except as hereinafter provided, in their present condition, ordinary wear and tear excepted, known as No. _____ and hereinafter called the Property.

_____
(Street Address, City, Zip)

2. The undersigned person(s) _____

_____ (as joint tenants/tenants in common), hereinafter called Purchaser, hereby agree(s) to buy the Property, and the undersigned owner(s), hereinafter called Seller, hereby agree(s) to sell the Property upon the terms and conditions stated herein.

3. The purchase price shall be U.S. $ _____ , payable as follows: $ _____ hereby receipted for;

4. Price to include any of the following items currently in said Unit: lighting, heating, plumbing, ventilating, and central air conditioning fixtures; attached TV antennas and/or water softener (if owned by Seller); window and porch shades, venetian blinds, storm windows, storm doors, screens, curtain rods, drapery rods, attached mirrors, linoleum, floor tile, awnings, fireplace screen and grate, built-in kitchen appliances, wall-to-wall carpeting _____

all in their present condition, conveyed free and clear of all taxes, liens and encumbrances except as provided in paragraph 11. Price shall also include use of the following parking facility(s): _____ ; and the following storage facility(s): _____

_____ . The following fixtures of a permanent nature within said Unit are excluded from this sale: _____

Contracts of Sale *(Continued)*

135

. Personal property shall be conveyed by bill of sale.

5. If a new loan is to be obtained by Purchaser from a third party, Purchaser agrees to promptly and diligently (a) apply for such loan, (b) execute all documents and furnish all information and documents required by the lender, and (c) pay the customary costs of obtaining such loan. Then if such loan is not approved on or before _____, 19 ____, or if so approved but is not available at time of closing, this contract shall be null and void and all payments and things of value received hereunder shall be returned to Purchaser.

6. If a note and trust deed or mortgage is to be assumed, Purchaser agrees to apply for a loan assumption if required and agrees to pay (1) a loan transfer fee not to exceed $ _____ and (2) an interest rate not to exceed _____ % per annum. If the loan to be assumed has provisions for a shared equity or variable interest rates or variable payments, this contract is conditioned upon the Purchaser reviewing and consenting to such provisions within _____ days after receipt of a copy of the loan documents containing such provisions. If the lender's consent to a loan assumption is required, this contract is expressly conditioned upon obtaining such consent without change in the terms and conditions of such loan except as herein provided.

7. If a note is to be made payable to Seller as partial or full payment of the purchase price, this contract shall not be assignable by Purchaser without written consent of Seller.

8. Cost of any appraisal for loan purposes to be obtained after this date shall be paid by _____.

9. An abstract of title to the Property, certified to date, or a current commitment for title insurance policy in an amount equal to the purchase price, at Seller's option and expense, shall be furnished to Purchaser on or before _____, 19 ____. If Seller elects to furnish said title insurance commitment, Seller will deliver the title insurance policy to Purchaser after closing and pay the premium thereon.

10. The date of closing shall be the date for delivery of deed as provided in paragraph 11. The hour and place of closing shall be as designated by _____.

11. Title shall be merchantable in Seller, except as stated in this paragraph and in paragraph 12. Subject to payment or tender as above provided and compliance by Purchaser with the other terms and provisions hereof, Seller shall execute and deliver a good and sufficient _____ warranty deed to Purchaser on _____, 19 ____, or, by mutual agreement, at an earlier date, conveying the Property free and clear of all taxes, except the general taxes for the year of closing, and except _____ ; free and clear of all liens for special improvements installed as of the date of Purchaser's signature hereon, whether assessed or not; free and clear of all liens and encumbrances except _____ ; subject to the benefits and burdens of any Declaration of Covenants (hereinafter "Declaration"), Articles of Incorporation of the Owners' Association (hereinafter "Articles"), Bylaws of the Owners' Association (hereinafter "Bylaws"), and party wall agreements; except the following restrictive covenants which do not contain a forfeiture or reverter clause: _____

except recorded and/or apparent easements for telephone, electricity, water, sanitary sewer, and easements for _____

12. Except as stated in paragraph 11, if title is not merchantable and written notice of defect(s) is given by Purchaser or Purchaser's agent to Seller or Seller's agent on or before date of closing, Seller shall use reasonable effort to correct said defect(s) prior to date of closing. If Seller is unable to correct said defect(s) on or before date of closing, at Seller's option and upon written notice to Purchaser or Purchaser's agent on or before date of closing, the date of closing shall be extended thirty days for the purpose of correcting said defect(s). If title is not rendered merchantable as provided in this paragraph, at Purchaser's option, this contract shall be void and of no effect and each party hereto shall be released from all obligations hereunder and all payments and things of value received hereunder shall be returned to Purchaser.

13. Any encumbrance required to be paid may be paid at the time of settlement from the proceeds of this transaction or from any other source.

14. General taxes for the year of closing, based on the most recent levy and the most recent assessment, prepaid rents, water rents, sewer rents, FHA mortgage insurance premiums, interest on encumbrances, and current regular Condominium or Owners' Association assessments, if any; and _____ shall be apportioned to date of delivery of deed. Regular Condominium or Owners' Association assessments paid in advance shall be credited to Seller at the time of closing. Cash reserves held out of the regular Condominium or Owners' Association assessments for deferred maintenance by the Condominium or Owners' Association (hereinafter "Owners' Association") shall not be credited to Seller except as may be otherwise provided by the Declaration, Articles, or Bylaws. Any special assessment by the Owners' Association for improvements that have been installed as of the date of Purchaser's signature hereon shall be the obligation of Seller. Any other special assessment assessed prior to date of closing by the Owners' Association shall be the obligation of _____ .

15. Possession of the Property shall be delivered to Purchaser on _____ subject to the following leases or tenancies:

_____

If Seller fails to deliver possession on the date herein specified, Seller shall be subject to eviction and shall be liable for a daily rental of $_____ until possession is delivered.

16. In the event the Property shall be damaged by fire or other casualty prior to time of closing, in an amount of not more than ten percent of the total purchase price, and in the event such damage is not or cannot be repaired within said time or if the damages exceed such sum, this contract may be terminated at the option of Purchaser, and all payments and things of value received hereunder shall be returned to Purchaser. Purchaser may elect to carry out this contract despite such damage. In that event, Purchaser shall be entitled to all the credit for the insurance proceeds resulting from damage to the Unit, not exceeding, however, the total purchase price. Should any fixtures or services in said Unit fail between the date of this contract and the date of possession or the date of delivery of deed, whichever shall be earlier, then Seller shall be liable for the repair or replacement of such fixtures or services with a unit of similar size, age and quality, or an equivalent credit, but only to the extent that the maintenance or replacement of such fixtures or services is not the responsibility of the Owners' Association.

17. Time is of the essence hereof. If any note or check received as earnest money hereunder or any other payment due hereunder is not paid, honored or tendered when due, or if any other obligation hereunder is not performed as herein provided, there shall be the following remedies:

(a) IF SELLER IS IN DEFAULT, (1) Purchaser may elect to treat this contract as terminated, in which case all payments and things of value received hereunder shall be returned to Purchaser and Purchaser may recover such damages as may be proper, or (2) Purchaser may elect to treat

and subject to building and zoning regulations.

this contract as being in full force and effect and Purchaser shall have the right to an action for specific performance or damages, or both.

(b) IF PURCHASER IS IN DEFAULT, (1) Seller may elect to treat this contract as terminated, in which case all payments and things of value received hereunder shall be forfeited and retained on behalf of Seller and Seller may recover such damages as may be proper, or (2) Seller may elect to treat this contract as being in full force and effect and Seller shall have the right to an action for specific performance or damages, or both.

(c) Anything to the contrary herein notwithstanding, in the event of any litigation arising out of this contract, the court may award to the prevailing party all reasonable costs and expense, including attorneys' fees.

18. Purchaser and Seller agree that, in the event of any controversy regarding the earnest money held by broker, unless mutual written instruction is received by broker, broker shall not be required to take any action, but may await any proceeding, or at broker's option and discretion, may interplead any moneys or things of value into the court and may recover court costs and reasonable attorneys' fees.

19. Within five calendar days of the date this instrument becomes a contract between the parties, Seller agrees to deliver to Purchaser or Purchaser's agent a current copy of the Declaration, Articles, Bylaws and rules and regulations, if any. If Purchaser shall give written notice of disapproval of any of these documents to Seller or to Seller's agent within _____ calendar days (not less than 5) after receipt of such documents, this contract shall be terminated and all payments and things of value received hereunder shall be returned to Purchaser. If no such timely written notice of disapproval is given, Purchaser shall be deemed to have accepted and approved the terms of said documents, and Purchaser's right to terminate this contract pursuant to this paragraph 19 shall be waived.

20. Seller represents that the amount of the regular Owners' Association assessment is currently $ _____ per _____ and that there are no unpaid regular or special assessments against the Property except the current regular assessments and except _____

_____

Such assessments are subject to change as provided in the Declaration, Articles, or By-Laws. Seller agrees to request, promptly and diligently, a statement of assessments against the Property, prepared and certified by the Board of Directors of the Owners' Association or its designated agent, and deliver said statement to Purchaser on or before time of closing unless not obtainable after due diligence. Any fees incident to the issuance of such statement of assessment shall be paid by _____

21. If the Declaration, Articles, or By-Laws require written approval of the sale contemplated by this contract or waiver of right of first refusal, Seller shall, within seven calendar days of the date this instrument becomes a contract, request such approval and/or waiver as may be required and shall deliver it to Purchaser on or before time of closing. If Seller shall be unable to obtain such approval and/or waiver on or before _____, 19 _____ , this contract shall be terminated and all payments and things of value received hereunder shall be returned to Purchaser. Purchaser agrees to cooperate with Seller in obtaining the approval and/or waiver and shall make available such information as the Owner's Association may reasonably require.

22. Additional provisions:

23. If this proposal is accepted by Seller in writing and Purchaser receives notice of such acceptance on or before _____ , 19 ____ , this instrument shall become a contract between Seller and Purchaser and shall inure to the benefit of the heirs, successors and assigns of such parties, except as stated in paragraph 7.

_____   Broker   _____
Purchaser   Date

_____   By: _____
Purchaser   Date

_____
Purchaser's Address

(The following section to be completed by Seller and Listing Agent)

24. Seller accepts the above proposal this _____ day of _____ , 19 ____ , and agrees to pay a commission of _____ % of the purchase price for services in this transaction, and agrees that, in the event of forfeiture of payments and things of value received hereunder, such payments and things of value shall be divided between listing broker and Seller, one-half thereof to said broker, but not to exceed the commission, and the balance to Seller.

_____   _____
                                                             Seller

_____
Seller's Address

Listing Broker's name and address _____
* This form may also be used for the sale of Townhouses, Planned Unit Developments and other residential building groups involving ownership of common elements.

Contracts of Sale *(Continued)*

18

The Closing: What to Expect

The closing or settlement meeting as it is sometimes called is the culmination of all your work and analysis. It is at the closing that the apartment actually becomes yours. At this point, the rest of the downpayment is made (assuming that you paid 10% on final offer) and the mortgage or loan is signed by you. Depending on the type of apartment you are acquiring, either a deed (condominium) or a stock certificate (cooperative) will also be signed, and other paperwork relevant to the passing of title will be taken care of. Also, if you are buying a condominium, a completed title search on the apartment will have been undertaken and you will get a copy of the search documents as well.

You had better have a full checking account when you go into the closing because you will be writing a lot of checks. For example, at the closing you will have to pay your attorney as well as any applicable survey or appraisal fees. There may be some recording and notarizing fees (depending on state law), credit report charges, and of course the lender's service charge (points), which will have to be settled at the closing. Because you will have to make all of these payments at one time, you should know exactly what all of these charges are going to be prior to the closing. You and your attorney should get together a few days prior to the closing to go over all the costs and procedures.

If you are getting a mortgage, lenders are required by federal law to send you an estimate of closing costs that are associated with the loan. Make sure that it is comprehensive. You might be wise to check with the lender before the date of closing to make sure that all figures given are totally accurate.

There may be some other expenses that may have to be taken care of at the closing, such as property taxes and insurance that might be transferred to you by the prior owner of the apartment.

DETAILS OF CLOSING COSTS

First-time home buyers are often surprised at the amount of money and time required to be spent on a closing. What follows are specific details on what you can expect at a closing. This information is keyed into worksheets reproduced from a booklet issued by the federal government entitled *Settlement Costs—A H.U.D. Guide*, published by the Office of Consumer Affairs and Regulatory Functions of the U.S.

Department of Housing and Urban Development. These worksheets follow this chapter.

You may be able to shop around for closing services. Although many vendors will charge similar fees in the same locale, you probably will be able to save money by comparison shopping. Obviously you should try to get the best service for the least money but remember—you are purchasing an apartment, not a loaf of bread. Don't sacrifice quality for price.

What is reproduced on pages 149–155 is the Uniform Settlement Statement developed by the Department of Housing and Urban Development for government-backed loans (such as VA and FHA mortgages), and it will be used here for illustrative purposes. If you follow the statement through step by step, you will know exactly what your costs of settlement will be before you walk into the closing room. Although this exact statement may not be used in your particular closing, a similar document may be used. Explanations made here will follow the section letters and numbers assigned to the Uniform Settlement Statement.

Pay particular attention to the first two pages of the settlement statement. There, in sections J and K, you are provided with a summary of all funds transferred or to be transferred between the buyer and the seller. The final line at the bottom of the second page is the important line. The left-hand column specifies the total net cash that must be paid by you, the borrower, while the right-hand column details the total cash due to the seller.

Section L of the form sets out a list of settlement services that "may be required and for which you may be charged." Those services with their appropriate numbers will be detailed now.

Typical Settlement Services

The first item in section L—700—refers to the sales commission due to the selling broker. That commission is paid by the seller in most cases. However, if you have hired a buying broker you might have to pay any balance due at this time. If no broker of any kind was used, obviously no commission is due. Selling brokers normally are paid in full at the closing.

Items 701–702 provide for the situation in which two or more selling brokers share the commission, as occurs where there is a multiple listing. What normally happens is that the listing broker takes a percentage of the commission and the broker who actually consummated the deal also takes a percentage.

Item 703 refers to an amount due and payable if part of the commission has already been paid. Occasionally, the earnest money that you pay to the seller at the time of signing the contract is retained by the broker as an advance on his or her commission. If that is in fact the case, the remainder of the commission is now due and payable.

Items 800–807 are for items payable in connection with the mortgage or loan you have obtained. One word here: Obviously, you can't change lenders at this point, but you may be able to negotiate with your lender on closing costs. Don't just accept the lender's list of charges for the closing; try to get a better deal for yourself, if possible.

Item 801 is the *loan origination fee*. All lenders will charge you a fee for the paperwork that they must do in connection with the loan; this is known as the loan origination fee. The amount of the fee is traditionally a percentage of the total loan granted. For example, if you have obtained a $50,000 loan or mortgage and the loan origination fee is 2% (not at all untypical) you would have to lay out an additional $1,000 for that service.

Item 802, the *loan discount* (or as it is sometimes called, *points*), is a similar one-time charge that the lender uses "to adjust the yield on the loan to what market conditions demand." Therefore, if you haven't locked in your interest rate commitment prior to closing, it will be locked in as of that date. Often, loans are given with an interest rate to be determined on the date of closing.

Normally, each point is equal to 1% of the loan. If you are granted a mortgage of $40,000 with three points, that means you must pay an additional 3% at the closing, or $1,200.

Item 803 is the *appraisal fee*. Every mortgage or loan backed by real property must be appraised as to its actual worth for collateral purposes. Usually the lender provides the appraiser and the buyer has to pay for the appraiser's services. These charges vary from locale to locale.

Item 804 is the *credit report fee*. As discussed elsewhere, the lender will undoubtedly run a credit check on you, and obtaining that report costs money. Normally the costs of a credit report are not large. Nevertheless, you are responsible for paying the fee to the lender no matter how large or small.

If you are buying an apartment in a newly built complex you may be subject to item 805, a *lender's inspection fee*. The loan officer may wish to go out to the construction site to check out the apartment in person. This will be in addition to an appraisal in most cases. This is normally a nominal charge.

Item 806 only comes into play if you purchase what is called private mortgage insurance, or mortgage insurance not provided by an insurer who normally works with your lender.

Item 807—an *assumption fee*—is a fee that the lender charges if you are assuming the seller's mortgage. You are essentially paying for the processing of the paperwork involved.

Advance Payments—Items 901–903

At the closing you will undoubtedly have to make some payments in advance for services for which you are obligated as a new owner.

Item 901 covers interest. Lenders usually require that borrowers pay at settlement the interest that will accrue on the mortgage from the date of closing to the beginning of the initial period covered by the first monthly mortgage payment. Thus, assume your closing takes place on September 16 and your first monthly mortgage payment is due November 1. You are responsible for paying interest (not principal) for the month of October. You must give a check to the lender for that interest payment at closing.

Item 902 is the *mortgage insurance*. Mortgage insurance, as distinguished from credit life insurance, protects the lender from any possible default on the mortgage by you. Often lenders will ask for you to pay the first premium payment at the closing. Credit life insurance is insurance you, the buyer, will be required to purchase. That insurance will protect your heirs from having to pay off the mortgage in the event of your death. However, item 902 refers to mortgage insurance, not credit insurance.

Even though *homeowners' insurance* (item 903) is bought by you as a separate item, you will most assuredly have to name the lender as a cobeneficiary of the policy. If your apartment is destroyed by fire, the lender has lost his collateral. Usually the lender requests that the buyer pay the first year's premium in advance at the time of the closing. If so, enter this amount on line 903.

Escrow Account—Items 1001–1005

When you receive a mortgage from a lender and you begin paying it off each month, not all of your payment goes to paying off the interest and principal of the loan. Part is also put into an escrow account. The escrow account is held by the lender to assure the payment of periodically recurring expenses, such as real estate taxes. Part of the lender's service (especially if it is a bank) is to pay your taxes for you. That way you are not billed directly by the local taxing authority; the bank remits the proper amount when due.

Item 1001 is *homeowners' insurance premiums*. Some lenders require that homeowner premiums be paid out of the escrow account. If so, any amount so required would be entered on line 1001.

If the lender requires that mortgage insurance (item 1002) be paid out of escrow, you would again enter the appropriate amount on line 1002.

Items 1003–1004 are the lines set aside for city and county taxes that will undoubtedly be due on a periodic basis. Here you enter the amounts assigned by the lender in the escrow account toward the payments of these taxes. The proper amounts should be indicated on your monthly mortgage statement.

Item 1005 is *annual assessments*. This is particularly applicable to condominium and cooperative apartment owners. You might be asked by your lender to make a contribution to the escrow account to cover any assessments that the condominium or cooperative governing board may require you to make once you are in residence. For example, if a large capital improvement is necessary, such as a new roof or new electric wiring, the reserve fund of the condominium or cooperative may not be enough to cover the cost. In that case, each owner will be asked to pay an assessment of a certain amount to pay for the work to be done. This is over and above the monthly charge that you normally make.

Title Charges—Items 1100–1110

Condominium owners will be subject to most of the charges to be detailed in this section. Cooperative buyers, on the other hand, will encounter fewer of these charges because no title needs to be searched in a cooperative apartment; shares in an apartment corporation change hands on a sale, not a deed and title as in the case of a condominium.

Item 1101 is the *settlement fee*. You can expect a bill for setting up the closing for anywhere between $200 and $400. This is a separate fee that you pay to the settlement agent, who may be an attorney, the bank, or a real estate broker.

Item 1102 is the *title search*. When real property changes hands, the history of ownership must be researched so that all parties to the transaction are sure that the buyer is getting what is called "clear title" to the property. The searcher of the title is looking for liens or any other legal actions that might have been filed against a previous owner.

Although uncommon, from time to time a *document preparation fee* (1103) will be added to a list of closing costs. If it is to be paid, it covers the cost of preparing the mortgage, note, and/or deed. Normally, however, these documents are prepared free of charge by the lender's staff or by your attorney.

Item 1106, the *notary fee*, if levied at all, is for the legal affixing of a notary public's signature on the various documents to authenticate them. In point of fact, there is normally someone available to do this right at the closing—either one of the attorneys, the real estate brokers, or a member of their staff who performs this function. A separate fee is ordinarily not required.

The *attorney's fee* (1107), however, is a different matter. If you use an attorney (see Chapter 11), you must pay your attorney any balance still owed at the time of the closing. Depending on the part of the country in which you are located, expect attorney fees to average between $500 and $1000 for the closing and all the work that must be done to prepare for it.

Items 1108–1110 are for *title insurance*. If you refer to the discussion under item 1102 (title search), it was noted that the purpose of a title search was to look for any defects in title which might prevent you from getting full legal ownership of the property. Title insurance protects you and the lender in case a mistake was made and you are sued by a previous owner who claims you do not have clear title. The cost of title insurance is minimal, and it is a one-time premium that must be paid.

Other Charges

There may be some other closing charges as well as the ones already mentioned, such as recording and transfer taxes or a tax stamp fee. But your attorney or real estate broker will apprise you of these prior to the closing.

Finally, all these charges are added together and the total is entered on line 1400 of the worksheet. That figure then is transferred to line 103 of Section J.

QUESTIONS CONCERNING CLOSING COSTS

1. Do you know all the expenses that you will have on the day of the closing?
2. Have you met with your lawyer to go over closing procedures and expenses?
3. Have you received a final list of closing charges from the lender?
4. Have you checked with the seller's attorney to see if there are any last-minute problems on their side?
5. Do you have enough money in your checking account to cover all closing expenses?

A.

U. S. DEPARTMENT OF HOUSING AND URBAN DEVELOPMENT

SETTLEMENT STATEMENT

B. TYPE OF LOAN
1. ☐ FHA   2. ☐ FmHA   3. ☐ CONV. UNINS.
4. ☐ VA   5. ☐ CONV. INS.
6. File Number: 7. Loan Number:
8. Mortgage Insurance Case Number:

C. **NOTE:** *This form is furnished to give you a statement of actual settlement costs. Amounts paid to and by the settlement agent are shown. Items marked "(p.o.c.)" were paid outside the closing; they are shown here for informational purposes and are not included in the totals.*

D. NAME OF BORROWER:	E. NAME OF SELLER:	F. NAME OF LENDER:

G. PROPERTY LOCATION:	H. SETTLEMENT AGENT:	
	PLACE OF SETTLEMENT:	I. SETTLEMENT DATE:

J. SUMMARY OF BORROWER'S TRANSACTION	
100. GROSS AMOUNT DUE FROM BORROWER.	
101. Contract sales price	
102. Personal property	
103. Settlement charges to borrower *(line 1400)*	
104.	
105.	
Adjustments for items paid by seller in advance	
106. City/town taxes	to	
107. County taxes	to	
108. Assessments	to	

K. SUMMARY OF SELLER'S TRANSACTION	
400. GROSS AMOUNT DUE TO SELLER:	
401. Contract sales price	
402. Personal property	
403	
404.	
405.	
Adjustments for items paid by seller in advance	
406. City/town taxes	to	
407. County taxes	to	
408. Assessments	to	

Settlement Statement

(Form Continues on Next Page)

109.	
110.	
111.	
112.	
120.	GROSS AMOUNT DUE FROM BORROWER

200. AMOUNTS PAID BY OR IN BEHALF OF BORROWER:

201.	Deposit or earnest money	
202.	Principal amount of new loan(s)	
203.	Existing loan(s) taken subject to	
204.		
205.		
206.		
207.		
208.		
209.		

Adjustments for items unpaid by seller

210.	City/town taxes	to	
211.	County taxes	to	
212.	Assessments	to	
213.		
214.		
215.		
216.		
217.		
218.		
219.		
220.	TOTAL PAID BY/FOR BORROWER	

300. CASH AT SETTLEMENT FROM/TO BORROWER

301.	Gross amount due from borrower (line 120)	
302.	Less amounts paid by/for borrower (line 220)	( )
303.	CASH (□ FROM) (□ TO) BORROWER	

409.	
410.	
411.	
412.	
420.	GROSS AMOUNT DUE TO SELLER

500. REDUCTIONS IN AMOUNT DUE TO SELLER:

501.	Excess deposit (see instructions)	
502.	Settlement charges to seller (line 1400)	
503.	Existing loan(s) taken subject to	
504.	Payoff of first mortgage loan	
505.	Payoff of second mortgage loan	
506.		
507.		
508.		
509.		

Adjustments for items unpaid by seller

510.	City/town taxes	to	
511.	County taxes	to	
512.	Assessments	to	
513.		
514.		
515.		
516.		
517.		
518.		
519.		
520.	TOTAL REDUCTION AMOUNT DUE SELLER	

600. CASH AT SETTLEMENT TO/FROM SELLER

601.	Gross amount due to seller (line 420)	
602.	Less reductions in amount due seller (line 520)	( )
603.	CASH (□ TO) (□ FROM) SELLER	

(Back of Form Continued on Next Page)

L. SETTLEMENT CHARGES

	PAID FROM BORROWER'S FUNDS AT SETTLEMENT	PAID FROM SELLER'S FUNDS AT SETTLEMENT
700. TOTAL SALES/BROKER'S COMMISSION *based on price $* @ % =		
Division of Commission (line 700) as follows:		
701. $ to		
702. $ to		
703. Commission paid at Settlement		
704.		
800. ITEMS PAYABLE IN CONNECTION WITH LOAN		
801. Loan Origination Fee %		
802. Loan Discount %		
803. Appraisal Fee to		
804. Credit Report to		
805. Lender's Inspection Fee		
806. Mortgage Insurance Application Fee to		
807. Assumption Fee		
808.		
809.		
810.		
811.		
900. ITEMS REQUIRED BY LENDER TO BE PAID IN ADVANCE		
901. Interest from to @ $ /day		
902. Mortgage Insurance Premium for months to		
903. Hazard Insurance Premium for years to		
904. years to		
905.		
1000. RESERVES DEPOSITED WITH LENDER		
1001. Hazard insurance months @ $ per month		
1002. Mortgage insurance months @ $ per month		
1003. City property taxes months @ $ per month		
1004. County property taxes months @ $ per month		
1005. Annual assessments months @ $ per month		
1006. months @ $ per month		
1007. months @ $ per month		

(Form Continues on Next Page)

Settlement Statement *(Continued)*

1008. _____ months @ $ _____ per month

1100. TITLE CHARGES

1101.	Settlement or closing fee	to
1102.	Abstract or title search	to
1103.	Title examination	to
1104.	Title insurance binder	to
1105.	Document preparation	to
1106.	Notary fees	to
1107.	Attorney's fees	to

(includes above items numbers;)

| 1108. | Title insurance | to |

(includes above items numbers;)

1109.	Lender's coverage	$
1110.	Owner's coverage	$
1111.		
1112.		
1113.		

1200. GOVERNMENT RECORDING AND TRANSFER CHARGES

1201.	Recording fees: Deed $; Mortgage $; Releases $
1202.	City/county tax/stamps: Deed $; Mortgage $
1203.	State tax/stamps: Deed $; Mortgage $
1204.	
1205.	

1300. ADDITIONAL SETTLEMENT CHARGES

1301.	Survey	to
1302.	Pest inspection	to
1303.		
1304.		
1305.		

1400. TOTAL SETTLEMENT CHARGES (enter on lines 103, Section J and 502, Section K)

HUD-1 Rev. 5/76

SETTLEMENT COSTS WORK SHEET (*Use this worksheet to compare the charges of various lenders and providers of settlement services.*)

	PROVIDER 1	PROVIDER 2	PROVIDER 3
800. ITEMS PAYABLE IN CONNECTION WITH LOAN			
801. Loan Origination Fee %			
802. Loan Discount %			
803. Appraisal Fee to			
804. Credit Report to			
805. Lender's Inspection Fee			
806. Mortgage Insurance Application Fee to			
807. Assumption Fee			
808.			
809.			
810.			
811.			
900. ITEMS REQUIRED BY LENDER TO BE PAID IN ADVANCE			
901. Interest from to @ $ 'day			
902. Mortgage Insurance Premium for months to			
903. Hazard Insurance Premium for years to			
904. years to			
905.			
1000. RESERVES DEPOSITED WITH LENDER			
1001. Hazard insurance months @ $ per month			
1002. Mortgage insurance months @ $ per month			
1003. City property taxes months @ $ per month			
1004. County property taxes months @ $ per month			
1005. Annual assessments months @ $ per month			
1006. months @ $ per month			
1007. months @ $ per month			
1008. months @ $ per month			

(Form Continues on Next Page)

Settlement Statement (*Continued*)

153

1100. TITLE CHARGES

1101.	Settlement or closing fee	to			
1102.	Abstract or title search	to			
1103.	Title examination	to			
1104.	Title insurance binder	to			
1105.	Document preparation	to			
1106.	Notary fees	to			
1107.	Attorney's fees	to			
	(includes above items numbers;				
1108.	Title insurance	to			
	(includes above items numbers;				
1109.	Lender's coverage	$			
1110.	Owner's coverage	$			
1111.					
1112.					
1113.					

1200. GOVERNMENT RECORDING AND TRANSFER CHARGES

1201.	Recording fees: Deed $	; Mortgage $	; Releases $		
1202.	City/county tax/stamps: Deed $	; Mortgage $			
1203.	State tax/stamps: Deed $	; Mortgage $			
1204.					
1205.					

1300. ADDITIONAL SETTLEMENT CHARGES

1301.	Survey	to			
1302.	Pest inspection	to			
1303.					
1304.					
1305.					

| 1400. TOTAL SETTLEMENT CHARGES *(enter on lines 103, Section J and 502, Section K)* | | |

Settlement Statement *(Continued)*

CALCULATING THE BORROWER'S TRANSACTIONS

A Sample Worksheet

This page is a sample worksheet for a family purchasing a $35,000 house and getting a new $30,000 loan. Line 103 assumes that their total settlement charges are $1,000. (This figure is the sum of all the individual settlement charges, which will be listed in detail in Section L, of their Uniform Settlement Statement.) The $1,000 figure is merely illustrative. The amount may be higher in some areas and for some types of transactions, and lower for others.

J. SUMMARY OF BORROWER'S TRANSACTION	
100. GROSS AMOUNT DUE FROM BORROWER:	
101. Contract sales price	35,000.00
102. Personal property	200.00
103. Settlement charges to borrower *(line 1400)*	1,000.00
104.	
105.	
Adjustments for items paid by seller in advance	
106. City/town taxes to	
107. County taxes to	
108. Assessments 6/30 to 7/31 (owners assn)	20.00
109. Fuel oil 25 to gal. @.50/gal	12.50
110.	
111.	
112.	
120. **GROSS AMOUNT DUE FROM BORROWER**	36,232.50
200. AMOUNTS PAID BY OR IN BEHALF OF BORROWER:	
201. Deposit or earnest money	1,000.00
202. Principal amount of new loan(s)	30,000.00
203. Existing loan(s) taken subject to	
204.	
205.	
206.	
207.	
208.	
209.	
Adjustments for items unpaid by seller	
210. City/town taxes to	
211. County taxes 1-1 to 6-30 @$600/yr	300.00
212. Assessments 1-1 to 6-30 @100/yr	50.00
213.	
214.	
215.	
216.	
217.	
218.	
219.	
220. **TOTAL PAID BY/FOR BORROWER**	31,350.00
300. CASH AT SETTLEMENT FROM/TO BORROWER	
301. Gross amount due from borrower *(line 120)*	36,232.50
302. Less amounts paid by/for borrower *(line 220)*	(31,350.00)
303. CASH (☐ FROM) (☒ TO) BORROWER	4,882.50

Settlement Statement (*Continued*)

Your Financial Worksheet

Once you have decided which providers you wish to use for your settlement services and have selected the lender who will make your loan, you can calculate the total estimated cash you will need to complete the purchase. The form below, which is a part of the Uniform Settlement Statement, can be used as a worksheet for this purpose.

J. SUMMARY OF BORROWER'S TRANSACTION	
100. GROSS AMOUNT DUE FROM BORROWER:	
101. Contract sales price	
102. Personal property	
103. Settlement charges to borrower (line 1400)	
104.	
105.	
Adjustments for items paid by seller in advance	
106. City/town taxes to	
107. County taxes to	
108. Assessments to	
109.	
110.	
111.	
112.	
120. *GROSS AMOUNT DUE FROM BORROWER*	
200. AMOUNTS PAID BY OR IN BEHALF OF BORROWER:	
201. Deposit or earnest money	
202. Principal amount of new loan(s)	
203. Existing loan(s) taken subject to	
204.	
205.	
206.	
207.	
208.	
209.	
Adjustments for items unpaid by seller	
210. City/town taxes to	
211. County taxes to	
212. Assessments to	
213.	
214.	
215.	
216.	
217.	
218.	
219.	
220. *TOTAL PAID BY/FOR BORROWER*	
300. CASH AT SETTLEMENT FROM/TO BORROWER	
301. Gross amount due from borrower (line 120)	
302. Less amounts paid by/for borrower (line 220)	( )
303. CASH (☐ FROM) (☐ TO) BORROWER	

Settlement Statement (*Continued*)

19

Managing Agents: Their Duties and Responsibilities

M ost larger building complexes, whether they are condominium or cooperative, end up hiring managing agents to run the buildings. That's because the owners or owner-tenants do not want to spend all their free time operating a business for which there is no pay. And running a building is certainly similar to operating a business. What do managing agents actually do?

CONDOMINIUMS

Some of the duties of managing agents in a condominium complex include the following.

1. Preparing budgets and other periodic financial statements.
2. Supervising the operation and maintenance of all common areas, such as hallways, roofs, and swimming pools.
3. Hiring and discharging of all building employees.
4. Recording up-to-date financial transactions, also known as "keeping the books."
5. Collecting all homeowners' dues and assessments.
6. Working closely with the homeowners' association to carry out policy.

These are typical duties; some agents may have more or less. Agents normally are paid a monthly fee for the service. The management firm is usually a local real estate company that specializes in this type of work. Some management firms do nothing but management; others combine management with real estate sales or mortgage activities. In any case, a potential buyer should inquire into the competence of the managing agents of the building prior to purchasing an apartment.

It would be wise to talk to the managing agent, just as you would talk to the homeowners' association or board of directors as mentioned earlier. Again, you are interested primarily in the agent's philosophy of management and the implementation of that philosophy.

You can assume that if the grounds and common areas are well maintained and the complex is well staffed with competent individuals, the managing agent is doing a good job. On the other hand, if repairs seem to have been put off and energy conservation is not of the utmost concern to the agent, you can assume just the opposite. Managing agents usually are hired under one- or two-year contracts, so replacement of an incompetent agent is always possible. However, often because of "special relationships" with homeowners' associations, some managing agents have been known to stay on and on even though they are doing only a mediocre job. The homeowners' association and the managing agent have to work together as a team; if they don't the property and therefore your investment will deteriorate.

COOPERATIVES

Managing agents of cooperative buildings usually have greater responsibilities than do those of condominiums because they have more fiduciary duties. Managing agents of cooperatives normally:

1. Pay mortgage charges to building lenders.
2. Remit any withholding taxes due on employees of the building.
3. Pay any local taxes that might be assessed.
4. Collect maintenance charges from all tenant-owners.
5. Purchase supplies for the proper maintenance of the building.
6. Keep payroll records.

All of this is in addition to the functions performed by condominium managing agents enumerated above.

Since the managing agents of cooperative buildings have more of a fiduciary role than their condominium counterparts, it is vital that the cooperative managing board hire agents with broad fiduciary and financial experience and with a record of honest dealings. References must be checked and double-checked in this regard, and a committee of the board (a finance committee, in all probability) should oversee the fiduciary functions of the managing agent. If such a committee does not exist in the cooperative you wish to buy in, be wary. The possibility of temptation is high for unsupervised managing agents, and financial losses could result to the detriment of all tenant-owners. Explore all this prior to purchase.

One more thing: Make sure that the managing agent for the complex—especially if it is newly built or converted—is totally independent of the developer or converter. Often developers like to keep their hands on a complex through a managing agent that they own a piece of. Such a situation permits the developer or converter "to get his way" on many important management functions after all of his interest is supposed to be gone. Sometimes the management company tries to keep secret its links to certain individuals, so be thorough in your investigations of this matter.

20

Refinancing Your
Condominium
or Cooperative Apartment

Some people buy an apartment and the first thing they think about is that they now have an asset which they can use as collateral for a loan. Since most apartments are mortgaged at the time of purchase, any subsequent mortgage would be a second mortgage. There is only one problem with that, however; some states—predominantly those in the West—do not permit second mortgages. These states are called *homestead* states, and they have homestead laws which prohibit one's home from being subjected to a second mortgage. The rationale behind these laws is that if a home has more than one mortgage on it, the chances of the homeowner losing his home through mortgage default are greater, and these states want to encourage home ownership and retention.

Most states, however, do permit homeowners to refinance or to put second mortgages on their condominium or cooperative apartments. Banks in these states often change their policies with regard to the granting of second mortgages depending on the economic situation at the time. How second mortgages are given varies quite often from state to state, so you should check with an attorney or financial advisor before you go ahead.

SHOULD YOU REFINANCE?

The answer to that question depends on the circumstances surrounding your particular situation. If, for instance, you need money to finance a child's education, to start or expand a business, or to make an investment, you may only be able to get the funds via the second mortgage or refinancing route. If interest rates are particularly high and other types of loans are hard to get, the equity you have built up in your apartment may be enough of an asset so that most lenders will loan you the money you need.

As you might imagine, a second mortgage will be given to you at a significantly higher rate of interest than your first mortgage was, because the risk for the lender is higher when he holds a second mortgage. If you were to go bankrupt or for some reason you were unable to pay your debts, the lender from whom you got your first mortgage would institute foreclosure proceedings against the apartment. Foreclosure means that your apartment would be sold, and the proceeds of the sale would go to the first mortgage holder. The second mortgage holder would be paid with what is left over, if anything. But there is usually little or nothing left over when an apartment or house is sold through foreclosure, so the lender giving the second mortgage incurs a big risk. For that risk he charges a higher interest rate.

It should be noted that any amount received as a result of refinancing is a nontaxable event. As a result you do not have to pay taxes on the refinancing proceeds. However, you should be aware that you may have to pay points (or a loan processing fee), and that amount is deductible as interest.

Refinancing requires that a new closing be held. That means, of course, more expenses. For example, you will probably have to pay lawyers' fees again as well as an appraisal charge, points, survey fees, and in some states a mortgage recording tax as well. The total amount you will have to pay depends on the state the apartment is located in and the amount of the second mortgage or refinancing. Since points are generally 1% of the mortgage for each point you will undoubtedly be paying several hundred dollars for points alone.

21

Buying a Condominium
or Cooperative Apartment
as an Investment

There are some people who buy condominium, and occasionally cooperative, apartments solely as investments—that is, they don't plan to live in them. Buyers will rent the unit out at a rental that they hope will cover the monthly homeowners' fee, taxes, and maintenance expenses, with some amount left over for a profit. Since condominium apartments are individually owned and the homeowners' association cannot keep a qualified renter out of the owned units, it is a fairly easy proposition to rent out a condominium apartment. The investor, however, must have experience in managing rental properties to make it worthwhile.

Renting out a cooperative apartment, on the other hand, is an entirely different matter. Normally, cooperative boards will have to pass on the suitability of a tenant who is subleasing from the proprietary lessee, and some boards have been known to be very picky about who is living in the building, whether they own or rent. A few cooperative complexes will not allow subleasing at all, so if you are thinking about investing in a cooperative apartment, be sure that subleasing is allowed and, if it is allowed, find out what the criteria are for subleasing.

However, there is a recent innovation that may make it easier for you if you want to invest in a condominium or cooperative apartment. Quite often now, landlords who convert their buildings from rental to condo or coop will sell already occupied units (apartments not purchased by an existing tenant) to interested investors. You may be able to pick up a bargain this way, but you must remember that your tenant, in most cases, is one who has lived in the apartment during the conversion process. This could sour that tenant on you, because you are now his landlord.

ADVANTAGES OF INVESTING IN A CONDOMINIUM OR COOPERATIVE

Investing in a condominium apartment has certain advantages over other types of investments. For example, in certain parts of the country, a condominium unit can be purchased with a downpayment of as little as 5%. So, if you have $20,000 available for investment conceivably you could buy four $100,000 apartments for your $20,000 investment. But, lenders are often reluctant to give mortgages at such low downpayments if they know that the purchaser is buying the unit strictly for investment purposes and not to live in. And, in addition, the mortgage rate may be set higher for the investor than for the owner-occupant.

Many builders of new condominiums adhere to the same guidelines. They will require a higher downpayment from the investor than from the live-in buyer. They may also erect other barriers to the investor, such as asking that a certain amount of money be put into escrow or the like.

The reason that some owners and builders are so strict with investors is that renters are thought of as not taking as good care of an apartment and the common areas as would an owner-resident. Whether this is a valid conclusion or not is beside the point. It is the reason given universally by lenders and others for the stricter requirements on "investor" apartments. However, there are enough successful people who invest in condominiums and cooperatives that they must think it worth the extra effort and monetary outlay.

Investors in apartments get two additional tax advantages besides getting those mentioned in Chapter 6. The first is that any amount spent on repairs and maintenance of the apartments is tax deductible because, according to the tax laws, the apartment is being held for profit-making purposes. Second, the investor gets a depreciation deduction that the ordinary buyer of an apartment cannot get.

Depreciation

Depreciation is only available as a deduction to investors who do not live in the apartments in which they invest. The tax laws state that property must be held for investment before depreciation can be deducted. Even if you purchase an apartment as an investment and you lose money on it, you can take depreciation as long as you intended to make profit when you bought the asset.

Now, what exactly can you depreciate? You can't depreciate the entire cost of the apartment. Since the cost of an apartment includes things such as the economic situation at the time the apartment is sold or bought and the particular status of the neighborhood at the time a deal is made, the IRS will not allow you to take the full worth of the apartment in depreciation. It is much more likely that you will be able to deduct only 70-80% of your cost. Still, a hefty deduction is available. So, if you purchase an apartment for $100,000 as an investment, the IRS will probably not challenge a depreciation deduction based, for instance, on a total of $75,000.

Most real estate professionals use one of two methods to determine the proper calculation for depreciation purposes. In the first, you can use the same figure used by the tax assessor when the apartment is assessed for tax purposes (only applicable in the case of a condominium) or, second, you can get a professional appraisal. An appraisal is the only way that investors in cooperative apartments can come up with an essentially unchallengable net worth for depreciation purposes.

Depreciation is based on the "useful life" of an asset, and recent tax legislation has set the useful life of real property at 15, 35, or 45 years. Which one you should choose depends on a number of factors. Suffice it to say that most investors will probably choose the 15-year period, because that way they will be able to write off the apartment more quickly. A decision will also have to be made whether the investor is going to use *straight-line depreciation*—which involves depreciating the asset at about the same rate for 15 years—or whether a new *accelerated depreciation* should be taken.

If you are getting the idea that investing in an apartment is a complicated way of investing, you are absolutely right. Read all you can about it and seek out the aid of real estate and tax professionals before you begin to invest.

However, apartment investors will tell you that they think the greatest advantage to this kind of investment is the possibility of tremendous appreciation in the worth of the apartment, especially if the apartment is located in an area that is just starting a resurgence. Some investors have been fortunate enough to double their money in three or four years. This is a risky game, however, because the investor is betting that apartment prices will continue to rise, and, of course, that is by no means guaranteed. It is not an investment for the faint of heart.

There is one other reason for investing in an apartment. When you purchase an apartment you can take a capital gain when you sell it if you have held the apartment for the requisite period of time— presently one year.

As far as seeking professional help is concerned, many professional investors and real estate agents hire themselves out as consultants on apartment investors. If you are a novice in this game, you should get all the advice you can afford.

22

The Prospectus and
Other Important Items

In many states, before you can buy a condominium or cooperative apartment you must be furnished with a prospectus or offering plan which details just about everything you and your attorney might want to know about the apartment and the building. Usually financial statements that show the fiscal condition of the developer are included in the prospectus, as are proposed budgets, engineer's reports, and other data. All of these are included so that you as a consumer can make an intelligent and informed decision.

COOPERATIVES

The importance of reading these documents cannot be overemphasized. They are gold mines of information that must be studied carefully. For example, if you are buying into a cooperative building you should study (or get an accountant to study) the mortgage that covers the building. Some questions to ask would be:

> Does the building mortgage require renegotiation after a few years?
> How much longer does the mortgage have to run?
> Is there a second or third mortgage on the building?
> Does the mortgage have a "balloon" payment which must be paid off at the end of the mortgage term?

The answers to all these questions are vital because they have a direct bearing on whether your maintenance payment will rise rapidly or slowly during the early years of your residency. If a new mortgage has to be renegotiated soon, or if it has a big balloon, the chances are that a new mortgage will cost more than the old one, which will necessitate a large increase in your monthly maintenance payments.

Another item to look for in the financial portion of the prospectus is how often (or, in the case of a newly built or converted building, how easily) the board can make special assessments to owner-shareholders. Some boards of directors keep maintenances artificially low and tack on special assessments on a fairly regular basis. If you are buying into a cooperative building that has been a coop for some years, ask for a history of special assessments.

An engineering report will give you clues as to the condition of the building. Pay particular attention to the age and condition of the heating and air conditioning system. Also you will want to know as much as possible about the roof and the plumbing. If any of these items are in poor repair, you can be pretty sure that a special assessment might be forthcoming soon to pay for these items.

CONDOMINIUMS

If you are buying into a condominium you won't have to worry about a mortgage, since condominium buildings don't have them. However, many of the other concerns are identical with coops, such as the history of assessments and the condition of the structure.

Advice was given earlier to the effect that every potential buyer should hire a home inspection specialist. Don't take the engineering report in the prospectus as gospel; after all, the developer hired the engineer who did the report. Despite the fact that the report is to be furnished (at least in most states) by an independent (i.e., unbiased) engineer, that may just not be the case.

Other items to check out that may have a bearing on increases in maintenance or homeowner dues:

If the building or development has a maintenance staff (including doormen and concierges), are they under a labor contract? If so, when is the contract due for renegotiation? A whopping increase in salaries will come out of your monthly charges.

Is the building you want to buy into heated by an oil burner? Again, a rise in oil bills will cause an increase in monthly charges.

Is some kind of major renovation or landscaping planned? If so, can the operating surplus in the accounts of the homeowners' association or the corporation handle it? Are any improvements presently in progress?

Buried in the paperwork someplace may be a clause holding the new owner of a condominium liable for the unpaid homeowners' dues of the previous owner of the unit. If there is such a clause in the bylaws or prospectus, make sure that the prior owner is up to date in his or her homeowner dues before you buy. Have your attorney look for this. If you buy from an owner who has defaulted, you could be in for an expensive surprise.

23

The Proprietary Lease and the Condominium Deed

The *proprietary lease* or occupancy agreement—one of the vital documents associated with the purchase of a cooperative apartment—is, as its name states, nothing more than a lease. As with any lease, the *lessee* (the tenant) lives in the apartment at the sufferance of the *lessor* (the apartment corporation). The lessor in the case of a cooperative apartment is the building corporation generally, and the governing board as its representative, in particular. If you violate a term of the lease, the board on behalf of the corporation can evict you, just as any landlord could do under an ordinary rental lease.

A condominium deed, on the other hand, is a deed that is practically identical to the deed you would get if you bought a single-family house, with the addition of a few clauses delineating the owner's share in the common areas of the condominium. As mentioned earlier, however, the homeowners' association cannot evict a troublesome owner very easily.

A TYPICAL PROPRIETARY LEASE

Immediately following this chapter is an example of a typical proprietary lease. Depending on state law, proprietary leases will vary in wording and content, but all proprietary leases contain some standard clauses which should be examined carefully before signing. A few of the standard clauses will be reproduced here, so that certain points already made can be reinforced. Here are some typical clauses (emphasis is the author's).

1. *An Assignment Clause.* "The shares may not be sold or the proprietary lease assigned, *or the apartment sublet,* without first obtaining the consent thereto duly authorized by resolution of the Board of Directors . . . by written consent or vote of shareholders owning at least 65% of the Apartment Corporation's outstanding shares. *Such consent may be arbitrarily refused,* provided such refusal is not based upon race, color, creed, or other ground prescribed by law. . . ." This clause shows the real power of the board of directors to refuse the right of a tenant-owner to sublet his or her apartment. Many boards feel that if a sublessee does not fit the "image" of the building, then that person should not be allowed to live in the bulding. A reason doesn't have to be given for turning down the sublessee.

174

2. *Alteration Clause*. "Shareholders will be responsible for the cost of interior repairs (including maintenance and replacement of all appliances, plumbing fixtures, and other fixtures and equipment) and decorating the apartment. *The consent of the Apartment Corporation is required before alterations or additions may be made in the apartment or to its fixtures and equipment* (which consent may not be unreasonably withheld)."

Because any alteration may affect the common areas, the consent of the board is required if you want to knock down a wall or redo the bathroom. Ask to see the proprietary lease before you buy, so that you can check this clause. Some are stricter than others.

3. *Occupation Use Clause*. "The apartment may be used for (*i*) any occupation use permitted under applicable zoning law, building code, or other rules and regulations of governmental authorities having jurisdiction and (*ii*) residential purposes, and for no other purpose *unless otherwise consented to in writing by the Apartment Corporation*." Some coop boards use this clause to keep out professionals such as physicians or psychologists who might have their patients coming to see them at all hours of the day and night.

4. *Pledge Clause*. "The lease and appurtenant shares may be pledged to a recognized lending institution." This refers to the pledging of shares as collateral for a loan. Some boards permit the pledge of shares and others don't. State laws may differ on the matter as well.

CONDOMINIUM DEED

The condominium deed, along with a document known in some states as the Declaration of Condominium, usually defines the owner's rights and proportionate share in the common elements. An example of a deed and declaration immediately follow.

One point must be made here: Each state requires that things be done differently, and some states may not require as detailed a set of papers be included as others. However, most require that the buyer be given some protection in this manner.

The Proprietary Lease, Condominium Deed, and Declaration of Condominium that follow relate to apartments in the State of New York; those in other states may differ substantially in content and wording.

PROPRIETARY LEASE

APARTMENT   SHARES

HOUSING CORPORATION, LESSOR
TO
LESSEE.

INDEX

PROPRIETARY LEASE

PROPRIETARY LEASE, made as of _____, 19 , by and between
_____ HOUSING CORPORATION, a New York Corporation, having
an office at 551 Fifth Avenue, New York, N.Y. 10176, hereinafter called the Lessor,
and _____ hereinafter called the Lessee.

WHEREAS, the Lessor is the Owner of _____, the land and the
building erected thereon in the County of _____, City and State of New York,
known as and by the street number _____, New York, hereinafter
called the building; and

WHEREAS, the Lessee is the owner of _____ shares of the Lessor, to which
this lease is appurtenant and which have been allocated to Apartment #_____ in
the building;

Demised Premises	NOW, THEREFORE, in consideration of the premises, the Lessor hereby leases to the Lessee, and the Lessee hires from the Lessor, subject to the terms and conditions hereof, Apartment #_____ in the building (hereinafter referred to as the apartment) for a term from _____, 1981, until _____ unless sooner
Term	terminated as hereinafter provided). As used herein "the apartment" means the rooms in the building as partitioned on the date of execution of this lease designated by the above stated apartment number, together with their appurtenances and fixtures and any closets, terraces, balconies, roof, or portion thereof outside of said partitioned rooms, which are allocated exclusively to the occupant of the apartment.
Rent (Maintenance) How Fixed	1.(a) The rent (sometimes called maintenance) payable by the Lessee for each year, or portion of a year, during the term shall equal that proportion of the Lessor's cash requirements for such a year, or portion of a year, which the number of shares of Lessor allocated to the apartment bears to the total number of shares of the Lessor issued and outstanding on the date of the determination of such cash requirements. Such maintenance shall be payable in equal monthly installments in advance on the first day of each month, unless the Board of Directors of the Lessor (hereinafter called Directors) at the time of its determination of the cash requirements shall otherwise direct. The Lessee shall also pay such additional rent as may be provided for herein when due.
Accompanying Shares to be Specified in Proprietary Lease	(b) In every proprietary lease heretofore executed by the Lessor there has been specified and in every proprietary lease hereafter executed by it there will be specified, the number of shares of the Lessor issued to a lessee simultaneously therewith.

183

Cash
Requirements
Defined

(c) "Cash requirements" whenever used herein shall mean the estimated amount in cash which the Directors shall from time to time in its judgment determine to be necessary or proper for (1) the operation, maintenance, care, alteration and improvement of the corporate property during the year or portion of the year for which such determination is made; (2) the creation of such reserve for contingencies as it may deem proper; and (3) the payment of any obligations, liabilities or expenses incurred or to be incurred, after giving consideration to (i) income expected to be received during such period (other than rent from proprietary lessees), and (ii) cash on hand which the Directors in its discretion may choose to apply. The Directors may from time to time modify its prior determination and increase or diminish the amount previously determined as cash requirements of the corporation for a year or portion thereof. No determination of cash requirements shall have any retroactive effect on the amount of the rent payable by the lessee for any period prior to the date of such determination. All determinations of cash requirements shall be conclusive as to all lessees.

Authority
Limited to
Board of
Directors

(d) Whenever in this paragraph or any other paragraph of this lease, a power or privilege is given to the Directors, the same may be exercised only by the Directors, and in no event may any such power or privilege be exercised by a creditor, receiver or trustee.

Issuance
of Additional
Shares

(e) If the Lessor shall hereafter issue shares (whether now or hereafter authorized) in addition to those issued on the date of the execution of this lease, the holders of the shares hereafter issued shall be obligated to pay rent at the same rate as the other proprietary lessees from and after the date of issuance. If any such shares be issued on a date other than the first or last day of the month, the rent for the month in which issued shall be apportioned. The cash requirements as last determined shall, upon the issuance of such shares, be deemed increased by an amount equal to such rent.

Paid-in
Surplus

(f) The Directors may from time to time as may be proper determine how much of the maintenance and other receipts, when received (but not more than such amount as represents payments on account of principal of mortgages on the property and other capital expenditures), shall be credited on the corporate accounts to "Paid-in Surplus." Unless the Directors shall determine otherwise, the amount of payments on account of principal of any mortgages shall be credited to Paid-in Surplus.

Failure to
Fix Cash
Requirements

(g) The omission of the Directors to determine the Lessor's cash requirements for any year or portion thereof shall not be deemed a waiver or modification in any respect of the covenants and provisions hereof, or a release of the Lessee from the obligation to pay the maintenance or any installment thereof, but the maintenance computed on the basis of the cash requirements as last determined for any year or portion thereof shall thereafter continue to be the maintenance until a new determination of cash requirements shall be made.

Lessor's
Repairs

2. The Lessor shall at its expense keep in good repair all of the building including all of the apartments, the sidewalks and courts surrounding the same, and its equipment and apparatus except those portions the maintenance and repair of which are expressly stated to be the responsibility of the Lessee pursuant to Paragraph 18 hereof.

Services by
Lessor

3. The Lessor shall maintain and manage the building as a first-class apartment building, and shall keep the elevators and the public halls, cellars and stairways clean and properly lighted and heated, and shall provide the number of attendants requisite, in the judgment of the Directors, for the proper care and service of the building, and shall provide the apartment with a proper and sufficient supply of hot and cold water and of heat, and if there be central air conditioning equipment supplied by the Lessor, air conditioning when deemed appropriate by the Directors. The covenants by the Lessor herein contained are subject, however, to the discretionary power of the Directors to determine from time to time what services and what attendants shall be proper and the manner of maintaining the operating of the building, and also what existing services shall be increased, reduced, changed, modified or terminated.

Damage to
Apartment or
Building

4.(a) If the apartment or the means of access thereto or the building shall be damaged by fire or other cause covered by multiperil policies commonly carried by cooperative corporations in New York City (any other damage to be repaired by Lessor or Lessee pursuant to Paragraphs 2 and 18, as the case may be), the Lessor shall at its own cost and expense, with reasonable dispatch after receipt of notice of said damage, repair or replace or cause to be repaired or replaced, with materials of a kind and quality then customary in buildings of the type of the building, the building, the apartment, and the means of access thereto, including the walls, floors, ceilings, pipes, wiring and conduits in the apartment.

Anything in this Paragraph or Paragraph 2 to the contrary, Lessor shall not be required to repair or replace, or cause to be repaired or replaced, equipment, fixtures, furniture, furnishings or decorations installed by the Lessee or any of his predecessors in title nor shall the Lessor be obligated to repaint or replace wallpaper or other decorations in apartments.

Rent Abatement

(b) In case the damage resulting from fire or other cause shall be so extensive as to render the apartment partly or wholly untenantable, or if the means of access thereto shall be destroyed, the rent hereunder shall proportionately abate until the apartment shall again be rendered wholly tenantable or the means of access restored; but if said damage shall be caused by the act of negligence of the Lessee or the agents, employees, guests or members of the family of the Lessee or any occupant of the apartment, such rental shall abate only to the extent of the rental value insurance, if any, collected by Lessor with respect to the apartment.

Expiration of Lease Due to Damage

(c) If the Directors shall determine that (i) the building is totally destroyed by fire or other cause, or (ii) the building is so damaged that it cannot be repaired within a reasonable time after the loss shall have been adjusted with the insurance carriers, or (iii) the destruction or damage was caused by hazards which are not covered under the Lessor's insurance policies then in effect, and if in any such case the record holders of at least 75% of the issued shares, at a shareholders' meeting duly called for that purpose held within 120 days after the determination by the Directors, shall vote not to repair, restore or rebuild, then upon the giving of notice pursuant to Paragraph 31 hereof, this Lease and all other proprietary leases and all right, title and interest of the parties thereunder and the tenancies thereby created, shall thereupon wholly cease and expire and rent shall be paid to the date of such destruction or damage. The Lessee hereby waives any and all rights under Section 227 of the Real Property Law and in no event shall the Lessee have any option or right to terminate this Lease.

Waiver of Subrogation

(d) Lessor agrees to use its best efforts to obtain a provision in all insurance policies carried by it waiving the right of subrogation against the Lessee; and, to the extent that any loss or damage is covered by the Lessor by any insurance policies which contain such waiver of subrogation, the Lessor releases the Lessee from any liability with respect to such loss or damage. In the event that the Lessee suffers loss or damage for which Lessor would be liable, and Lessee carries insurance which covers such loss or damage and such insurance policy or policies contain a waiver of subrogation against the Landlord, then in such event Lessee releases Lessor from any liability with respect to such loss or damage.

Inspection of Books of Account Annual Report

5. The Lessor shall keep full and correct books of account at its principal office or at such other place as the Directors may from time to time determine, and the same shall be open during all reasonable hours to inspection by the Lessee or a representative of the Lessee. The Lessor shall deliver to the Lessee within three months after the end of each fiscal year, an annual report of corporate financial affairs, including a balance sheet and a statement of income and expenses, certified by an independent certified public accountant.

Changes in Terms and Conditions of Proprietary Leases

6. Each proprietary lease shall be in the form of this lease, unless a variation of any lease is authorized by lessees owning at least two-thirds of the Lessor's shares then issued and executed by the Lessor and Lessee affected. The form and provisions of all the proprietary leases then in effect and thereafter to be executed may be changed by the approval of Lessees owning at least 75% of the Lessor's shares then issued, and such changes shall be binding on all lessees even if they did not vote for such changes except that the proportionate share of rent or cash requirements payable by any lessee may not be increased nor may his right to cancel the lease under the conditions set forth in Paragraph 35 be eliminated or impaired without his express consent. Approval by lessees as provided for herein shall be evidenced by written consent or by affirmative vote taken at a meeting called for such purpose.

Penthouses, Terraces and Balconies

7. If the apartment includes a terrace, balcony, or a portion of the roof adjoining a penthouse, the Lessee shall have and enjoy the exclusive use of the terrace or balcony or that portion of the roof appurtenant to the penthouse, subject to the applicable provisions of this lease and to the use of the terrace, balcony or roof by the Lessor to the extent herein permitted. The lessee's use thereof shall be subject to such regulations as may, from time to time, be prescribed by the Directors. The Lessor shall have the right to erect equipment on the roof, including radio and television aerials and antennas, for its use and the use of the lessees in the building and shall have the right of access thereto for such installations and for the repair thereof. The Lessee shall keep the terrace, balcony, or portion of the roof appurtenant to his apart-

ment clean and free from snow, ice, leaves and other debris and shall maintain all screens and drain boxes in good condition. No planting, fence, structures or lattices shall be erected or installed on the terraces, balconies, or roof of the building without the prior written approval of the Lessor. No cooking shall be permitted on any terraces, balconies or the roof of the building, nor shall the walls thereof be painted by the Lessee without the prior written approval of the Lessor. Any planting or other structures erected by the Lessee or his predecessor in interest may be removed and restored by the Lessor at the expense of the Lessee for the purpose of repairs, upkeep or maintenance of the building.

Assignment of Lessor's Rights Against Occupancy

8. If at the date of commencement of this lease, any third party shall be in possession or have the right to possession of the apartment, then the Lessor hereby assigns to the Lessee all of the Lessor's rights against said third party from and after the date of the commencement of the term hereof, and the Lessee by the execution hereof assumes all of the Lessor's obligations to said third party from said date. The Lessor agrees to cooperate with the Lessee, but at the Lessee's expense, in the enforcement of the Lessee's rights against said third party.

Cancellation of Prior Agreements

9. If at the date of the commencement of this lease, the Lessee has the right to possession of the apartment under any agreement or statutory tenancy, this lease shall supersede such agreement or statutory tenancy which shall be of no further effect after the date of commencement of this lease, except for claims theretofore arising thereunder.

Quiet Enjoyment

10. The Lessee, upon paying the rent and performing the covenants and complying with the conditions on the part of the Lessee to be performed as herein set forth, shall, at all times during the terms hereby granted, quietly have, hold and enjoy the apartment without any let, suit, trouble or hindrance from the Lessor, subject, however, to the rights of present tenants or occupants of the apartment, and subject to any and all mortgages and underlying leases of the land and building.

Indemnity

11. The Lessee agrees to save the Lessor harmless from all liability, loss, damage and expense arising from injury to person or property occasioned by the failure of the Lessee to comply with any provision hereof, or due wholly or in part to any act, default or omission of the Lessee or of any person dwelling or visiting in the apartment, or by the Lessor, its agents, servants or contractors when acting as agent for the Lessee as in this lease

provided. This paragraph shall not apply to any loss or damage when Lessor is covered by insurance which provides for waiver of subrogation against the Lessee.

**Payment
of Rent**

12. The Lessee will pay the rent to the Lessor upon the terms and at the times herein provided, without any deduction on account of any set-off or claim which the Lessee may have against the Lessor, and if the Lessee shall fail to pay any installment of rent promptly, the Lessee shall pay interest thereon at the maximum legal rate from the date when such installment shall have become due to the date of the payment thereof, and such interest shall be deemed additional rent hereunder.

House Rules

13. The Lessor has adopted House Rules which are appended hereto, and the Directors may alter, amend or repeal such House Rules and adopt new House Rules. This lease shall be in all respects subject to such House Rules which, when a copy thereof has been furnished to the Lessee, shall be taken to be part hereof, and the Lessee hereby covenants to comply with all such House Rules and see that they are faithfully observed by the family, guests, employees and subtenants of the Lessee. Breach of the House Rules shall be a default under this Lease. The Lessor shall not be responsible to the Lessee for the nonobservance or violation of House Rules by any other lessee or person.

**Use of
Premises**

·14. The Lessee shall not, without the written consent of the Lessor on such conditions as Lessor may prescribe, occupy or use the apartment or permit the same or any part thereof to be occupied or used for any purpose other than as a private dwelling for the Lessee and Lessee's spouse, their children, grandchildren, parents, grandparents, brothers and sisters and domestic employees, and in no event shall more than one married couple occupy the apartment without the written consent of the Lessor. In addition to the foregoing, the apartment may be occupied from time to time by guests of the Lessee for a period of time not exceeding one month, unless a longer period is approved in writing by the Lessor, but no guests may occupy the apartment unless one or more of the permitted adult residents are then in occupancy or unless consented to in writing by the Lessor.

Subletting

15. Except as provided in Paragraph 38 of this lease, the lessee shall not sublet the whole or any part of the apartment or renew or extend any previously authorized sublease, unless consent thereto shall have been duly authorized by a resolution of the Directors, or given in writing by a majority of the Directors or, if the Directors

shall have failed or refused to give such consent, then by lessees owning at least 75% of the then issued shares of the Lessor. Consent by lessees as provided for herein shall be evidenced by written consent or by affirmative vote taken at a meeting called for such purpose. Any consent to subletting may be subject to such conditions as the Directors or lessees, as the case may be, may impose. There shall be no limitation on the right of Directors or lessees to grant or withhold consent, for any reason or for no reason to a subletting.

Assignment

16(a). The Lessee shall not assign this lease or transfer the shares to which it is appurtenant or any interest therein, and no such assignment or transfer shall take effect as against the Lessor for any purpose, until

(i) An instrument of assignment in form approved by Lessor executed and acknowledged by the assignor shall be delivered to the Lessor; and

(ii) An agreement executed and acknowledged by the assignee in form approved by Lessor assuming and agreeing to be bound by all the covenants and conditions of this lease to be performed or complied with by the Lessee on and after the effective date of said assignment shall have been delivered to the Lessor, or, at the request of the Lessor, the assignee shall have surrendered the assigned lease and entered into a new lease in the same form for the remainder of the term, in which case the Lessee's lease shall be deemed cancelled as of the effective date of said assignment; and

(iii) All shares of the Lessor to which this lease is appurtenant shall have been transferred to the assignee, with proper transfer taxes paid and stamps affixed; and

(iv) All sums due from the Lessee shall have been paid to the Lessor, together with a sum to be fixed by the Directors to cover reasonable legal and other expenses of the Lessor and its managing agent in connection with such assignment and transfer of shares; and

(v) A search or certification from a title or abstract company as the Directors may require; and

(vi) Except in the case of an assignment, transfer or bequest to the Lessee's spouse, of the shares and this lease, and except as provided in Paragraph 38 of this lease, consent to such assignment shall have been authorized by resolution of the Directors, or given in writing by a majority of the Directors, or, if the Directors shall have failed or refused to give such consent within 30 days after submission of references to them or Lessor's agent, then

by lessees owning of record at least 75% of the then issued shares of the Lessor. Consent by lessees as provided for herein shall be evidenced by written consent
or by affirmative vote taken at a meeting called for such
purpose in the manner as provided in the by-laws.

Consents:
On Death
of Lessee

(b) If the Lessee shall die, consent shall not be unreasonably withheld to an assignment of the lease and shares to
a financially responsible member of the Lessee's family
(other than the Lessee's spouse as to whom no consent is
required).

Consents Generally:
Stockholders'
and Directors'
Obligations to Consent
Release of
Lessee Upon
Assignment
Further
Assignment
or Subletting

(c) There shall be no limitation, except as specifically
provided, on the right of Directors or lessees to grant or
withhold consent, for any reason or for no reason, to an
assignment.

(d) If the lease shall be assigned in compliance herewith,
the Lessee-assignor shall have no further liability on any
of the covenants of this lease to be thereafter performed.

(e) Regardless of any prior consent theretofore given,
neither the Lessee nor his executor, nor administrator,
nor any trustee or receiver of the property of the Lessee,
nor anyone to whom the interests of the Lessee shall
pass by law, shall be entitled further to assign this lease,
or to sublet the apartment, or any part thereof, except
upon compliance with the requirements of this lease.

Statement
by Lessor

(f) If this lease is then in force and effect, Lessor will,
upon request of Lessee, deliver to the assignee a written
statement that this lease remains on the date thereof in
force and effect; but no such statement shall be deemed
an admission that there is no default under the lease.

Pledge of
Shares
and Lease

17.(a) A pledge of this lease and the shares to which it is
appurtenant shall not be a violation of this lease, but neither the pledgee nor any transferee of the pledged security shall be entitled to have the shares transferred of record on the books of the Lessor, nor to vote such shares,
nor to occupy or permit the occupancy by others of the
apartment, nor to sell such shares or this lease, without
first obtaining the consent of the Lessor in accordance
with and after complying with all of the provisions of Paragraphs 14, 15, 16, as the case may be. The acceptance
by Lessor of payments by the pledgee or any transferee
of the pledged security on account of rent or additional
rent shall not constitute a waiver of the aforesaid provisions. The provisions of this subparagraph (a) shall be
subject to sub-paragraph (b) of this paragraph 17.

(b) The Lessee may pledge and assign this lease and the
shares of the Lessor allocated to the apartment as security for a loan made to the Lessee by a bank, trust com-

pany, insurance company or other recognized lending institution ("the Lender") provided, however, that the certificate representing the shares allocated to the apartment and this lease may be assigned to the Lender only as security repayment of the loan. In the event of a default by the Lessee in any of the terms, covenants, provisions or conditions of this lease, the Lessor will give written notice thereof to the Lender if written notice of the name and address of the Lender has been given by registered or certified mail to the Lessor prior to the date of any such default.

If the Lessee shall fail to cure said default within the time and in the manner provided for in this lease, then the Lender shall have an additional period of time equal to the time originally given the Lessee to cure said default, and the Lessor will not act upon said default until the time of the Lender to cure said default has elapsed and the Lender has not cured said default. In the event of a default by the Lessee in any of the terms, covenants, provisions or conditions of this lease, or in the payment to the Lender of any installment or principal or interest or in the performance of any other obligation of the Lessee to the Lender, the Lessor after written notice thereof from the Lender will exercise the right of termination of this lease granted to the Lessor pursuant to Paragraph 31 hereof (Right to Terminate Lease on Lessee's Default) and if the Lessee shall fail to vacate the apartment, will institute summary dispossess proceedings against the Lessee and take all steps and do all acts thereafter required in order to obtain possession of the apartment, all at the expense of the Lender, provided, however, that the Lender shall meanwhile pay all maintenance charges and other charges becoming due hereunder until this lease and the shares allocated to the apartment are acquired for personal occupancy.

If Lessor shall fail to exercise its right to terminate and/or to commence summary proceedings or to take all steps or do all acts required to be done pursuant hereto, then and in that event, Lessor shall execute and deliver to the Lender a power of attorney coupled with an interest to act in the name of the Lessor in any of the ways provided for herein at the Lender's sole expense, and if the Lessor shall fail to execute and deliver such power of attorney within five days after demand, such power of attorney may be executed by the Lender on behalf of any as the agent for the Lessor. The Lessee agrees that until any such loan is repaid to the Lender in full with interest, the Lessee shall not have any right to cancel this lease as provided in Paragraph 35 hereof and the Lessor agrees that until it receives written notice from the Lender that the entire amount of the loan with interest has been paid in full or discharged, the Lessor will not accept any surrender of this lease by the Lessee under paragraph 35 hereof.

If this lease is terminated at the Lender's request by reason of a default by the Lessee in any of the terms, covenants, provisions or in the payment to the Lender of any installment of principal or interest or in the performance of any other obligation of the Lessee to the Lender, the Lender may sell and assign the shares of the Lessor allocated to the apartment and this lease, or sublet the apartment, for the account of the Lender to a reputable person subject only to the approval of then managing agent of the Lessor (which approval shall not be unreasonably withheld or delayed). If written notice of any such loan has been given to the Lessor by the Lender as aforesaid, the Lender may assign all of its rights thereto and to the shares of Lessor allocated to the apartment and this lease by giving written notice to the Lessor by certified or registered mail setting forth the name and address of the assignee, and such assignee and any subsequent assignee or assignees shall thereupon have all the rights of the Lender under this Paragraph 17(b).

Repairs by
the Lessee

18.(a). The Lessee shall keep the interior of the apartment (including interior walls, floors and ceilings, but excluding windows, window panes, window frames, sashes, sills, entrance and terrace doors, frames and saddles) in good repair, shall do all of the painting and decorating required for his apartment, including the interior of window frames, sashes and sills and shall be solely responsible for the maintenance, repair and replacement of plumbing, gas and heating fixtures and equipment and such refrigerators, dishwashers, removable and through-the-wall air conditioners, washing machines, ranges and other appliances, as may be in the apartment. Plumbing, gas and heating fixtures as used herein shall include exposed gas, steam and water pipes attached to fixtures, appliances and equipment and the fixtures, appliances and equipment to which they are attached, and any special pipes or equipment which the Lessee may install within the wall or ceiling, or under the floor, but shall not include gas, steam, water or other pipes or conduits within the walls, ceilings or floors or air conditioning or heating equipment which is part of the standard building equipment. The Lessee shall be solely responsible for the maintenance, repair and replacement of all lighting and electrical fixtures, appliances, and equipment, and all meters, fuse boxes or circuit breakers and electrical wiring and conduits from the junction box at the riser into and through the Lessee's apartment. Any ventilator or air conditioning device which shall be visible from the outside of the building shall at all times be painted by the Lessee in a standard color which the Lessor may select for the building.

Odors and Noises

(b) The Lessee shall not permit unreasonable cooking or other odors to escape into the building. The Lessee shall not permit or suffer any unreasonable noises or anything which will interfere with the rights of other lessees or unreasonably annoy them or obstruct the public halls or stairways.

Equipment and Appliances

(c) If, in the Lessor's sole judgment, any of the Lessee's equipment or appliances shall result in damage to the building or poor quality or interruption of service to other portions or the building, or overloading of, or damage to facilities maintained by the Lessor for the supplying of water, gas, electricity or air conditioning to the building, or if any such appliances visible from the outside of the building shall become rusty or discolored, the Lessee shall promptly, on notice from the Lessor, remedy the condition and, pending such remedy, shall cease using any appliance or equipment which may be creating the objectionable condition.

Rules and Regulations and Requirements of Mortgage

(d) The Lessee will comply with all the requirements of the Board of Fire Underwriters, insurance authorities and all governmental authorities and with all laws, ordinances, rules and regulations with respect to the occupancy or use of the apartment. If any mortgage affecting the land or the building shall contain any provisions pertaining to the right of the Lessee to make changes or alterations in the apartment, or to remove any of the fixtures, appliances, equipment or installations, the Lessee herein shall comply with the requirements of such mortgage or mortgages relating thereto. Upon the Lessee's written request, Lessor will furnish Lessee with copies of applicable provisions of each and every such mortgage.

Lessor's Right to Remedy Lessee's Defaults

19. If the Lessee shall fail for 30 days after notice to make repairs to any part of the apartment, its fixtures or equipment as herein required, or shall fail to remedy a condition which has become objectionable to the Lessor for

reasons above set forth, of if the Lessee or any person dwelling in the apartment shall request the Lessor, its agents or servants to perform any act not hereby required to be performed by the Lessor, the Lessor may make such repairs, or arrange for others to do the same or remove such objectionable condition or equipment, or perform such act, without liability on the Lessor; provided that, if the condition requires prompt action notice of less than 30 days, or, in case of emergency, no notice need be given. In all such cases the Lessor, its agents, servants and contractors shall, as between the Lessor and Lessee, be conclusively deemed to be acting as agents of the Lessee and all contracts therefor made by the Lessor shall be so construed whether or not made in the name of the Lessee. If Lessee shall fail to perform or comply with any of the other covenants or provisions of this lease within the time required by a notice from Lessor (not less than 5 days), then Lessor may, but shall not be obligated to, comply therewith, and for such purpose may enter upon the apartment of Lessee. The Lessor shall be entitled to recover from the Lessee all expenses incurred or for which it has contracted hereunder, such expenses to be payable by the Lessee on demand as additional rent.

Increase
in Rate of
Fire Insurance

20. The Lessee shall not permit or suffer anything to be done or kept in the apartment which will increase the rate of fire insurance on the building or the contents thereof. If, by reason of the occupancy or use of the apartment by the Lessee, the rate of fire insurance on the building or an apartment or the contents of either shall be increased, the Lessee shall (if such occupancy or use continues for more than 30 days after written notice from the Lessor specifying the objectionable occupancy or use) become liable for the additional insurance premiums incurred by Lessor or any lessee or lessees of apartments in the building on all policies so affected, and the Lessor shall have the right to collect the same for its benefit or the benefit of any such lessees as additional rent for the apartment due on the first day of the calendar month following written demand therefor by the Lessor.

Alterations

21.(a) The Lessee shall not, without first obtaining the written consent of the Lessor, which consent shall not be unreasonably withheld, make in the apartment or building, or on any roof, penthouse, terrace or balcony appurtenant thereto, any alteration, enclosure or addition or any alteration of or addition to the water, gas, or steam risers or pipes, heating or air conditioning system or units, electrical conduits, wiring or outlets, plumbing fixtures, intercommunication or alarm system, or any other installation or facility in the apartment or building. The performance by Lessee of any work in the apartment shall be in accordance with any applicable rules and regulations of the Lessor and governmental agencies having jurisdiction thereof. The Lessee shall not in any case install any appliances which will overload the existing wires or equipment in the building.

Removal of Fixtures

(b) Without Lessor's written consent, the Lessee shall not remove any fixtures, appliances, additions or improvements from the apartment except as hereinafter provided. If the Lessee, or a prior lessee, shall have heretofore placed, or the Lessee shall hereafter place in the apartment, at the Lessee's own expense, any additions, improvements, appliances or fixtures, including but not limited to fireplace mantels, lighting fixtures, refrigerators, air conditioners, dishwashers, washing machines, ranges, woodwork, wall paneling, ceilings, special doors or decorations, special cabinet work, special stair railings or other built-in ornamental items, which can be removed without structural alterations or permanent damage to the apartment, then title thereto shall remain in the Lessee and the Lessee shall have the right, prior to the termination of this lease, to remove the same at the Lessee's own expense, provided: (i) that the Lessee at the time of such removal shall not be in default in the payment of rent or in the performance or observance of any other covenants or conditions of this lease; and (ii) that the Lessee shall, at the Lessee's own expense, prior to the termination of this lease, repair all damage to the apartment which shall have been caused by either the installation or removal of any of such additions, improvements, appliances or fixtures; (iii) that if the Lessee shall have removed from the apartment any articles or materials owned by the Lessor or its predecessor in title, or any fixtures or equipment necessary for the use of the apartment, the Lessee shall either restore such articles and materials and fixtures and equipment and repair any damage resulting from their removal and restoration, or replace them with others of a kind and quality customary in comparable buildings and satisfactory to the Lessor; and (iv) that if any mortgagee had acquired a lien on any such property prior to the execution of this lease, Lessor shall first procure from such mortgagee its written consent to such removal.

Surrender on Expiration of Term

(c) On the expiration or termination of this lease, the Lessee shall surrender to the Lessor possession of the apartment with all additions, improvements, appliances and fixtures then included therein, except as hereinabove provided. Any additions, improvements, fixtures or appliances not removed by the Lessee on or before such expiration or termination of this lease, shall, at the option of the Lessor, be deemed abandoned and shall become the property of the Lessor and may be disposed of by the Lessor without liabililty or accountability to the Lessee.

Lease Subordinate to Mortgages and Ground Leases

22. This lease is and shall be subject and subordinate to all present and future ground or underlying leases and to any mortgages now or hereafter liens upon such leases or on the land and building, or buildings, and to any and all extensions, modifications, consolidations, renewals and replacements thereof. This clause shall be self-operative and no further instrument of subordination shall be required by any such mortgagee or ground or underlying lessee. In confirmation of such subordination the Lessee shall at any time, and from time to time, on demand, execute any instruments that may be required by any mortgagee, or by the Lessor, for the purpose of more formally subjecting this lease to the lien of any such mortgage or mortgages or ground or underlying leases, and the duly elected officers, for the time being, or the Lessor are and each of them is hereby irrevocably appointed the attorney-in-fact and agent of the Lessee to execute the same upon such demand, and the Lessee hereby ratifies any such instrument hereafter executed by virtue of the power of attorney hereby given.

In the event that a ground or underlying lease is executed and delivered to the holder of a mortgage or mortgages on such ground or underlying lease or to a nominee or designee of or a corporation formed by or for the benefit of such holder, the Lessee hereunder will attorn to such mortgagee or the nominee or designee of such mortgagee or to any corporation formed by or for the benefit of such mortgagee.

Mechanic's Lien

23. In case a notice of mechanic's lien against the building shall be filed purporting to be for labor or material furnished or delivered at the building or the apartment to or for the Lessee, or anyone claiming under the Les-

see, the Lessee shall forthwith cause such lien to be discharged by payment, bonding or otherwise; and if the Lessee shall fail to do so within ten days after notice from the Lessor, then the Lessor may cause such lien to be discharged by payment, bonding or otherwise, without investigation as to the validity thereof or of any offsets or defenses thereto, and shall have the right to collect, as additional rent, all amounts so paid and all costs and expenses paid or incurred in connection therewith, including reasonable attorneys' fees and disbursements, together with interest thereon from the time or times of payment.

Cooperation

24. The Lessee shall always in good faith endeavor to observe and promote the cooperative purposes for the accomplishment of which the Lessor is incorporated.

Right of Entry

25. The Lessor and its agents and their authorized workmen shall be permitted to visit, examine, or enter the apartment and any storage space assigned to Lessee at any reasonable hour of the day upon notice, or at any time and without notice in case of emergency, to make or facilitate repairs in any part of the building or to cure any default by the Lessee and to remove such portions of the walls, floors, and ceilings of the apartment and storage space as may be required for any such purpose, but the Lessor shall therefore restore the apartment and storage space to its proper and usual condition at Lessor's expense if such repairs are the obligation of Lessor, or at Lessee's expense if such repairs are the obligation of Lessee or are caused by the act or omission of the Lessee or any of the Lessee's family, guests, agents, key employees or subtenants. In order that the Lessor shall at all times have access to the apartment or storage rooms for the purposes provided for in this lease, the Lessee shall provide the Lessor with a key to each lock providing access to the apartment or the storage rooms, and if any lock shall be altered or new lock installed, the Lessee shall provide the Lessor with a key thereto immediately upon installation. If the Lessee shall not be personally present to open and permit an entry at any time when an entry therein shall be necessary or permissible hereunder and shall not have furnished a key to Lessor, the Lessor or the Lessor's agents (but, except in an energency only when specifically authorized by an officer of the Lessor or an officer of the Managing Agent) may forcibly enter the apartment or storage space without liability for damages by reason thereof (if during such

entry the Lessor shall accord reasonable care to the Lessee's property), and without in any manner affecting the obligations and covenants of this lease. The right and authority hereby reserved do not impose, nor does the Lessor assume by reason thereof, any responsibility or liability for the care or supervision of the apartment, or any of the pipes, fixtures, appliances or appurtenances therein contained, except as herein specifically provided.

Waivers

26. The failure of the Lessor to insist, in any one or more instances, upon a strict performance of any of the provisions of this lease, or to exercise any right or option herein contained, or to serve any notice, or to institute any action or proceeding, shall not be construed as a waiver, or a relinquishment for the future, of any such provisions, options or rights, but such provision, option or right shall continue and remain in full force and effect. The receipt by the Lessor of rent, with knowledge of the breach of any covenant hereof, shall not be deemed a waiver of such breach, and no waiver by the Lessor of any provision hereof shall be deemed to have been made unless in a writing expressly approved by the Directors.

Notices

27. Any notice by or demand from either party to the other shall be duly given only if in writing and sent by registered mail; if by the Lessee, addressed to the Lessor at the building with a copy sent by regular mail to the Lessor's Managing Agent; if to the Lessee, addressed to the building. Either party may by notice served in accordance herewith designate a different address for service of such notice or demand. Notices or demands shall be deemed given on the date when mailed.

Reimbursement of Lessor's Expenses

28. If the Lessee shall at any time be in default hereunder and the Lessor shall incur any expense (whether paid or not) in performing acts which the Lessee is required to perform, or in instituting any action or proceeding based on such default, or defending, or asserting a counterclaim in, any action or proceeding brought by the Lessee, the expense thereof to the Lessor, including reasonable attorneys' fees and disbursements, shall be paid by the Lessee to the Lessor, on demand, as additional rent.

Lessor's Immunities

29.(a) The Lessor shall not be liable, except by reason of Lessor's negligence, for any failure or insufficiency of heat, or of air conditioning (where air conditioning is supplied or air conditioning equipment is maintained by the Lessor), water supply, electric current, gas, telephone, or elevator service or other service to be supplied by the Lessor hereunder, or for interference with light, air, view or other interests of the Lessee. No abatement of rent or other compensation or claim of eviction shall be made or allowed because of the making or failure to make or delay in making any repairs, alterations or decorations to the building, or any fixtures or appurtenances therein, or for space taken to comply with any law, ordinance or governmental regulation, or for interruption or curtailment of any service agreed to be furnished by the Lessor, due to accidents, alterations or repairs, or to difficulty or delay in securing supplies or labor or other cause beyond Lessor's control, unless due to Lessor's negligence.

Storage Space and Laundry

(b) If the Lessor shall furnish to the Lessee any storage bins or space, the use of the laundry, or any facility outside the apartment, including but not limited to a television antenna, the same shall be deemed to have been furnished gratuitously by the Lessor under a revocable license. The Lessee shall not use such storage space for the storage of valuable or perishable property and any such storage space assigned to Lessee shall be kept by Lessee clean and free of combustibles. If washing machines or other equipment are made available to the Lessee, the Lessee shall use the same on the understanding that such machines or equipment may or may not be in good order and repair and that the Lessor is not responsible for such equipment, nor for any damage caused to the property of the Lessee resulting from the Lessee's use thereof, and that any use that Lessee may make of such equipment shall be at his own cost, risk and expense.

Automobiles and Other Property

(c) The Lessor shall not be responsible for any damage to any automobile or other vehicle left in the care of any employee of the Lessor by the Lessee, and the Lessee hereby agrees to hold the Lessor harmless from any liability arising from any injury to person or property caused by or with such automobile or other vehicle while in the care of such employee. The Lessor shall not be responsible for any property left with or entrusted to any employee of the Lessor, or for the loss of or damage to any property within or without the apartment by theft or otherwise.

Window Cleaning

30. The Lessee will not require, permit, suffer or allow the cleaning of any window in the premises from the outside (within the meaning of Section 202 of the New York

Labor Law) unless the equipment and safety devices required by law, ordinance, rules and regulations, including, without limitation, Section 202 of the New York Labor Law, are provided and used, and unless the industrial code of the State of New York is fully complied with and the Lessee hereby agrees to indemnify the Lessor and its employees, other lessees, and the managing agent, for all losses, damages or fines suffered by them as a result of the Lessee's acquiring, permitting, suffering or allowing any window in the premises to be cleaned from the outside in violation of the requirements of the aforesaid laws, ordinances, regulations and rules.

Termination of Lease by Lessor

31. If upon, or at any time after, the happening of any of the events mentioned in subdivisions (a) to (i) inclusive of this Paragraph 31, the Lessor shall give to the Lessee a notice stating that the term hereof will expire on a date at least five days thereafter, the term of this lease shall expire on the date so fixed in such notice as fully and completely as if it were the date herein definitely fixed for the expiration of the term, and all right, title and interest of the Lessee hereunder shall thereupon wholly cease and expire, and the Lessee shall thereupon quit and surrender the apartment to the Lessor, it being the intention of the parties hereto to create hereby a conditional limitation, and thereupon the Lessor shall have the right to re-enter the apartment and to remove all persons and personal property therefrom, either by summary dispossess proceedings, or by any suitable action or proceeding at law or in equity, or by force or otherwise, and to repossess the apartment in its former estate as if this lease has not been made, and no liabililty whatsoever shall attach to the Lessor by reason of the exercise of the right of re-entry, repossession and removal herein granted and reserved:

Lessee Ceasing to Own Accompanying Shares Lessee Becoming a Bankrupt

(a) If the Lessee shall cease to be the owner of the shares to which this lease is appurtenant, or if this lease shall pass or be assigned to anyone who is not then the owner of all of said shares;

(b) If at any time during the term of this lease (i) the then holder hereof shall be adjudicated a bankrupt under the laws of the United States; or (ii) a receiver of all of the property of such holder or of this lease shall be appointed under any provision of the laws of the State of New York, or under any statute of the United States, or any statute of any State of the United States and the order appointing such receiver shall not be vacated within thirty days; or (iii) such holder shall make a general assignment for the benefit of creditors; or (iv) any of the shares owned by such holder to which this lease is appurtenant shall be duly levied upon under the proceeds of any court whatever unless such levy shall be discharged within thirty days; or (v) this lease or any of the shares to which it is appurtenant shall pass by operation of law or otherwise to anyone other than the Lessee herein named or a person to whom such Lessee has assigned this lease in the manner herein permitted, but this subsection (v) shall not be applicable if this lease shall devolve upon the executors or administrators of the Lessee and provided that within eight (8) months (which period may be extended by the Directors) after the death said lease and shares shall have been transferred to any assignee in accordance with Paragraph 16 hereof;

Assignment, Subletting or Unauthorized Occupancy

(c) If there be an assignment of this lease, or any subletting hereunder, without full compliance with the requirements of Paragraphs 15 or 16 or 38 hereof, or if any person not authorized by Paragraph 14 shall be permitted to use or occupy the apartment, and the Lessee shall fail to cause such unauthorized person to vacate the apartment within ten days after written notice from the Lessor;

Default in Rent

(d) If the Lessee shall be in default for a period of one month in the payment of any rent or additional rent or of any installment thereof and shall fail to cure such default within ten days after written notice from the Lessor;

Default in Other Covenants

(e) If the Lessee shall be in default in the performance of any covenant or provision hereof, other than the covenant to pay rent, and such default shall continue for thirty days after written notice from the Lessor;

Lessee's Objectionable Conduct

(f) If at any time the Lessor shall determine, upon the affirmative vote of two-thirds of its then Board of Directors, at a meeting duly called for that purpose, that because of objectionable conduct on the part of the Lessee, or of a person dwelling or visiting in the apartment, repeated after written notice from Lessor, the tenancy of the Lessee is undesirable;

Termination of all Proprietary Leases

(g) If at any time the Lessor shall determine, upon the affirmative vote of two-thirds of its then Board of Directors at a meeting of such directors duly called for that purpose, and the affirmative vote of the record holders of at least 75% in amount of its then issued shares, at a shareholders' meeting duly called for that purpose, to terminate all proprietary leases;

Destruction
of Building

Condemnation

Lessor's
Rights
After
Lessee's
Default

(h) If the building shall be destroyed or damaged and the shareholders shall decide not to repair or rebuild as provided in Paragraph 4;

(i) If at any time the building or a substantial portion thereof shall be taken by condemnation proceedings.

32. (a) In the event the Lessor resumes possession of the apartment, either by summary proceedings, action of ejectment or otherwise, because of default by the Lessee in the payment of any rent or additional rent due hereunder, or on the expiration of the term pursuant to a notice given as provided in Paragraph 31 hereof upon the happening of any event specified in subsections (a) to (f) inclusive of Paragraph 31, Lessee shall continue to remain liable for payment of a sum equal to the rent which would have become due hereunder and shall pay the same in installments at the time such rent would be due hereunder. No suit brought to recover any installment of such rent or additional rent shall prejudice the right of the Lessor to recover any subsequent installment. After resuming possession, the Lessor may, at its option, from time to time (i) relet the apartment for its own account, or (ii) relet the apartment as the agent of the Lessee, in the name of the Lessee or in its own name, for a term or terms which may be less than or greater than the period which would otherwise have constituted the balance of the term of this lease, and may grant concessions or free rent, in its discretion. Any reletting of the apartment shall be deemed for the account of the Lessee, unless within ten days after such reletting the Lessor shall notify the Lessee that the premises have been relet for the Lessor's own account. The fact that the Lessor may have relet the apartment as agent for the Lessee shall not prevent the Lessor from thereafter notifying the Lessee that it proposes to relet the apartment for its own account. If the Lessor relets the apartment as agent for the Lessee, it shall, after reimbursing itself for its expenses in connection therewith, including leasing commissions, and a reasonable amount for attorneys' fees and expenses, and decorations, alterations and repairs in and to the apartment, apply the remaining avails of such reletting against the Lessee's continuing obligations hereunder. There shall be a final accounting between the Lessor and the Lessee upon the earliest of the four following dates: (A) the date of expiration of the term of this lease as stated on page 1 hereof; (B) the date as of which a new proprietary lease covering the apartment shall have be-

come effective; (C) the date the Lessor gives written notice to the Lessee that it has relet the apartment for its own account; (D) the date upon which all proprietary leases of the Lessor terminate. From and after the date upon which the Lessor becomes obligated to account to the Lessee, as above provided, the Lessor shall have no further duty to account to the Lessee for any avails of reletting and the Lessee shall have no further liability for sums thereafter accruing hereunder, but such termination of the Lessee's liability shall not affect any liabilities theretofore accrued.

Collection
of Rent
from Subtenants

(b) If the Lessee shall at any time sublet the apartment and shall default in the payment of any rent or additional rent, the Lessor may, at its option, so long as default shall continue, demand and receive from the subtenant the rent due or becoming due from such subtenant to the Lessee, and apply the amount to pay sums due and to become due from the Lessee to the Lessor. Any payment by a subtenant to the Lessor shall constitute a discharge of the obligation of such subtenant to the Lessee, to the extent of the amount so paid. The acceptance of rent from any subtenant shall not be deemed a consent to or approval of any subletting or assignment by the Lessee, or a release or discharge of any of the obligations of the Lessee hereunder.

Sale of
Shares

(c) Upon the termination of this lease under the provisions of subdivisions (a) to (f) inclusive of Paragraph 31, the Lessee shall surrender to the corporation the certificate for the shares of the corporation owned by the Lessee to which his lease is appurtenant. Whether or not said certificate is surrendered, the Lessor may issue a new proprietary lease for the apartment and issue a new certificate for the shares of the Lessor owned by the Lessee and allocated to the apartment when a purchaser therefor is obtained, provided that the issuance of such shares and such lease to such purchaser is authorized by a resolution of the Directors, or by a writing signed by a majority of the Directors or by lessees owning, of record at least a majority of the shares of the Lessor accompanying proprietary leases then in force. Upon such issuance the certificate owned or held by the Lessee shall be automatically cancelled and rendered null and void. The Lessor shall apply the proceeds received for the issuance of such shares towards the payment of the Lessee's indebtedness hereunder, including interest, attorneys' fees and other expenses incurred by the Lessor, and, if the proceeds are sufficient to pay the same, the Lessor shall pay over any surplus to the Lessee, but, if insufficient, the Lessee shall remain liable for the balance of the indebtedness. Upon the issuance of any such new proprietary lease and certificate, the Lessee's liability hereunder shall cease and the Lessee shall only be liable for rent and expenses accrued to that time. The Lessor shall not, however, be obligated to sell such shares and appurtenant lease or otherwise make any attempt to mitigate damages.

Waiver of Right of Redemption

33. The Lessee hereby expressly waives any and all right of redemption in case the Lessee shall be dispossessed by judgment or warrant of any court or judge. The words "enter", "re-enter" and "re-entry" as used in this lease are not restricted to their technical legal meaning.

Surrender of Possession

34. Upon the termination of this lease under the provisions of subdivisions (a) to (f) of Paragraph 31, the Lessee shall remain liable as provided in Paragraph 32 of this lease. Upon the termination of this lease under any other of its provisions, the Lessee shall be and remain liable to pay all rent, additional rent and other charges due or accrued and to perform all covenants and agreements of the Lessee up to the date of such termination. On or before any such termination the Lessee shall vacate the apartment and surrender possession thereof to the Lessor or its assigns, and upon demand of the Lessor or its assigns, shall execute, acknowledge and deliver to the Lessor or its assigns any instrument which may reasonably be required to evidence the surrendering of all estate and interest of the Lessee in the apartment, or in the building of which it is a part.

Lessee's Option to Cancel

35.(a) This lease may be cancelled by the Lessee on any September 30th after the third anniversary of the consummation of the Offering Statement-Plan of Cooperation Organization pursuant to which proprietary leases were originally issued, upon complying with all the provisions hereinafter set forth. Irrevocable written notice of intention to cancel must be given by the Lessee to the Lessor on or before April 1 in the calendar year in which such cancellation is to occur. At the time of the giving of such notice of intention to cancel there must be deposited with the Lessor by the Lessee:

Deposits Required

(i) the Lessee's counterpart of this lease with a written assignment in form required by the Lessor, in blank, effective as of August 31 of the year of cancellation, free from all subleases, tenancies, liens, encumbrances and other charges whatsoever.

(ii) the Lessee's certificate for his shares of the Lessor,

endorsed in blank for transfer, and with all necessary transfer tax stamps affixed and with payment of any transfer taxes due thereon.

(iii) a written statement setting forth in detail those additions, improvements, fixtures or equipment which the Lessee has, under the terms of this lease, the right to and intends to remove.

Removal
of Fixtures
Possession

(b) All additions, improvements, appliances and fixtures which are removable under the terms of this lease and which are enumerated in the statement made as provided in subdivision (iii) above shall be removed by the Lessee prior to August 31st of the year of cancellation, and on or before said August 31st the Lessee shall deliver possession of the apartment to the Lessor in good condition with all required equipment, fixtures and appliances installed and in proper operating condition and free from all subleases and tenancies, liens, encumbrances and other charges and pay to the Lessor all rent, additional rent and other charges which shall be payable under this lease up to and including the following September 30th.

Permission to Show
and Occupy
Premises

(c) The Lessor and its agents may show the apartment to prospective lessees, contractors and architects at reasonable times after notice of the Lessee's intention to cancel. After August 31st or the earlier vacating of the apartment, the Lessor and its agents, employees and lessees may enter the apartment, occupy the same and make such alterations and additions therein as the Lessor may deem necessary or desirable without diminution or abatement of the rent due hereunder.

Effective
Date of
Cancellation

(d) If the Lessee is not otherwise in default hereunder, and if the Lessee shall have timely complied with all of the provisions of subdivisions (a) and (b) hereof, then this lease shall be cancelled and all rights duties and obligations of the parties hereunder shall cease as of the September 30th fixed in said notice, and the shares of Lessor shall become the absolute property of the Lessor, provided, however, that the Lessee shall not be released from any indebtedness owing to the Lessor on said last mentioned date.

Rights on
Lessee's
Default

(e) If the Lessee shall give the notice but fail to comply with any of the other provisions of this paragraph, the Lessor shall have the option at any time prior to September 30th (i) of returning to the Lessee this lease, the certificate for shares and other documents deposited, and thereupon the Lessee shall be deemed to have withdrawn the notice of intention to cancel this lease, or (ii) of treating this lease as cancelled as of the September 30th named in the notice of intention to cancel as the date for the cancellation of such lease, and bringing such proceedings and actions as it may deem best to enforce the covenants of the Lessee hereinabove contained and to collect from the Lessee the payments which the Lessee is required to make hereunder, together with reasonable attorneys' fees and expenses.

Extension
of Option
to Cancel

36.(a) If on April 1st in any year the total number of shares owned by lessees holding proprietary leases, who have given notice pursuant to Paragraph 35 of intention to cancel such proprietary leases on September 30th of said year, shall aggregate ten percent (10%) or more of the Lessor's outstanding shares, exclusive of treasury shares, then the Lessor shall, prior to April 30th in such year, give a written notice to the holders of all issued shares of the Lessor, stating the total number of shares then outstanding and in its treasury and the total number of shares owned by lessees holding proprietary leases who have given notice of intention to cancel. In such case the proprietary lessees to whom such notice shall have been given shall have the right to cancel their leases in compliance with the provisions of Paragraph 35 hereof, provided only that written notice of the intention to cancel such leases shall be given on or before July 1st instead of April 1st.

Right of
Lessees
to Cancel

(b) If lessees owning at least 80% of the then issued and outstanding shares of the Lessor shall exercise the option to cancel their leases in one year, then this and all other proprietary leases shall thereupon terminate on the September 30th of the year in which such options shall have been exercised, as though every lessee had exercised such option. In such event none of the lessees shall be required to surrender his shares to the Lessor and all certificates for shares delivered to the Lessor by those who had, during that year, served notice of intention to cancel their leases under the provisions hereof, shall be returned to such lessees.

Continuance of
Cooperative
Management
of Building
After All
Leases Terminated

37. No later than thirty days after the termination of all proprietary leases, whether by expiration of their terms or otherwise, a special meeting of shareholders of the Lessor shall take place to determine whether (a) to continue to operate the building as a residential apartment building, (b) to alter, demolish or rebuild the building or any part thereof, or (c) to sell the building and liquidate

the assets of the Lessor, and the Directors shall carry out the determination made at said meeting of shareholders of the Lessor, and all of the holders of the then issued and outstanding shares of the Lessor shall have such rights as enure to shareholders of corporations having title to real estate.

Unsold Shares

38.(a) The term "Unsold Shares" means and has exclusive reference to the shares of the Lessor which were issued to the Sponsor or individuals produced by the Sponsor pursuant to the Offering Statement-Plan of Cooperative Organization or Contract of Sale under which the Lessor acquired the Leasehold to the building, and, all shares which are Unsold Shares retain their character as such (regardless of transfer) until (a) such shares become the property of a purchaser for bonafide occupancy (by himself or a member of his family) of the apartment to which such shares are allocated, or (2) the holder of such shares (or a member of his family) becomes a bonafide occupancy of the apartment. This Paragraph 38 shall become inoperative as to this lease upon the occurrence of either of said events with respect to the Unsold Shares held by the Lessee named herein or his assignee.

Subletting Apartment and Sale of Shares

(b) Neither the subletting of the apartment nor the assignment of this lease, by the Lessee who is the holder of the block of Unsold Shares allocated thereto, shall require the consents of the Directors or shareholders, as provided in Paragraphs 15 and 16, but the consent only of the Sponsor.

Change in Form of Lease

(c) Without the Lessee's consent, no change in the form, terms or conditions of this proprietary lease, as permitted by Paragraph 6, shall (1) affect the rights of the Lessee who is the holder of the Unsold Shares accompanying this lease to sublet the apartment or to assign this lease, as provided in this paragraph, or (2) eliminate or modify any rights, privileges or obligations of such Lessee.

(d) The provisions of Paragraph 35 are not applicable to a Lessee who is the holder of a block of the Unsold Shares accompanying this lease.

(e) A lessee who is the holder of a block of unsold shares shall not have the following paragraphs of this lease applicable to them: Paragraph 11, unless the action is due to the negligent conduct of the holder of proprietary shares himself: Paragraph 14; the first six lines of Paragraph 18(a) through the words "sashes and sills"; Paragraph 21(a), insofar as said alteration comports with the filed building plans.

Foreclosure
Receiver of
Rents

39. Notwithstanding anything contained in this lease, if any action shall be instituted to foreclose any mortgage on the land or the building or the leasehold of the land or building, the Lessee shall, on demand, pay to the receiver of the rents appointed in such action, rent, if any, owing hereunder on the date of such appointment and shall pay thereafter to such receiver in advance, on the first day of each month during the pendency of such action, as rent hereunder, the rent for the apartment as last determined and established by the Directors prior to the commencement of said action, and such rent shall be paid during the period of such receivership, whether or not the Directors shall have determined and established the rent payable hereunder for any part of the period during which such receivership may continue. The provisions of this Paragraph are intended for the benefit of present and future mortgages of the land or the building or the leasehold of the land or building and may not be modified or annulled without the prior written consent of any such mortgage holder.

To Whom
Covenants
Apply

40. The references herein to the Lessor shall be deemed to include its successors and assigns, and the references herein to the Lessee or to a shareholder of the Lessor shall be deemed to include the executors, administrators, legal representatives, legatees, distributees and assigns of the Lessee, except as hereinabove stated.

Waiver of
Trial
by Jury

41. To the extent permitted by law, the respective parties hereto shall and they hereby do waive trial by jury in any action, proceeding or counterclaim brought by either of the parties hereto against the other on any matters whatsoever arising out of or in any way connected with this lease, the Lessee's use or occupancy of the apartment, or any claim of damage resulting from any act or omission of the parties in any way connected with this lease or the apartment.

Lessee's
Additional
Remedies

42. In the event of a breach or threatened breach by Lessee of any provision hereof, the Lessee shall have the right of injunction and the right to invoke any remedy at law or in equity, as if re-entry, summary proceedings and other remedies were not herein provided for, and the election of one or more remedies shall not preclude the Lessor from any other remedy.

Lessee
More Than
One Person

43. If more than one person is named as Lessee hereunder, the Lessor may require the signatures of all such persons in connection with any notice to be given or action to be taken by the Lessee hereunder, including, without limiting the generality of the foregoing, the surrender or assignment of this lease, or any request for consent to assignment or subletting. Each person named as Lessee shall be jointly and severally liable for all of the Lessee's obligations hereunder. Any notice by the Lessor to any person named as Lessee shall be sufficient, and shall have the same force and effect, as though given to all persons named as Lessee.

Effect of
Partial
Invalidity

44. If any clause or provision herein contained shall be adjudged invalid, the same shall not affect the validity of any other clause or provision of this lease, or constitute any cause of action in favor or either party as against the other.

Marginal
Headings
Changes to
be in
Writing

45. The marginal headings of the several paragraphs of this lease shall not be deemed a part of this lease.
46. The provisions of this lease cannot be changed orally.
IN WITNESS WHEREOF, the parties have executed this lease.

HOUSING CORPORATION, Lessor

By _____

President
(L.S.)

By:_____

Lessee. (L.S.)

STATE OF NEW YORK   )
) ss.:

COUNTY OF NEW YORK)

On the   day of   in the year   before me personally appeared   to me known, who being by me duly sworn, did depose and say that he resides at   that he is the President of HOUSING CORPORATION, the corporation described in and which executed the foregoing instrument; that he knows the seal of said corporation; that the seal affixed to said instrument is such corporate seal; that it was so affixed by order of the Board of Directors of said corporation, and that he signed his name thereto by like order

----

STATE OF NEW YORK   )
) ss.:

COUNTY OF NEW YORK)

On the   day of   in the year   before me personally appeared   to me personally known and known to me to be the individual described in and duly acknowledged to me that he executed the same.

UNIT DEED

THIS INDENTURE made the   day of   , 1981, between W & W ASSOCIATES, a New York Limited Partnership with offices c/o Raphael & Marcus, P. C., 551 Fifth Avenue, Suite 1419, New York, New York 10176, ("Grantor"), and residing at   ("Grantee").

WITNESSETH

That the Grantor, in consideration of Ten ($10.00) Dollars and other valuable consideration paid by the Grantee, does hereby grant and release unto the Grantee, and the heirs or successors and assigns of the Grantee forever:

The unit (the "Unit") designated and described as Unit No. XXXXX in the declaration (the "Declaration") establishing a plan for condominium ownership of the land (the "Land") and building (the "Building") comprising Belle Harbor Condominium I , a condominium (collectively, the "Property") made by the Grantor under Article 9-B of the New York Real Property Law, dated 19   , and recorded in the Office of the County Clerk of Queens County on   , 19 in Queens.

The Land is comprised of all that certain lot, piece or parcel of land, situate, lying and being in the County of Queens, and State of New York and more particularly bounded and described in Exhibit A [not shown] annexed hereto and made a part hereof.

TOGETHER with an undivided   percent interest in the Common Elements (as defined in the Declaration);

TOGETHER with an easement for the continuance of all encroachments by the Unit on any other Units or Common Elements now or hereafter existing as a result of construction of the Building, settling or shifting of the Building, repair or restoration of the Building or of the Unit after damage or destruction by fire or other casualty or after taking in condemnation or eminent domain proceedings, or by reason of an alteration or repair to the Common Elements made by Grantor or by or with the consent of the Board of Manager, so that any such encroachments may remain so long as the Building or any section thereof shall stand;

TOGETHER with an easement in common with the owners of other Units to use any pipes, wires, ducts, cables, conduits, public utility lines, and other Common Elements located in any of the other Units or elsewhere on the Property and serving the Unit;

TOGETHER with the appurtenances and all the estate and rights of the Grantor in and to the Unit;

TOGETHER with and SUBJECT to all easements of necessity in favor of the Unit or in favor of other Units or the Common Elements;

SUBJECT to easements in favor of other Units and in favor of the Common Elements for the continuance of all encroachments or such other Units or Common Elements on the Unit, now or hereafter existing as a result of construction of the Building, settling or shifting of the Building, repair or restoration of the Building or of any other Unit or of the Common Elements after damage or destruction by fire or other casualty or after taking in condemnation or eminent domain proceedings, or by reason of an alteration or repair to the Common Elements made by Grantor or by or with the consent of the Board of Managers, so that any such encroachments may remain so long as the Building or any section thereof shall stand;

SUBJECT also to an easement in favor of the other Units to use the pipes, wires, ducts, conduits, cables, public utility lines and other Common Elements located in the Unit or elsewhere on the Property and serving such other Units;

TOGETHER with the rights and easements in favor of the Unit contained in, and SUBJECT to the provisions of, and the easements, restrictions, covenants, agreements and limitations set forth in the Declaration, By-Laws (and the Rules and Regulations annexed thereto) and Floor Plans (each as defined in the Declaration) as the same may be amended from time to time by instruments recorded or filed in the Office of the Clerk of Queens County, State of New York, which, together with any amendments thereto, shall constitute covenants running with the land and shall bind any person having at any time any interest or estate in the Unit, as though such were recited and stipulated at length herein, including, without limitation, the provisions of Article VIII, Section 1 of the By-Laws which provide in part that the sale or lease of a Unit is subject to the right of first refusal in favor of the Board of Managers (as defined in the By-Laws) and the Grantor, as Sponsor under the Declaration.

TO HAVE AND TO HOLD the same unto the Grantee, and the heirs or successors and assigns of the Grantee, forever.

Grantee has examined the Unit and is purchasing the same "as is" and in its existing condition.

The use for which the Unit is intended is that of a one-family residence except that a Unit may be used as a professional office, subject, however, to the applicable governmental regulations and with respect to future conveyances of the Unit, the prior written permission of the Board of Managers and restrictions contained in the Declaration and/or the By-Laws.

The Grantor, in compliance with Section 13 of the Lien Law, covenants that the Grantor will receive the consideration for this conveyance and will hold the right to receive such consideration as a trust fund for the purpose of paying the cost of the improvement and will apply the same first to the payment of the cost of the improvement before using any part of the same for any other purpose.

And the Grantor covenants that it has not done or suffered anything whereby the said premises have been encumbered in any way whatever, except as aforesaid.

This conveyance is made in the regular course of business actually conducted by the Grantor, and is not a substantial portion of the assets of the Grantor.

IN WITNESS WHEREOF, the Grantor has duly executed this deed the day and year first above written.

W & W ASSOCIATES

By _____

STATE OF NEW YORK)
) ss.:
COUNTY OF NEW YORK)

   On the   day of   , nineteen hundred and
known, who being by me duly sworn, did depose and say: that he resides at
            that he is   of W & W Associates, the limited partnership
described in and which executed the foregoing instrument; that he knows the seal of
said corporation; that the seal affixed to said instrument is such corporate seal; that it
was so affixed by order of the board of directors of said corporation; and that he signed
his name thereto by like order.

                                           _____
                                                   Notary Public

DECLARATION
OF
BELLE HARBOR CONDOMINIUM I
(Pursuant to Article 9-B of the Real Property Law
of the State of New York)

W & W Associates, a New York Limited Partnership having an office at 180 East End Avenue, New York, New York 10028 (herein referred to as the "Sponsor"), does hereby declare as follows:

1. *Submission of the Property*. The Sponsor hereby submits the Land and Buildings (each as hereinafter defined) and all other property, real, personal or mixed, intended for use in connection therewith (collectively the "Property") to the provisions of Article 9-B of the Real Property Law of the State of New York (the "New York Condominium Act") and pursuant thereto does hereby establish a condominium regime to be known as Belle Harbor Condominium I (the "Condominium").

2. *The Land*. The Property consists in part of all that certain tract, plot, piece and parcel of land (the "Land) situate, lying and being in the   County of Queens   and State of New York   , and more particularly described in Schedule A [not shown] annexed hereto and made a part hereof. The Land is owned by the Sponsor in fee simple, subject only to the conditions of title set forth on Schedule A.

3. *The Property*. The Property consists, in part, of one building (the "Building") , containing a total of 6 apartments consisting of two and three bedroom apartments (the "Units"). The owners of the Units are herein referred to as "Unit Owners".

4. *The Building*. The Owner owns the following property situated in the County of Queens, City and State of New York, being more particularly bounded and described as follows:

5. *The Units*. Schedule B [not shown] annexed hereto and made a part hereof sets forth the following data with respect to each Unit necessary for the proper identification thereof: Unit Number; building designation; approximate square foot area; number of rooms; the portions of the Common Elements (as hereinafter defined) to which the Unit has immediate access or the right to exclusive use; and the percentage interest in the Common Elements. The location of each Unit is more clearly designated on the Floor Plans (as hereinafter defined) and reference should be made thereto for the statement of the location of each Unit.

As shown on the floor plans of the Building (the "Floor Plans"), certified by Marlo and Dechiara, Architects and intended to be filed in the Office of the County Clerk of Queens   County simultaneously with the recording of this Declaration, the physical dimensions of each Unit consist of the area enclosed horizontally by the unexposed faces of the dry walls at the exterior walls of the Building and the unexposed faces of the dry walls of the Unit side of the dry walls dividing the Units from corridors, stairs or other Units. Vertically each Unit consists of the space between the upper face of the sub-floor and the upper face of the dry wall ceiling. Doors and windows which open from a Unit shall be deemed part of the Unit. To the extent that all or portions of the dry walls or ceilings in Units have been substituted for by

215

sheetrock walls, the term "dry" as used in this Declaration shall be deemed to mean dry or sheetrock, as the case may be.

6. *Common Elements*. The common elements of the Condominium (the "Common Elements") consist of the entire Property, including all parts of the Buildings and improvements thereon, other than the Units. The Common Elements include, without limitation, the following:

(a) The Land, including, without limitation, the portions of the Land on which the buildings are erected, all lawn, garden and sitting areas, streets, roads, drives, walks, parking areas and all other improved or unimproved areas forming a part of the Land and not within the Units together with all easements, rights and privileges appurtenant thereto;

(b) All foundations, columns, girders, beams, supports, those portions of the exterior walls beyond the outside face of the dry wall, those portions of the walls and partitions dividing the Units from corridors and stairs located beyond the unexposed face of the dry wall enclosing the Unit, those portions of the walls and partitions located between the unexposed faces of both dry walls enclosing the respective Units, the sub-floors those portions of the ceilings of first-floor Units from the upper face of the dry wall to the upper face of the sub-floor of the Unit above, those portions of the ceilings of second-floor Units above the upper face of the plaster wall, roofs, corridors, halls and stairs;

(c) All installations outside the Units for services such as heat, power, light, telephone and water;

(d) All sewer and drainage pipes and facilities;

(e) The apartment designated for use by the resident superintendent;

(f) All storage rooms, meter rooms, cellar space, carriage rooms and laundry room;

(g) All other apparatus and installations existing in the Buildings for common use or necessary or convenient to the existence, maintenance or safety of the Buildings; and

(h) The Limited Common Elements consisting of the balcony or patio, if any, solely accessible from the interior of a Unit.

7. *Use of the Units*. Each of the Units may be used only as a residence for a single family by the Unit Owner thereof or his permitted lessees and the members of their immediate families, except that any Unit may be used as a professional office, subject however, to applicable governmental regulations and the prior written permission of the Board of Managers. Notwithstanding the foregoing, the Sponsor may without the permission of the Board of Managers (i) grant permission for the use of any Unit as a professional office and/or (ii) retain ownership of one or more Units for use as models, sales and/or production offices in connection with the sale or rental of the Units.

8. *Person to Receive Service*. Any person serving as a member of the Board of Managers of the Condominium and residing on the Property is hereby designated to receive service of process in any action which may be brought against the Condominium.

9. *Determination of Percentages in Common Elements*. The percentage interest of the respective Units in the Common Elements has been determined upon the ba-

sis of the relative square foot area of each Unit as compared to the total square foot area of all Units.

10. *Encroachments*. If (a) any portion of the Common Elements encroaches upon any Unit; (b) any Unit encroaches upon any other Unit or upon any portion of the Common Elements; or (c) any encroachment shall hereafter occur as a result of (i) construction or renovation of the Buildings; (ii) settling or shifting of the Buildings; (iii) any alteration or repair to the Common Elements made by Sponsor or by or with the consent of the Board of Managers; (iv) any repair or restoration of the Buildings or any Unit after damage by fire or other casualty of any taking by condemnation or eminent domain proceedings of all or any portion of any Unit or the Common Elements, then, in any such event, a valid easement shall exist for such encroachments and for the maintenance of the same so long as the Buildings or any Building shall stand.

11. *Pipes, Wires, Ducts, Cables, Conduits, Public Utility Lines and All Other Common Elements Located Inside of Units*. Each Unit shall have an easement in common with all other Units to use all pipes, wires, ducts, cables, conduits, public utility lines and all other Common Elements located in any of the other units or elsewhere on the Property and serving such Unit. Each Unit shall be subject to an easement in favor of all Units to use the pipes, wires, ducts, cables, conduits, public utility lines and all other Common Elements located in such Unit or elsewhere on the Property and serving other Units. The Board of Managers shall have a right of access to each Unit to inspect the same to remove violations therefrom and to maintain, repair or replace the Common Elements contained therein or elsewhere in the Buildings or on the Land.

12. *Power of Attorney of Board of Managers*. Each Unit Owner shall grant to the persons who shall from time to time constitute the Board of Managers jointly an irrevocable power of attorney, coupled with an interest, to acquire title to, interest in or lease of any Unit whose owner desires to surrender, sell or lease the same or which may be the subject of a foreclosure or other judicial sale, in the name of the Board of Managers or its designee, on behalf of all Unit Owners, and to convey, sell, lease, mortgage (but not to vote the votes appurtenant thereto) or otherwise deal with any such Unit so acquired or to sublease any Unit so leased by the Board of Managers.

13. *Acquisition of Units by Board of Managers*. If (a) any Unit Owner shall surrender his Unit, together with: (i) the undivided interest in the Common Elements appurtenant thereto; (ii) the interest of such Unit Owner in any other Units theretofore acquired by the Board of Managers of its designee, on behalf of all Unit Owners or the proceeds of the sale or lease thereof, if any; and (iii) the interest of such Unit Owner in any other assets of the Condominium (collectively the "Appurtenant Interests") pursuant to the provisions of Section 339-x of the Real Property Law of the State of New York; (b) the Board of Managers shall purchase from any Unit Owner, who has elected to sell the same, a Unit, together with the Appurtenant Interests, pursuant to Sec. 1 of Art. VIII of the By-Laws of Belle Harbor Condominium (the "By-Laws"); or (c) the Board of Managers shall purchase, at a foreclosure or other judicial sale, a Unit, together with the Appurtenant Interests, then, in any such event, title to such Unit, together with the Appurtenant Interests, as the case may be, shall be held by the Board of Managers or its designee, on behalf of all Unit Owners, in proportion to their respective interests in the Common Elements.

14. *Covenants with the Land*. The walks now or hereafter constructed on the Land shall be repaired and maintained by and at the cost and expense of the Condominium.

The Sponsor does hereby reserve (a) an easement in, over, under and across the streets, roads, drives, walks and parking areas now or hereafter constructed upon the Land for all street purposes, including, without limitation, the right to transport construction equipment and materials across and temporarily to store said equipment and materials on said streets, roads, drives, walks, and parking areas for use in connection with the development of the Condominium; and (b) an easement, right, license and privilege to connect to and make use of any utility lines, wires, pipes, conduits, sewers and drainage lines (collectively the "Utilities") now or hereafter installed in all or any part of the Land and to build, relocate and install thereon such additional Utilities as the Sponsor shall deem necessary or desirable to provide adequate drainage and utility facilities for or in connection with the development of the Condominium.

The Sponsor does hereby reserve an easement to erect and maintain one or more signs for the purpose of advertising the development of the Condominium.

All provisions of this Declaration, the By-Laws and the Rules and Regulations annexed hereto (true copies of which are annexed hereto as Schedule C [not shown] and made a part hereof), including, without limitation, the provisions of this Article 14, shall, to the extent applicable and unless otherwise expressly herein or therein provided to the contrary, be perpetual and be construed to be covenants running with the land and with every part thereof and interest therein, and all of the provisions thereof shall be binding upon and inure to the benefit of the owner of all or any part thereof, or interest and assigns, but the same are not intended to create nor shall they be construed as creating any rights in or for the benefit of the general public.

15. *Amendment of Declaration*. This Declaration may be amended by the vote of at least 66-⅔% in number and in common interest of all Unit Owners, cast in person or by proxy at a meeting duly held in accordance with the provisions of the By-Laws, or in lieu of a meeting, any amendment may be approved in writing by 66-⅔% in number and in common interest of all Unit Owners; provided, however, that any such amendment shall have been approved in wiring by all mortgagees who are the holders of mortgages comprising first liens on   or more Units and Sponsor so long as Sponsor owns any Units. No such amendment shall be effective until recorded in the Office of the County Clerk of Queens County.

16. *Changes in the Condominium*. Except to the extent prohibited by law, Sponsor or its designee shall have the right, without the vote or consent of the Board of Managers or other Unit Owners, to: (a) make alterations, additions or improvements, whether structural or non-structural, interior or exterior, ordinary or extraordinary, in, to and upon Units owned by Sponsor or its designee ("Unsold Units"); (b) change the layout of, or number of rooms in, any Unsold Units by subdividing one or more Unsold Units into two or more separate Units, combining separate Unsold Units (including those resulting from such subdivision or otherwise) into one or more Units altering the boundary walls between any Unsold Units or otherwise; and (d) if appropriate, reapportion among the Unsold Units affected by such change in size or number pursuant to the preceding clause (e) their percentage interests in the Common Elements; provided, however, that the percentage interest in the Common Ele-

ments of any other Units (other than Unsold Units) shall not be changed by reason thereof unless the owners of such Units shall consent thereto and, provided further that Sponsor or its designee shall comply with all laws, ordinances and regulations of all governmental authorities having jurisdiction and shall agree to hold the Board of Managers and all other Unit Owners harmless from any liability arising therefrom. The provisions of this Article 16 may not be added to, amended, modified or deleted without the prior written consent of Sponsor or its designee; provided, however, that wherever the consent, approval or satisfaction of Sponsor or its designee is required under this Declaration or the By-Laws, such consent approval or satisfaction shall not be required when there are no Unsold Units. Notwithstanding the other provisions of this Article 16, no reapportionment of the interests in the Common Elements appurtenant to any Unit shall be made unless there is first delivered to the Board of Managers a written certification stating that the percentage interests of the respective Units in the Common Elements, immediately after such reapportionment, will be based upon floor space and the overall dimensions of the respective Units. The certification referred to in the preceding sentence shall be delivered, at Sponsor's election, by Sponsor, the managing agent of the Condominium or any other person reasonably acceptable to the Board of Managers, in the case of any Unsold Units.

17. *Waiver*. No provision contained in this Declaration shall be deemed to have been abrogated or waived by reason of any failure to enforce the same, irrespective of the number of violations or breaches which may occur.

18. *Captions*. The captions herein are inserted only as a matter of convenience and for reference, and in no way define, limit or describe the scope of this Declaration nor the intent of any provision hereof.

19. *Gender*. The use of the masculine gender in this Declaration shall be deemed to refer to the feminine gender and the use of the singular shall be deemed to refer to the plural, and vice versa, whenever the context so requires.

20. *Severability*. If any provision of this Declaration, or any section, sentence, clause, phrase or word, or the application thereof shall in any circumstances be judicially held in conflict with the laws of the State of New York then the said laws shall be deemed controlling and the validity of the remainder of this Declaration and the application of any such provision, section, sentence, clause, phrase or word in other circumstances shall not be affected thereby.

IN WITNESS WHEREOF, the Sponsor has caused this Declaration to be executed by its duly authorized officers and its corporate seal to be hereunto affixed this day of   , 198

W & W ASSOCIATES

By _____

Attest:

_____

Partner

PART 2

SELLING

INTRODUCTION TO SELLING

As the following chapters indicate, selling an apartment requires almost as much planning and decision making as buying one does. The decisions that must be made are different from the ones buyers must make, but they are just as important if the seller plans to get the maximum return from his or her apartment investment.

In the material that follows, selling will be examined from all its aspects, including the tax consequences of the sale, the use of real estate brokers, creative financing techniques, and other vital considerations.

For every buyer there must be a seller, and in many cases there are far more sellers than there are buyers. To give yourself the edge, you should read the chapters on pricing your apartment and on preparing it for sale especially carefully. Potential buyers may also want to read this section, as it will give them insights into how the seller will be approaching the sale and the problems that must be faced.

Selling—Step by Step

1. Decide to sell.

   a. What will you do with the money you receive from the sale?

2. Can the buyer assume your mortgage?
3. Are there any special requirements that you must comply with before selling?

   a. If so, have you considered and solved the problems involved?

4. Decide on a viable selling price.
5. Investigate giving financing to your buyer, if buyer asks.

   a. Know the advantages and disadvantages of purchase money mortgages.

6. Hire an experienced broker and attorney.
7. Negotiating the deal.
8. The closing.

24

Deciding to Sell

S elling an apartment, a house, or other residence means making a number of decisions that can profoundly affect your way of life. Selling is probably easier than buying because fewer decisions have to be made. However, the decisions are just as important as the ones involved in buying. For instance, as a seller you will have to determine:

1.   Whether in fact you really want to sell. That may be harder to ascertain than it sounds. Some people sell for the wrong reasons, such as just wanting to make a profit. They give little thought to the fact that they must have an alternative housing plan if in fact they do sell. It is necessary to decide exactly where you are going to live once you sell, whether you are going to rent or buy, and the effects of all this on those people who will be living with you. It must be emphasized that all of this should be determined before you decide to put your apartment on the market.

2.   What price are you going to ask for the apartment? Many sellers make the mistake of strictly adhering to one price and not deviating from it. The result is usually an unsold apartment. You should determine a range within which you will sell. For example, you should figure out, with the help of a real estate professional, what is the highest price you can expect to get and what is the lowest you can possibly accept, and then you must stick to that range once negotiations begin. If, for instance, it is determined that you may be able to get $100,000 for your apartment but you may have to settle for $85,000, that should be your range. Obviously you will hope to get closer to the $100,000 than the $85,000, but economic conditions and the law of supply and demand may be working against you in this matter. Don't be greedy; get a fair price, but don't look for an excessive one.

3.   Another important decision that will have to be made early on is what you are going to do with the money you will get from the sale of the apartment. Are you going to sink it all in the purchase of another residence? Will you have enough left over to invest in something else? If so, how will you invest it? Or, alternatively are you going to rent, and in that case where are you going to rent and at what price?

4.   If you do decide to sell, are you going to use a broker or brokers to sell the apartment? If not, are you prepared for the aggravation of dealing with buyers yourself?

5. Should you take the money in one lump sum or would it be wiser to have the buyer pay you in monthly installments over a set number of years? There may be, as we shall see, valid reasons for doing it either way.

What all of this adds up to is that you must formulate a plan or a strategy before you make the final decision to sell your apartment. The chapters that follow will give you specifics on these and other matters pertaining to selling. From time to time, it will be recommended that you read a chapter in the Buying section of this book. You should do that because it will put many of the ideas put forth in the Selling section into a different, and hopefully an instructive, perspective.

25

Preparing to Sell

Once the decision has been made to sell your apartment, a number of other decisions have to be made before you actually put the apartment on the market.

ASSUMPTION OF YOUR MORTGAGE—CONDOMINIUMS

The most vital thing you must check on if you are selling a condominium is whether or not the mortgage you presently hold is assumable. Call your lender, tell him or her that you want to sell, and ask about the possibility of a qualified buyer assuming your mortgage. If a buyer can assume and the lender permits it, you will probably have a much easier time selling your apartment than if it is not assumable. However, the option of assumability lies with the lender, not with you.

You should be aware, however, that if someone else assumes your mortgage and he or she defaults on it, you may still be held liable to pay off the mortgage. The chances of your actually having to pay, though, are reduced by the fact that the apartment still stands as collateral for the mortgage loan and, if necessary, the lender will most likely sell the apartment rather than go against you. If, however, the bottom were to fall out of the condominium market and prices declined substantially, then the bank would go after you, the seller, and you would still be held liable. Some banks may release you from personal liability if your mortgage is assumed by someone else. It is vital that you ask about this *before* you permit a buyer to assume your mortgage.

Many lenders will permit assumption but they reserve the right to charge an assumption fee, to raise the interest rate, or to extend the time of the mortgage on the new debtor. If this is the case with your mortgage, the chances of getting someone new to assume your obligation will be very limited. Be sure you know all these restrictions before you opt for assumption.

What are the factors the bank or other lender will look at in determining whether or not to permit assumption? It depends on the interest rate prevalent at the time the assumption request is made, the interest rate of the mortgage you have, the length of time the mortgage has to run, and the qualifications of the individual assuming your mortgage. Some lenders put more emphasis on one of these factors than others and some will weigh all of them equally, but one thing is certain, you usually can't predict what a lender will do about assumption.

There is also the possibility that when you call the lender you will be told that your mortgage is not assumable and, furthermore, that if you do sell you will have to pay off your mortgage totally out of the proceeds of the sale. You might even have to pay a prepayment penalty as well. That depends on the type of mortgage or deed of trust and its provisions. Before you put the apartment up for sale you should take your mortgage to an attorney (the one who is going to help you sell your apartment) and seek his or her advice on assumability and whether or not and at what point, if any, you must pay off your mortgage. Obviously, if you are fortunate enough to have an assumable, low-interest mortgage you will probably have little trouble finding qualified buyers for your apartment. On the other hand, if your mortgage is not assumable, your selling task will be much more difficult.

SPECIAL REQUIREMENTS

It is at this point as well that you should check with the board of managers of the building as to any special requirements that must be considered before you sell. As indicated in Chapter 29, you may have to offer your apartment to the board first and exclusively for some period of time before you can offer it to the general public. Known as the *right of first refusal,* such provisions are becoming more and more commonplace these days. Typically, the board has a period of three months to decide whether or not to purchase the apartment. You probably will not get much more than the bare market value for the apartment if you must sell it to the board of managers, but unfortunately you will have little or no choice in the matter.

Similarly, if a right of first refusal is not required you may have to turn back a portion of the profit you make to the board. Profit turnbacks can be as high as 8–10% of the total profit you make, minus brokers' fees and fix-up expenses. Under one of these provisions you are free to sell to whomever you wish, but you must return part of your profit to the board, which uses it for ongoing operating expenses.

Profit turnbacks and right of first refusal provisions should enter into your thinking at the time you are making your sell decision. They should be explored thoroughly with an attorney before you make up your mind fully whether or not to sell.

PROBLEM FOR SELLERS OF COOPERATIVE APARTMENTS

If you own a cooperative apartment you probably know that the managing board of the cooperative can accept or reject any prospective buyer for your apartment. *Before you begin the selling process you should get together with the board to find out what type of person they will accept and what type they will reject. If you begin negotiating with somebody and they are turned down by the board, you have wasted time and you may have lost other potential deals in the interim period. So, for example, if you know in advance that the board is not willing to accept a couple with children under the age of 5, you would not bother working with a buyer who fell into that category. You and your real estate broker should be totally aware of the managing board's requirements and history with regard to rejections so that a loss of time and possible embarrassment to all parties can be avoided.

QUESTIONS CONCERNING PREPARATIONS FOR SALE

1. Is my mortgage assumable?
2. If so, under what conditions?
3. Must I pay a prepayment penalty if I decide to pay off the mortgage early?
4. Is it a necessity that I offer my apartment to the building first before I offer it to the general public?
5. Will I have to turn back a portion of my profit to the board of managers when I sell?
6. Knowing all the limitations involved, am I still willing to sell my apartment?

*Some states may vary in their approach to these matters because of differences in local laws, but on the whole these statements apply.

26

The Sales Price: How Is It Determined?

Pricing an apartment properly is certainly much more of an art than a science, and it is definitely not a job for amateurs. Arriving at a viable sales price for your apartment involves the interplay of five main factors.

1. The most important factor is the price the market can bear at the moment you put the apartment up for sale. What the market can bear is determined most commonly by a recent sale of a similar apartment in the same neighborhood. Assume for a moment that you are selling a one-bedroom apartment. If a one-bedroom apartment down the street in the same or a similar complex went for $100,000 last week, then that is a base figure with which you can start. Your apartment, however, would have to be quite comparable in many respects to get the same $100,000. Of course this factor varies as the economy ebbs and flows. If the economy is good and people are working, the price that the market can bear will probably be higher than in times of recession and high unemployment.

Accurate information about area sales prices can usually be obtained from local real estate professionals. All sales price determinations should be made in consultation with an active, experienced real estate agent.

2. Timing is vital. One week can make a difference in determining a sales price. For example, if interest rates have risen and lenders are charging more for mortgages (in the case of condominiums) or personal loans (in the case of cooperative apartments), potential buyers may decide that rates are too high and they will delay looking for an apartment to buy. Some lenders may have pulled out of the market altogether thereby resulting in fewer potential buyers. Or, a natural calamity may have occurred causing great damage to a condominium or cooperative complex. Much of timing involves luck.

3. The location of the apartment includes not only the geographic site of the apartment within a certain neighborhood, but also its location relative to other apartments in the building complex. If, for instance, the apartment is in a high-rise building it is a well-known fact that apartments on higher floors are usually worth more than are the same apartments on the lower floors. Apartments on higher floors normally have more light and better views than do those on lower floors, and light and views are items that buyers will pay a premium to get.

232

Neighborhood location is also important. Just one or two blocks in a city or town can make a big difference in price. If the apartment happens to be located in a fringe area, it will command less money than one located in a more luxurious neighborhood.

4. The next factor is the condition of the apartment itself. Obviously, if the apartment you want to sell is in poor condition you will not get as much for it as if it were in good condition. To make the apartment more salable you may have to spend some money fixing it up.

5. The final consideration is the price you paid for the apartment when you bought it.

All of these factors interact in the minds of real estate professionals when they come up with a sales price quote. It is an axiom among real estate brokers that every seller thinks his property is worth a fortune, when in reality it is undoubtedly worth a great deal less. Unless you are a real estate professional let a knowledgeable broker appraise your apartment and give you a realistic sales price. You should consult with a broker on this *prior* to putting the apartment on the market. Sellers who disregard the advice of brokers with regard to price usually find that they have priced their apartments too high, and they end up lowering the price significantly to make a sale.

When an apartment, house, or any other piece of real estate is initially put up for sale, brokers will usually price the property at 10–15% more than they ultimately expect to get for it. That's because buyers usually want and expect to bargain the price down. So, if your apartment is appraised at $100,000, expect it to be offered at $110,000 or even a bit higher. That price gives both the buyer and you, the seller, a little room to maneuver. Few, if any, apartments or houses go for their asking price. Just as you probably wouldn't pay the sticker price for a new car, you can't expect a buyer to pay the first quoted price for a home.

You will want to include in your calculations the broker's commission. You as the seller of course are responsible for the payment of the commission if a broker sells your apartment for you (see Chapter 30). Since the commission is usually in the area of 6% of the total purchase price, you should figure that amount into your sales price as well. Therefore, our $100,000 apartment will probably be offered for $116,000 ($10,000 for the 10% bargaining and $6,000 for a commission).

Don't overprice your apartment. A savvy real estate broker will not allow you to do that. If you do overprice the apartment it will probably go unsold until you come to your senses and lower the price. Be flexible during negotiations with a potential buyer. If you decide you want and can accept $100,000 and you are offered $95,000 as a final price, consider it seriously, especially if the apartment has gone unsold for a length of time. Take the advice of your broker. If the broker thinks that $95,000 is all you will get considering the state of the market, take the $95,000. If you are too greedy you'll probably lose out in the end.

You would be wise, then, to work with a real estate broker in determining your sales price and in selling the apartment for a reasonable price for both you and the buyer. Remember, the broker will try to sell the apartment for as much as possible because his commission is fixed as a percentage of the sales price (except in the case of flat-fee brokers). Therefore, you can be fairly confident that if a broker tells you to make a deal at the price offered, you should close the deal at that price. A broker will not waste his or her time with a seller who is unrealistic. The apartment that has gone unsold for a year or more is probably owned by a seller who has decided that he knows more than his broker and who tries to go it alone.

27

Tax Considerations
for Sellers

A ny seller of a condominium or cooperative apartment must be aware of the tax implications of the sale. Fortunately, the Internal Revenue Code favors home ownership, and sellers and buyers of homes and apartments are given some large tax breaks.

CAPITAL ASSETS AND CAPITAL GAINS

A residence, whether it is a house or an apartment, is defined by the tax laws as a *capital asset*. As such, when you sell this asset you do not pay an ordinary tax; you pay capital gains, which has a lower tax rate than does ordinary income. But, and this is vital, if the apartment you are selling is your *main* residence (not a weekend or vacation home) and you buy another chief residence within two years from the sale, and if its price is the same or higher than the sales price of your old home (less some adjustments such as real estate brokers' fees and other sales expenses), you can postpone paying any capital gains or any type of tax until you sell the second home. The gain is actually postponed by subtracting the gain on the first residence from the cost basis of the second residence. This postponement of gain can occur again and again if new residences are bought periodically.

If you do not build or buy a replacement home within the 24-month period, or if the new home costs less than the old one, you must pay tax on the gain that you made.

It is important, then, to try to sell your apartment as quickly as possible. Ideally, if you can sell it before you move out you will not have to worry about paying any tax on the gain now, if you purchase another home within two years. As indicated, if the apartment you plan to sell is a weekend retreat or a vacation home and you have not established a permanent residence there, you may take the capital gains.

There are two different time periods that are of importance as far as capital gains are concerned: short term and long term. To take full advantage of the lower capital gains tax rate, a capital asset must be held for one year or longer. If you have owned the apartment and you sell it before 12 months have passed, that would be a short-term capital gain and you would then be subject to the short-term capital gains rate, which is nothing more than the ordinary income rate. Many sellers, especially those who buy into a conversion, wait the full year before they sell so that they can take advantage of the long-term capital gains rate.

The concept of capital gains is actually an easy one to grasp. Think of it this way. When you sell a capital asset such as an apartment or house that you own, only 40% of the profit that you receive is added to your other income, and that amount constitutes your taxable income for the year. The remaining 60% of the profit that you receive is excluded forever from your income.

A specific example would be in order here: Suppose you purchase an apartment in Miami Beach on July 23, 1982, for $125,000 and you sell it on October 17, 1984, for $165,000. Your profit is $40,000. Since you held the property for more than a year you will only have to include 40% of that profit in your taxable income for 1984 (40% of $40,000 is $16,000). Depending on your tax bracket, you figure your tax from that. If you are in the 50% tax bracket you would have to pay $8,000 in taxes on the $40,000 profit.

If the sale of your apartment results in a capital gain, you must report it on Schedule D on your federal tax return. A copy of Schedule D is reproduced at the end of this chapter.

$125,000 EXCLUSION

If you are over 55 years of age, the good news is you can ignore the entire discussion just given. The law now provides that if you are over 55 and you file either an individual or joint tax return, and you have used the apartment as your principal residence for at least three of the last five years, you exclude totally (not just postpone) any gain earned, up to $125,000.

The bad news is that this is a once-in-a-lifetime tax break. In addition, if your gain is under $125,000—say, for instance, $50,000—you or your spouse can never use the remaining $75,000. Nevertheless, the elimination of any tax on any gain should be welcome to an older person who may be planning and saving for retirement.

INSTALLMENT SALES

Sellers who take back purchase money mortgages from buyers should know about the installment sales provisions of the Internal Revenue Code. If you have made a gain on the sale of your apartment (and you don't qualify for the $125,000 exclusion because you are under 55 years of age) and you have taken back a purchase money mortgage, you can elect to either report the total amount of the gain you will receive in the year you sell the apartment, or you can spread the taxable gain over the period of the mortgage so that you pay a portion of the tax in installments rather than all at once. Depending on your own personal tax situation, you might opt for one of these alternatives. In any case, you should get together with a finanical advisor to work out which option is better for you.

The purchase money mortgage, by the way, need not be structured in any particular fashion nor is there any particular period of time over which payments must be received. See Chapter 28 for more on purchase money mortgages.

Another tax item for sellers: If you paid off your mortgage early (applicable to condominiums only) so that you could sell the apartment free and clear, and if you had to pay a prepayment penalty, you can deduct the full amount of the penalty from your individual income tax return for the year of the sale. This can amount to a savings of several hundred dollars, so don't overlook it. The bank or other lending institution that held your mortgage should have given you some written documentation with regard to the penalty. If not, ask the lender for it so that you can deduct it. For a fuller discussion of all these matters, study Appendix A.

FIGURING PROFIT AND BASIS

Knowing how much tax to pay depends on how much profit you make when you sell a house or apartment. The rules are the same for both, so, in the following quote from the *New York Times* of July 18, 1982, whenever the word *house* is used you can substitute *apartment*.

"Good record-keeping is the key to figuring out how much of a gain you realize on the sale of a dwelling. To determine this figure, divide your records into three groups: records of purchase of the old house and any improvements to it, records of the sale of your old house, and records of the purchase of the new house.

"Information in the first category enables you to figure out the 'basis' or tax cost of your old house. The starting point is the purchase price of the dwelling. To that, add fees paid for title insurance, recording fees, transfer taxes, and legal fees.

"Included in those calculations should be the cost of any capital improvements made during the period of your residency. Capital improvements cover such items as room additions, new landscaping and swimming pools, or central heating or air conditioning units. However, you must subtract from the basis any tax credits you may have claimed in past years for energy-saving improvements or for property-related casualty deductions.

"The second set of records should enable you to ascertain the gain on your old house when you sold it. Obviously you begin with the selling price of the house and you subtract from that brokers' commissions and legal fees. Your gain is the amount you realize from the sale. This is the net figure of all the items in the second group minus the basis of the house, or the net figure of all the items in the first group.

"Now to figure taxable gain you must turn to the third set of records. First take the amount realized from the sale and subtract any fix-up costs—such as wallpapering and painting—that were incurred to make the house salable. Only work done within a 90-day period ending on the day that the sales contract is entered into, and paid for within 30 days after the sale, can be deducted. The resulting figure is the adjusted sales price of the old house."

At this point you must figure out the cost of the new house or apartment you are purchasing. These costs include downpayment, plus any mortgages assumed, as well as legal fees and real estate brokers' commissions.

"If the cost of the new house is the same or greater than the adjusted sales price of the old house, none of the actual gain is taxed immediately. But if the cost of the new house is less than the adjusted sales price, you are taxed on the difference." There is a way that cooperative apartment buyers can avoid paying tax on any difference however. That is detailed in the Buying section entitled Special Tax Break for Homeowners who Trade Down to a Cooperatives, on page 39.

SCHEDULE D
(FORM 1040)
Department of the Treasury
Internal Revenue Service (0)

Capital Gains and Losses (Examples of property to be reported
on this Schedule are gains and losses on stocks, bonds, and similar investments,
and gains (but not losses) on personal assets such as a home or jewelry.)
▶ Attach to Form 1040.   ▶ See Instructions for Schedule D (Form 1040).

1981

14

Name(s) as shown on Form 1040

Your social security number

| **Part I** | Short-term Capital Gains and Losses—Assets Held One Year or Less | | | | | | **D** |

a. Kind of property and description (Example, 100 shares 7% preferred of "Z" Co.)	b. Date acquired (Mo., day, yr.)	c. Date sold (Mo., day, yr.)	d. Gross sales price less expense of sale	e. Cost or other basis, as adjusted (see instructions page 23)	f. LOSS If column (e) is more than (d) subtract (d) from (e)	g. GAIN If column (d) is more than (e) subtract (e) from (d)
1						

2a Gain from sale or exchange of a principal residence held one year or less, from Form 2119, lines 7 or 11 . . . .

b Short-term capital gain from installment sales from Form 6252, line 19 or 27 . . .

3 Enter your share of net short-term gain or (loss) from partnerships and fiduciaries .

4 Add lines 1 through 3 in column f and column g . . . . ( )

5 Combine line 4, column f and line 4, column g and enter the net gain or (loss) . . .

6 Short-term capital loss carryover from years beginning after 1969 . . . . ( )

7 Net short-term gain or (loss), combine lines 5 and 6 . . . .

| **Part II** | Long-term Capital Gains and Losses—Assets Held More Than One Year | | | | | | |

8						

9a Gain from sale or exchange of a principal residence held more than one year, from Form 2119, lines 7, 11, 16 or 18 . . . .

b Long-term capital gain from installment sales from Form 6252, line 19 or 27 . . .

10 Enter your share of net long-term gain or (loss) from partnerships and fiduciaries .

11 Add lines 8 through 10 in column f and column g . . . . ( )

12 Combine line 11, column f and line 11, column g and enter the net gain or (loss) . . . .

13 Capital gain distributions . . . .

14 Enter gain from Form 4797, line 5(a)(1) . . . .

15 Enter your share of net long-term gain from small business corporations (Subchapter S) . . . . .

16 Combine lines 12 through 15 . . . .

17 Long-term capital loss carryover from years beginning after 1969 . . . . ( )

18 Net long-term gain or (loss), combine lines 16 and 17 . . . .

Note: *Complete this form on reverse. However, if you have capital loss carryovers from years beginning before 1970, do not complete Parts III or V. See Form 4798 instead.*

For Paperwork Reduction Act Notice, see Form 1040 Instructions

Schedule D

Part III　Summary of Parts I and II

19　Combine lines 7 and 18, and enter the net gain or (loss) here . . . .
　　NOTE: *If line 19 is a gain complete lines 20 through 22. If line 19 is a loss complete lines 23 and 24.*

20　If line 19 shows a gain, enter the smaller of line 18 or line 19. Enter zero if there
　　is a loss or no entry on line 18 . . . .

21　Enter 60% of line 20 . . . .
　　If line 21 is more than zero, you may be liable for the alternative minimum tax. See Form 6251.

22　Subtract line 21 from line 19. Enter here and on Form 1040, line 12 . . . .

23　If line 19 shows a loss, enter one of the following amounts:
　　(i)　If line 7 is zero or a net gain, enter 50% of line 19,
　　(ii)　If line 18 is zero or a net gain, enter line 19; or,
　　(iii)　If line 7 and line 18 are net losses, enter amount on line 7 added to 50% of the amount on line 18 . .

24　Enter here and as a loss on Form 1040, line 12, the smallest of:
　　(i)　The amount on line 23;
　　(ii)　$3,000 ($1,500 if married and filing a separate return); or,
　　(iii)　Taxable income, as adjusted . . . .

Part IV　**Computation of Alternative Tax**
　　(Complete this part if line 20 (or Form 4798, line 8) shows a gain and your tax rate is above 50%. See instructions page 23.)

25　Net short-term gain or (loss) from line 5, from sales or exchanges after June 9, 1981 . . . .

26　Net long-term gain or (loss) from line 16, from sales or exchanges after June 9, 1981 . . . .

27　If line 26 shows a gain, combine line 25 and line 26. If line 26 or this line shows a loss or zero, enter zero
　　and do not complete rest of this part . . . .

28　Enter the smaller of line 26 or line 27 . . . .

29　Enter the smaller of line 20 (or Form 4798, line 8) or line 28 . . . . . .

30　Enter your Taxable Income from Form 1040, line 34 . . . .

31　Enter 40% of line 29 . . . .

32　Subtract line 31 from line 30. If line 31 is more than line 30, enter zero . . . .

33　Tax on amount on line 32. ☐ Tax Rate Schedule X, Y, or Z; ☐ Schedule G. (See instructions page 23) . .

34　Enter 20% of line 29 . . . .

35　Add lines 33 and 34. If the result is less than your tax using other methods, enter this amount on Form
　　1040, line 35 and check Schedule D box . . . .

Part V　**Computation of Post-1969 Capital Loss Carryovers from 1981 to 1982**
　　(Complete this part if the loss on line 23 is more than the loss on line 24)

Section A.—Short-term Capital Loss Carryover

36　Enter loss shown on line 7; if none, enter zero and skip lines 37 through 41—then go to line 42 . . . .

37　Enter gain shown on line 18. If that line is blank or shows a loss, enter zero . . . .

38　Reduce any loss on line 36 to the extent of any gain on line 37 . . . .

39　Enter amount shown on line 24 . . . .

40　Enter smaller of line 38 or 39 . . . .

41　Subtract line 40 from line 38. This is your short-term capital loss carryover from 1981 to 1982 . . . . .

Section B.—Long-term Capital Loss Carryover

42　Subtract line 40 from line 39 (Note: *If you skipped lines 37 through 41, enter amount from line 24)* . . .

43　Enter loss from line 18; if none, enter zero and skip lines 44 through 47 . . . .

44　Enter gain shown on line 7. If that line is blank or shows a loss, enter zero . . . .

45　Reduce any loss on line 43 to the extent of any gain on line 44 . . . .

46　Multiply amount on line 42 by 2 . . . .

47　Subtract line 46 from line 45. This is your long-term capital loss carryover from 1981 to 1982 . . . . .

Part VI　Complete this Part Only if You are Electing Out of the Installment Method And are Reporting a Note or Other Obligation at Less Than Full Face Value

☐　Check here if you elect out of the installment method.
　　Enter the face amount of the note or other obligation ▶ ....
　　Enter the percentage of valuation of the note or other obligation ▶

☆ U.S. GOVERNMENT PRINTING OFFICE : 1981—O— 343 412 13 560b244

Schedule D (*Continued*)

241

28

Seller Financing:
The Purchase Money
Mortgage

As a seller you can provide financing for a potential buyer by giving a *purchase money mortgage*. What is a purchase money mortgage? Simply stated, it is a mortgage given by the seller to the buyer. Instead of applying to a bank, a savings and loan, or a private mortgage lender for financing, the buyer asks the owner of the apartment (or house or other piece of real estate) if he or she will take back a mortgage for the purchase price of the apartment minus, of course, an agreed-upon downpayment. Essentially, then, the seller stands in the same position as a bank would if a bank held the mortgage. The buyer makes his monthly payments to the seller instead of to a bank. Of course, an interest rate is agreed to between the buyer and seller just as one would be between the bank and the buyer.

Purchase money mortgages are becoming more common these days because of the fact that fewer and fewer lending institutions are getting in or staying in the condominium loan business. Therefore, sellers are turning to purchase money mortgages as a way of making mortgages available to good, qualified buyers. Purchase money mortgages are part of the creative financing movement that you may have been reading about. There are certain advantages and disadvantages to giving purchase money mortgages that every seller contemplating giving one should be aware of. Here are the considerations.

ADVANTAGES

1. It may make it easier to sell your apartment. Because mortgage money is tight in certain parts of the country, financing by way of a purchase money mortgage may be the only way to sell your apartment.

2. The seller gets to structure the deal any way he or she wishes. You can ask for any downpayment you deem necessary, and you can require an interest rate commensurate with the risk you are taking.

3. The seller gets steady income over a set number of years, which is particularly important if the seller has retired and needs supplementary income to support himself and his family. Also, cash flow is improved for the seller.

4. There are certain tax advantages that the seller gets as well, such as access to the installment sales provisions of the tax code. Since the entire purchase price does not come to the seller in one lump

sum, but is paid over a number of years, the seller need not declare a large sum of money as taxable income in the year of the sale. If the seller has retired and his or her income is lower than when the seller was working, he or she is probably in a lower tax bracket and, therefore, will be paying substantially less taxes.

DISADVANTAGES

1.   If you as the seller want to "trade up" to a more expensive apartment, a purchase money mortgage may not provide you with the necessary funds to do so. Assume for the moment that you are selling your apartment for $100,000 and you want to buy a $200,000 apartment to replace it. The only amount you will be getting in a lump sum at the closing on the sale of your $100,000 apartment is the amount of the downpayment. Let's further assume that the amount of the downpayment you get is $20,000. If you expect to take that $20,000 and use it as the downpayment on your $200,000 apartment, it may not be enough. You may have to dig into your savings or cash in some investments to get the required downpayment for your new home.

2.   The buyer who is actively seeking a purchase money mortgage may not be as creditworthy as one who looks for financing through the more traditional sources. It is a fact that some buyers who have poor credit histories and know that they can't get bank financing try to make up for that deficiency by asking for a purchase money mortgage. Sellers who give purchase money mortgages to such buyers are assuming a very large risk. And that leads to the next disadvantage.

3.   If the buyer defaults on his purchase money mortgage to you, you will have to foreclose on the apartment. That can be an expensive and time-consuming process, to say nothing of the aggravation involved.

What does all this mean then? It means that you now know the pluses and minuses of giving a purchase money mortgage, and you should, with the help of competent experts, assess your own situation and decide whether or not giving a purchase money mortgage is a wise course for you to follow. A lot depends on the type of buyer. The bottom line is, if you can't sell your apartment without granting a purchase money mortgage, make sure that you get the most creditworthy buyer you can. Your lawyer should be able to check out any prospective buyer very carefully. If for some reason the buyer does not check out, don't get involved with him or her in any kind of financial transaction.

As just discussed, there is some risk involved in the taking back of a purchase money mortgage: the buyer might default and you will have to foreclose to get the property back. That is a time-consuming and expensive procedure. But you can reduce the risk in the following manner:

> With properly executed seller financing, the seller can insure his money against default with a mortgage underwriter—just as a bank does in a conventional mortgage. But more important, the seller can now get his money out if he should need it before the term of the loan expires.
>
> The key to a safe transaction is to have the mortgage agreement drawn up by a bank, a savings and loan association or a mortgage company.*

Here is what they will do for you. "For a fee ranging from $200 to one-half of 1 percent of the mortgage, the bank or S&L will process the loan agreement, check the buyer's credit, provide access to mortgage insurance and utilize standard loan forms and documents."†

Some banks and savings and loans also offer a service whereby they will, if you wish, collect all payments from the buyer, pay all taxes, and so on, and will even collect delinquent payments from the buyer. The standard fee for this service is, according to experts, one-half of one percent of the monthly interest, or 6% of the annual interest. In other words, you need do nothing. You will just receive a check every month. This is becoming an increasingly popular service but you might have to search for a bank or savings and loan that offers it in your area.

---

*"Reducing the Risk in Owner-Financed Home Sales," *Home*, May 1982.
†Ibid.

29

Restrictions on the Sale
of Your Apartment

Unfortunately for sellers, a unique phenomenon has recently spread across the country which can restrict your freedom of action as well as your profit. These are the twin strategies of *right of first refusal* and *profit turnback*. These are unique because they are only relevant and applicable to sellers of cooperative and condominium apartments, not to sellers of single-family homes. It should be noted, however, that not every state allows right of first refusal or profit turnback. If your state prohibits them, then freedom of choice will be enhanced greatly.

RIGHT OF FIRST REFUSAL

Simply stated, right of first refusal means that you as the seller cannot offer your apartment for sale to the general public until you offer it first to the managing board or homeowners' association of the cooperative or condominium. This offer, in most cases, must stay open for a designated period of time, normally three months.

The result is that you will probably be restricted in the amount of profit you make if the board or association purchases the apartment. Most boards and homeowners' associations will buy the apartment for what they call the "market price," but it will probably be quite a bit less than what you could get for it if you sold to an outsider. You will undoubtedly have not as much bargaining room with a homeowners' group or governing board as you would with an individual buyer.

Why would a managing board want to buy an apartment in the first place? The answer is rather simple, really. Boards and homeowners' associations are always looking for ways to build up their reserve funds or to increase their cash flow. If they buy an apartment and sell it at a later time they may be able to make a hefty profit on the deal, and the profit can be put into the reserve fund or into present operating funds to keep the building or buildings going. Also, in the period between their purchase from you and a future sale, the board or homeowners' association can rent the apartment out as a landlord and the rental income can increase the cash flow of the complex.

These right of first refusal clauses are usually enacted during periods of economic stress for the condominium or cooperative, and they are rarely changed after the hard times have improved.

If you are governed by such a clause in the bylaws or house rules of your condominium or cooperative, there is not much you can do except comply. Some clauses are worded in such a way that you, as the seller, do not have to accept the first offer made and there is some room for negotiation. However, most clauses restrict your right to sell to an outsider exclusively for a set period of time. Obviously you should consult legal counsel if you want to break one of these clauses.

One further note: The good news is that just because such a clause exists does not mean that the board or homeowners' association will enforce it in every case and will try to buy every apartment that comes up for sale within a certain period. The board may feel, for instance, that it has enough cash flow or that its reserve fund is sufficiently flush that it needn't bother with buying your apartment. Some concern with building image is important to some governing boards as well, and if they are known as a board that always enforces the right of first refusal clause few buyers will buy into the building if their resale rights are going to be severely restricted.

PROFIT TURNBACKS

Yet another restriction on the sale of your apartment is the profit turnback. Here you can sell your apartment in an unfettered fashion, but you must turn back a portion of your profit to the homeowners' association or cooperative board. The amount of the turnback varies with the complex involved, but after deducting sales expenses such as brokers' fees and lawyers' charges, the norm is a turnback of 8–10% of the profit you make on the sale. Once again the rationale used is that the turnback keeps the condominium or cooperative complex running smoothly and without having to raise homeowners' dues or maintenance charges nearly so often.

The practice of asking for a profit turnback is usually strictly enforced in those complexes where it is present. If you must turn back a portion of your profit to a board of managers, you might consider raising your asking price for the apartment by the amount of the turnback percentage. Since all sellers in the complex will probably be subject to the same procedure, you will probably not lose any potential buyers for your apartment because apartments within the complex will undoubtedly be priced accordingly.

If, however, you find that your apartment is overpriced in relation to apartments outside your complex, you may just have to eat the profit turnback and settle for a lower profit for yourself. For more on this read Chapter 8 in the Buying Section.

OTHER RESTRICTIONS

You may have to abide by other restrictions as well when it comes time to sell. Many apartment complexes, especially the garden apartment type, prohibit sellers from putting up For Sale signs anywhere on the property. Although this may seem to be a minor inconvenience, it could make a big difference to those sellers who want to try to sell their apartments without the aid of a real estate agent.

Some sellers reason that if they can't sell their apartments within a certain time they can always rent them out. But a large number of apartment complexes these days will not allow tenant-owners to lease or sublease their apartments, no matter what the circumstances.

The upshot of all this is that you should ask about any and all restrictions that would cover all eventualities before you finally put your apartment up for sale. Restrictions on the sale can affect your sales strategy enormously, and you should know what you are getting into before you start to wheel and deal.

30

Hiring and Dealing
with Real Estate Brokers

Once you have decided to sell your apartment you must make one further decision; that is, whether you wish to sell it yourself or whether you should hire a broker to sell it for you. Many sellers think that they can sell their apartments themselves but later regret their decision. As an individual seller you must make yourself available at all times, especially weekends when most buyers are looking. If you have run an ad in a local paper you can expect to get calls at all hours of the day and night, even if the ad has specified that calls will only be accepted during certain hours.

Also, selling an apartment requires more than just showing it to anybody who calls on the phone. Believe it or not, many people who call to look at an apartment have no intention of buying; they are just curious and nosy. Some individuals actually make a pastime out of looking at other people's apartments or houses. Another thing, highly developed sales skills are a necessity in selling some hard-to-move apartments. Unless you are a "supersalesperson," why hassle with people who may not really be interested in buying in the first place?

Remember, most brokers are skilled in the art of negotiation, and their function is to get you the best price possible for your property. Most sellers don't have this kind of expertise and that is another good reason to consider hiring a broker.

The worst thing you can do is to try to sell your apartment just to avoid paying a sales commission. If you have the time and patience to devote to selling your apartment by all means do it, but wise sellers employ experienced and knowledgeable brokers to do it for them. Despite some belief to the contrary, brokers usually do earn their money.

PICKING A BROKER

Picking a broker does not mean going down to the corner realty office to let them know that you wish to sell your apartment. The corner realty might be very good, but they may not have ever sold a condominium or cooperative. You want to choose a broker who is experienced in the sale of condominiums and cooperatives. Some brokers may advertise in the Yellow Pages that they specialize in condominium and cooperative apartment sales. That is your first source of leads to a broker. Also, if your complex has a managing agent, ask for a recommendation. Many managing agents of buildings also sell apartments within the buildings that they manage. They might be a good choice after all, because they do know the building.

Also, ask others in the complex who have recently purchased apartments about brokers with whom they might have dealt. If you hear consistently good things about one broker in particular, contact him or her as well.

Once you have narrowed down your broker choices, question the brokers about how they plan to present your apartment to prospective buyers. You will also want to know whether or not they have shown other apartments in you building. All in all, you should feel comfortable with the broker or brokers you choose. Some sellers give brokers keys to their apartments so that they can show them in the seller's absence. If you plan to do that, you had better feel very comfortable with the broker you are using.

One of the things you want to be sure to discuss with a prospective broker is his or her view of the financing options available to you. If the broker seems tentative or totally uninformed about purchase money mortgages or other creative financing vehicles (see Chapter 7), he or she has not done any homework, and you would be well-advised to go on to the next broker candidate. It should be emphasized again that few deals are being completed using the old-fashioned conventional mortgage, and the broker who is relying on techniques employed years ago should be shunted aside.

One more thing: Brokers are fiduciaries; that is, they have a duty to keep any money received by a buyer for a seller in a safe place such as an escrow account. It is important, therefore, that the broker be honest and trustworthy, as well as competent. In most states, real estate brokers and their salespeople are licensed by the state, and any hanky-panky as regards other people's money will cause revocation of their right to practice in that profession. If you smell anything at all rotten about a broker, cease doing business with him or her and go on to another.

Let's assume you have hired the broker, and he or she is working for you and is looking out for your best interests. Remember, however, that a great deal of money is at stake, and if you make the wrong choice of broker it can cost you a great deal. Don't be afraid to change brokers if things don't work out. Keep your relations with your broker on a purely business level and let the broker know early on that you expect total commitment and professionalism from him and his staff throughout the entire transaction.

Once you have settled on a broker, sit down with that person and discuss how you want to handle the deal. Let the broker know exactly how far you are willing to go in your asking price, how much of a downpayment you expect, and what concessions you might be willing to make to complete the deal. You might want to include some items, such as wall-to-wall carpeting or a chandelier that is in the apartment for the right buyer as part of the purchase price. In any event, be sure you cover all this with the broker before he or she starts to work.

SALES AGREEMENTS

Once you pick a broker he or she will probably ask you to sign a sales agreement. There are three main types of agreements.

1. *The Exclusive Sales or Exclusive Agency Agreement.* This agreement allows the broker you have picked to be your exclusive sales agent to the exclusion of all other brokers. Important: You as the seller *can* sell the apartment on your own and you will not be liable for the payment of a broker's commission. You are not allowed to give the listing out to any other broker, however, during the period when the exclusive agency is in effect.

Exclusive sales agreements usually run for a limited period of time—normally four to six weeks. After that period of time expires, you can renew the exclusive agency, if you wish, or you can let the agreement lapse and you can give the listing out to other brokers. The apartment then would become what is known as an *open listing*. As an open listing the first broker that comes up with a buyer who is ready, willing and able to buy would earn the commission.

2. *The Exclusive Right to Sell Agreement.* Here the broker earns his commission no matter who produces a ready, willing, and able buyer during the period of the agreement. So, if you as the seller would induce somebody to buy your apartment and they do, you will have to pay the broker a commission even though the broker had nothing to do with procuring the customer for you. Obviously, you should think long and hard before you sign an exclusive right to sell. If a broker insists on your signing such an agreement, you might at

that point say No, thank you, and go on to another broker who makes no such demands. Exclusive right to sell agreements can be written for a limited period of time and need not be renewed.

3. *Multiple Listing Agreements.* Some brokers are members of groups of brokers who share listings with one another. Any member of the group can sell the apartment, and then the brokers split the sales commission among themselves based on a formula worked out in advance by the group. Normally, the broker who brings in the listing and the one who sells it share the commission. Multiple-listing brokers will have more than one broker aware of the property, so your apartment may get wider exposure to more buyers than if you listed the apartment with just one broker who is not a member of a multiple-listing group.

FOLLOW-UP

Many sellers make the bad mistake of not following up on their real estate brokers. If a broker is not showing your apartment or is not advertising it, demand to know why. If you are not satisfied with the broker, you can change, or you can make your apartment an open listing where many brokers will work on it. Don't ignore follow-up; after all the broker is supposed to be working for you.

FEES

No matter where you live, be prepared to pay about 6% as a sales commission. That is 6% of the total sales price of the apartment, so if the apartment sells for $100,000 you must pay the broker $6,000 if he or she has produced the buyer.

However, some brokers as an inducement for you to sign an exclusive agency agreement will lower their commission to 5% or possibly even lower, especially if the apartment is a particularly high-priced one. As a seller you can use this as a bargaining chip with a broker who does not want to take a cut in his commission but wants you to sign an exclusive sales agreement. Tell the broker that you will be happy to sign a sales agreement if he or she will drop the commission. If the broker balks, go on to another experienced broker who will accept the deal. There are a good number of brokers out there who are anxious for your business, so you needn't worry that you won't be able to find another.

Commissions earned are normally paid at the time of the closing. If a broker asks you for some payments up front or prior to the closing, you are under no obligation to make such a payment and you would be terribly unwise to do so.

Brokers do not earn their commission until they produce a buyer who is ready, willing and able to buy. But, as a seller you have a responsibility to the broker as far as the terms of the sale are concerned. If you have accepted an offer from a buyer you cannot at that point change the terms of the deal and ask for a higher down payment or an increased sales price. If you do change the terms of the agreed upon deal after an offer has been accepted you may be liable to pay the commission to the broker who produced the buyer, because that broker produced a buyer who was ready, willing and able to buy under the original terms set out. If you renege on the original agreement with the buyer, the broker who brought you the buyer can sue you for the commission due even if the original deal is never consummated.

QUESTIONS CONCERNING REAL ESTATE BROKERS

1. Is he or she a specialist in condominium or cooperative sales?
2. How many years' experience does the broker have?
3. Is the broker fully conversant with all alternative and creative financing options?
4. How experienced and knowledgeable are the salespeople who will show your apartment?
5. How do they plan to present your apartment to prospective buyers?
6. What kind of sales agreement, if any, will you be required to sign?
7. Is the broker's fee negotiable?

31

Should You Have
an Attorney Represent You?

There might be some argument made that a buyer doesn't need an attorney when buying an apartment, but there can be no question that a seller needs one. It is the seller's attorney who traditionally draws up the contract of sale, so it is imperative that a seller be represented by competent legal counsel.

TYPE OF ATTORNEY

Attorneys tend to specialize in certain areas of the law. Knowing that, you would be wise to seek out an attorney who specializes in real estate transactions generally, and cooperatives or condominiums specifically. An attorney who conducts a general practice may not be suitable for this purpose. Although most real estate contracts are relatively straightforward and uncomplicated legal documents, problems can always develop that might have unforeseen consequences. You want to have the best people on your side.

FINDING AN ATTORNEY

If lawyers are good, that reputation will usually have preceded them. If you have a good relationship with a bank or savings and loan, ask loan officers for a referral. They see a lot of attorneys in action at closings, and they have probably formed some opinions as to which ones are the best in the locality where you are selling. Similarly, title guarantee companies see attorneys at work and they may have a suggestion or two as well. Of course, if friends or relatives have had good experiences with a fine real estate attorney, take their recommendations as well. Narrow your choice down to two or three lawyers and interview them. In the end, you should pick the one with whom you feel most comfortable. By the way, most lawyers will not charge you for the interview visit.

FEES

The typical nationwide lawyer's fee for a real estate transaction is approximately 1% of the total purchase price of the apartment. That fee, by the way, holds whether you are the buyer or the seller of an apartment. However, since the seller's attorney draws up the contract, the fee might be somewhat higher if the contract is a tricky or unusual one. Additional duties may add to the fee. For example, if the attorney conducts the negotiations on price with the buyer for you in the absence of a real estate agent, the fee might be higher. Upon occasion and if you are lucky and if the buyer really wants your apartment desperately, you might get him or her to pay your lawyer's fee; but don't expect it to happen very often.

DUTIES OF THE ATTORNEY

Besides drawing up the contract of sale, you should use your attorney as the person your real estate agent calls if the negotiations become especially sticky. If you can stay out of the negotiations on a day-to-day basis, and you can leave the details to the real estate agents and lawyers, you will probably be better off. Of course, you should inform your attorney and broker of the parameters of the deal you want to make and let them negotiate with prospective buyers.

If the attorney is a good one, he or she will undoubtedly counsel you on the tax consequences of the sale. If, in fact, that happens, be sure that you are charged separately for the tax advice. Why? Any tax advice received from an attorney, accountant, or other tax professional is tax deductible in the year in which it is given. So, if you get a bill from the attorney charging you $1,000, $800 of which is for drawing the contract and $200 for tax advice, you can deduct $200 on your federal income tax return in that year.

QUESTIONS CONCERNING ATTORNEYS

1. Is he or she fully experienced in cooperative and condominium legal matters?
2. How many contracts of sale has he or she drawn up in the course of his or her real estate practice?
3. Will the attorney have sufficient time to devote to your particular sale?
4. Who will actually do the bulk of the work, the attorney you are interviewing or a less experienced associate?

5. What is the fee you will be charged?

6. Is the fee all-inclusive for total services rendered, or will you be charged separately for drawing up the contract and his or her attendance at the closing?

7. Will the attorney be representing any other party in the transaction?

32

Preparing the Apartment for Showing

J ust as you would clean and wax a car before you tried to sell it, you should prepare an apartment properly to be shown to prospective buyers. Much of this may sound somewhat frivolous, but real estate brokers and salespeople in all parts of the country agree that a house or apartment that shows well is much more salable.

Some of the following suggestions and tips have been garnered from people who have had unusual success selling apartments quickly and for the price they wanted.

By far the most important thing is to have the apartment totally cleaned from top to bottom. Nothing turns a prospective buyer off faster than dirt, especially in the kitchen and bathroom areas. Some sellers have hired professional cleaning services to come in and do the job.

Strive to make the apartment as homey as possible. One very successful seller made sure that bread was baking in the oven when prospects came. The smell from the baking bread was very pleasing and enhanced the chances of making the sale. To complete the picture, the seller had coffee perking and flowers had been placed in vases throughout the apartment.

Emphasize the special features of the apartment in a subtle way. For example, if it is winter and the apartment has a working fireplace, have a fire going; or if the apartment is a particularly bright one, have the shades up so that the sun can come streaming in.

Fully furnished apartments show better than totally empty ones. Real estate salespeople will tell you that prospects tend to underestimate sizes of rooms when there is no furniture. If possible, try to show your apartment while it is furnished and while you are still living in it.

If any major work has to be done in the apartment—such as adding counterspace in the kitchen or a retiling of the bathroom—try, if possible, to make sure that it is completed before prospects see the apartment.

Don't forget some of the little repairs as well. For instance, leaky faucets should be fixed, and constantly running toilets should be adjusted. Also, don't neglect cleaning the windows. Most buyers will turn on faucets and look out windows to check the views.

If you don't already have one handy, buy a tape measure. Have it ready if the prospect needs it. Savvy real estate agents will often carry a tape measure with them at all times, but you should have one handy just in case. Serious buyers always want to know the exact sizes of rooms, windows, and walls.

If you can get a copy of the floor plan for your apartment have it handy to give to the serious prospect. Heady sellers will have 8, 10, or more copies available so that they don't give away their only copy.

Finally make sure that all television sets are turned off and stereos and radios are not blaring when prospects come to see the apartment. Noise is almost as much of a turn-off as dirt.

If you are using a selling agent, he or she may have some other tips and suggestions for you about showing your apartment.

SHOWING THE APARTMENT

Most apartments or houses tend to be shown on weekends or on weekday evenings. The question usually arises as to whether or not the seller should be there when the agent brings a prospective buyer. Most agents would probably say that it is better for the seller to be there.

The main reason to be present is to answer questions that the agent may not be able to answer. You might be asked, for instance, about the conduct of neighbors or the type of people who comprise the board of managers. You would be wise, however, not to interrupt the agent while the sales pitch is being given, but you should make yourself available to answer those tough questions that almost inevitably get asked. By the way, listen to the sales pitch if you can. Agents sometimes get carried away and make inaccurate statements that you might want to correct.

Try to control overly active pets or children while the apartment is being shown. You need not lock them up in a room, but you don't want the buyers to remember your apartment as the one where the cat scratched them or the child was constantly screaming.

To sum up, show off every advantage your apartment has, give it a homey look, and stay in the background in a controlled environment while the prospect is looking at the apartment. Your reward will be an eager buyer willing to meet most of your sales goals.

DOCUMENTS THE SELLER SHOULD HAVE FOR THE BUYER

As a seller you can help the prospective purchase of your apartment enormously by having a number of documents at hand that you can give, once a serious offer is made. The following documents should suffice:

1. A copy of the current income statement for the complex.
2. The latest balance sheet.
3. An up-to-date copy of the house rules and regulations.
4. A current budget.
5. Any proposed budgets.
6. In the case of a cooperative apartment, a prospectus or offering plan no matter how long ago it was issued.
7. A written history of assessments or other special payments that have been made over the past five years.
8. The master deed, if a condominium apartment.
9. Copies of ground or recreational leases, if any.
10. A reasonably up-to-date engineer's report. This is especially vital if the apartment you are selling has recently been converted from a rental unit.
11. Finally, for condominium apartments only, an accurate listing of real estate, water, and other local tax payments made during the period of your ownership.

33

Negotiating Bids, Offers, and Earnest Money

Negotiating normally involves much more than arriving at an agreed-upon price. Often other factors and considerations are negotiated before a deal can be struck. For example, you may have to add your wall-to-wall carpeting to the deal or the nice chandelier in the dining room may become part of the negotiations.

Similarly, and very importantly, both the buyer and the seller may negotiate over move-in and move-out dates. For instance, you might be buying another apartment that you can't move into for another four months, but the buyer of your apartment may want to move in three months. These differences will have to be negotiated. If you can be flexible concering this problem, by all means be flexible. But if you have constraints because of when you are moving, that should become part and parcel of the ultimate agreement. Probably as many deals get hung up on these ancillary kinds of problems as they do on price considerations. But, if you get into the situation where the buyer has to sell his home before he or she has enough money to buy yours, you would do well to have another buyer as a back-up. Almost inevitably, buyers never seem to sell their homes in time to meet a deadline to buy another.

Prior to getting into negotiations, you should have made decisions as to exactly what will be included in the apartment when you sell and what you will take with you. In almost every case, all kitchen appliances remain in apartments and become part of the deal, but if you want to take one of the appliances with you be sure that all parties to the transaction know about it.

A good attorney will ask you if time is of the essence in regard to the sale. The attorney for the buyer may also be interested in the same thing, so be prepared to discuss it before negotiations are concluded.

Negotiating is a two-way street; there are certain things that you will want and, of course, the buyer will insist on others. Obviously, compromising on both sides will probably be required, and no one side should expect to get everything he or she wants. That is why it is recommended that an intermediary—whether it be a real estate broker or an attorney—conduct the negotiations. An intermediary— usually one who is neutral and not as emotionally involved in the situation—is clearly preferable to your doing your own negotiating.

OFFERS

One point that can't be emphasized enough, especially for those sellers who decide to sell their apartments on their own, is that anything to do with a real estate transaction should be in writing, and that includes offers. Whenever an offer is made, be sure that you get it in writing. Not only will you have a record of the offer in case a dispute arises, but the buyer will treat his offer much more seriously if it is written out. You might accept oral interim offers, but final offers should always be in writing.

By the way, real estate brokers can get careless about this sort of thing. If you are using a broker, make sure that the final offer that is communicated to you from the buyer is in writing. Just because a broker is involved does not mean that you should be any less cautious.

COUNTER-OFFERS

You should, of course, keep yourself open to all offers. You may find during the course of the negotiations that you want to make a counter offer. How much you counter offer in any situation should be decided in consultation with your intermediary. Since each negotiation will have a life of its own, there are no general guidelines that can be given with regard to counter offers.

EARNEST MONEY

Once a final price has been agreed to, the potential buyer will probably give a deposit of $1,000 or more to seal the deal at that time. This deposit is sometimes termed *earnest money* and, as the word *earnest* implies, the deposit reflects the seriousness of the buyer in going ahead with the deal.

Whether your broker, your attorney, or you take the deposit, the money *must under all states' laws be placed in an escrow account*. If the deal goes forward, the earnest money is applied toward the purchase price of the apartment.

If the earnest money is not placed in an escrow account, there is a possibility that you could be sued by the buyer, so be extremely careful when you accept an earnest money deposit. Ask your intermediary (if you are using one) whether or not the earnest money has been placed in escrow. This is of utmost importance and must be adhered to strictly.

At this point all prospective sellers should read and study Chapter 17 in the Buying section to find out what the contract of sale should include and how it is used.

34

Choosing Among Buyers

If you find yourself in the fortunate position of having two or more viable bids with equal downpayments offered, how do you choose which buyer to deal with? This is especially important if the buyer is assuming your mortgage or if you have agreed to give a purchase money mortgage.

Short of outright discrimination, you do have quite a bit of freedom in choosing a buyer. Initially, you should consider the recommendation of your real estate broker. A good broker will have accumulated a great deal of financial, social, and personal information about the buyer, usually through credit checks, references, and other information sources. For a rule of thumb, you can't go wrong if you base your decision on the financial strength of the applicant. The applicant with the best financial credentials—the one having the highest income, the best credit references, and financial stability—should be the one chosen.

As indicated in Chapter 29, the managing board may have some particular prohibitions against certain individuals buying into specific cooperative complexes. For example, if your complex caters to mature adults, it would be poor strategy to present to the board an application of a young couple with children. So far, these kinds of prohibitions are legal in almost all parts of the country, so you have little to worry about if the couple with children threatens you with a lawsuit for not selling to them.

In cooperative buildings, the board can accept or reject a potential buyer for any reason at all, and in some locales they don't have to divulge the reason for the rejection. If you are fully aware of the policies of the board, you shouldn't send up an unqualified buyer; you will be doing nothing more than wasting your own and the board's time.

If a buyer is going to assume your mortgage or if you are going to give a purchase money mortgage, you would be wise to have an accountant and/or a lawyer check out the potential buyer. The buyer's financial situation, credit history and future earning potential should be checked most carefully. Remember, if you give a purchase money mortgage to an individual who later defaults, you will end up the loser, so extreme caution is the rule.

Cooperative boards have been known to reject potential buyers for such disparate reasons as the applicant was extremely obese or he was overbearing and obnoxious during the pre-sale interview. But board memberships change and acceptance policies are frequently altered as those changes occur, so you should be totally conversant with the latest board requirements. That way, the chances of your presenting a candidate who doesn't meet board requirements are significantly reduced.

Of course, condominium buyers do not have to run the gauntlet of an unreasonable board of directors. If you own a condominium you can usually sell to whomever you please, so there is even more need for you or your representative to conduct the necessary checks in a thorough and competent manner.

The bottom line here is, if you have a choice among buyers, the one with the strongest financial credentials should be the one given the first crack at making a deal.

APPENDIX A

Condominiums,
Cooperative Apartments,
and Homeowners Associations
(IRS Publication 588)

Department of the Treasury
Internal Revenue Service

Publication 588
(Rev. Nov. 81)

Condo-
miniums,
Cooperative
Apartments,
and
Homeowners
Associations

For use in preparing
1981 Returns

You can get the tax forms and publications referred to in this publication by writing to the IRS Forms Distribution Center listed in your Form 1040 or 1040A Instructions. Or, you can call the Tax Information number in the phone book listed under "United States Government, Internal Revenue Service."

Introduction

If you own a condominium or a cooperative apartment, you generally receive the same tax treatment as other homeowners. However, some special rules apply to you. In some ways, condominiums are treated differently from co-operatives.

This publication gives information about ownership of a condominium or a cooperative apartment and federal taxes. This publication explains how to figure your basis in the property, and whether to deduct or to add to your basis real estate taxes and interest paid at the time you buy your property. There is a discussion on itemizing deductions for interest paid on the mortgage, real estate taxes, casualty and theft losses, etc., and the tax results of making repairs and improvements to your property. Some items, such as depreciation, which you may deduct only if you rent or use your property in business, are also explained. Information on the residential energy credit and how to claim it is provided. There is a discussion on homeowners associations and how they may qualify to be tax-exempt.

For tax information on selling your condominium or cooperative apartment, see Publication 523, *Tax Information on Selling Your Home.* If you are using your condominium or cooperative apartment for rental purposes, see Publication 527, *Rental Property.* If you use part of your home for business purposes, see Publication 587, *Business Use of Your Home.*

Types of Ownership

In a *condominium* arrangement, you own outright a dwelling unit in a multi-unit structure. You also own a share of the common elements of the structure, such as land, lobbies, elevators, and service areas. You and the other condominium owners usually pay dues or assessments to a service corporation that is organized to take care of the common elements. In some cases the service corporation is operated on a nonprofit basis with the condominium owners as shareholders, and in other cases it is a profit-making enterprise.

In a *cooperative* housing arrangement, you own shares of stock in a corporation that owns or leases housing facilities. As a shareholder, you are entitled to occupy a dwelling unit in housing controlled by the corporation. The dwelling unit may be either a house or an apartment in a building, but it must include facilities for cooking, sleeping, and sanitation normally found in a person's home.

Basis

Whether you bought your condominium or cooperative apartment, received it as payment for services, as a gift or inheritance, in payment of a debt, or in trade for other property, you must know its basis to figure gain or loss when you sell or otherwise dispose of your property.

Cost as basis. The cost of property is the amount you pay for it in cash or other property.

Other basis. Sometimes, you must use a basis other than cost such as fair market value. For a complete discussion of original basis and adjustments to basis, see Publication 551, *Basis of Assets.*

Adjusted basis is your original basis *increased* or *reduced* by certain amounts. You must increase your basis during the period you own

the property for improvements, additions, and other capital expenses. You must reduce your basis for losses from fire or other casualty, payments for any easements or rights-of-way granted, and allowable depreciation if you use your home for business or rental purposes.

You must know your adjusted basis at the time of a casualty to figure your deductible loss from the casualty. If you change your home, in whole or in part, to business or rental property, your basis for depreciation is its fair market value or adjusted basis at the time you changed it, whichever is less.

Acquiring Your Property

The way you acquired your home determines its original basis.

Purchase. The original basis of a condominium you bought is the purchase price or cost of the property to you. This includes your down payment and any debt, such as a first or second mortgage, or notes you gave to the seller. You also add to or deduct certain settlement or closing costs from your basis, as explained later.

The basis of a cooperative apartment is the amount you paid for your shares in the corporation owning or controlling the property. This amount includes any purchase commissions or other costs of acquiring the shares. If you are entitled to occupy more than one apartment, you must divide the cost of your shares among your apartments by some reasonable method, such as the relative floor space of the apartments or their appraised value.

Compensation. If you received your property as payment for services, your basis is its fair market value when you received it. You also must include this amount in your income.

Gift. If someone gave you your property, its original basis to you is whatever the donor's adjusted basis was when the gift was made. However, if the donor's adjusted basis was more than the fair market value of the property when it was given to you, you must use that fair market value as your basis for determining any possible loss if you later sell or exchange the property.

For gifts made *before 1977,* if the fair market value was more than the donor's adjusted basis at the time of the gift, increase your basis by any federal gift tax paid on the gift. Do not raise the basis to more than the fair market value of the property when it was given to you. If you received the property as a gift before 1921, your original basis is the fair market value of the property at the time of the gift.

For gifts made *after 1976,* add only part of the gift tax paid to the basis. The part of the gift tax which you add to the basis is an amount which is in the same proportion to the total tax paid as the net appreciation in value of the gift is to the total value of the gift. Net appreciation in value of a gift is the amount by which the fair market value of the gift exceeds the donor's adjusted basis immediately before the gift.

Inheritance. If you inherited your condominium or your stock in a cooperative housing corporation, its original basis generally is its fair market value at the date of the decedent's death or the later alternate valuation date if chosen for federal estate tax valuation purposes. If an estate tax return was.filed, the value listed there for the property is generally your basis. If no return was filed, you should use the best available objective evidence of fair market value, such as a competent appraisal.

Publication 588

The requirements for filing a federal estate tax return are explained in Publication 559, *Tax Information for Survivors, Executors, and Administrators.*

Trade. If you acquired your property in a trade for other property, the original basis of your condominium or co-op shares is the adjusted basis of the property you gave up, plus any recognized gain or cash difference you paid, and minus any recognized loss or cash difference you received. If you traded your old home for your present one and realized a gain, see Publication 523, *Tax Information on Selling Your Home.*

Settlement or Closing Costs

If you bought your property, you probably paid an amount for settlement or closing costs in addition to the contract price. Various incidental expenses connected with the sale are not included in the selling price, but are divided between the buyer and seller, according to the sales contract, local custom, or understanding of the parties. You may deduct some of these costs in the year of the purchase if you itemize your deductions on Schedule A (Form 1040). You add others to the basis of your property. Some costs you neither deduct nor add to the basis.

Division of real estate taxes. When you buy a condominium or co-op apartment, real property tax usually is divided so that you and the seller each pay tax for the part of the property tax year that each owned the property.

For federal income tax purposes, the seller pays the property taxes up to, but not including, the date of the sale, and the buyer pays the taxes beginning with the date of sale, regardless of the property tax accrual or lien dates under local law. You and the seller are each considered to have paid your share of the tax. Each of you may deduct that amount for the year the property is sold, even if one of you pays the entire amount.

Example. You bought your condominium on September 1, 1980. The property tax year in your locality is the calendar year, and payment of the tax is due on August 15. The tax for the year on the property you bought was $730, and had been paid by the seller on August 15. Your settlement costs included $244, representing your share of the property taxes from September 1 through December 31 (122/365 of $730).

You may deduct this $244 on your return for the year if you itemize your deductions. You are considered to have paid this amount, and would be permitted to deduct it on your return, even if you were not required under the contract to reimburse the seller for your share of the year's property tax.

If you did not reimburse the seller for your share of the year's property tax, you would reduce the basis of your property by the $244 the seller paid for you. Conversely, if you had agreed to reimburse the seller for the entire year's property taxes under the terms of your contract, you would be permitted to deduct only $244. The seller may claim a deduction of $486 (243/365 of $730). Under these circumstances, you would add $486, the amount of the taxes you paid for the seller, to your basis of the property.

Interest. Another deductible item that normally appears on a settlement or closing statement is interest. Interest charged to the seller on the

mortgage up to the date of settlement or closing is deductible by the seller.

If your records do not clearly show the interest paid, you should get a statement from the holder of your mortgage showing that information. You should determine if interest paid at settlement or closing is included in the statement.

Example. You bought a new condominium on May 4, and sold your old home on May 6 of this year. During the year you made mortgage payments which included $625 of interest on your old home and $1,920 interest on your new condominium. The settlement sheet for the sale of the old house showed $25 interest owed by you for the 5-day period in May up to, but not including, the date of sale. The sum of these three amounts, $2,570, is your mortgage interest deduction for this year.

Prepaid interest. If you pay interest in advance for a period that goes beyond the end of the tax year in which paid, you must spread the interest over the tax years to which it belongs. You may deduct in each year only the interest for that year.

"Points" paid by a borrower. The term "points" is sometimes used to describe the charges paid by a borrower to a lender as loan origination fees, maximum loan charges, or premium charges. If the payment of any of these charges is solely for the use of money, it is interest.

You may deduct the amount you pay as points in full in the year of payment only if:

1) You are a cash method taxpayer,
2) You pay the points in buying or improving your principal home,
3) The debt is secured by your home, and
4) The charging of points is an established business practice in the area where the loan was incurred.

The deduction may not be more than the number of points generally charged in the area.

If these conditions are not met, points are treated as prepaid interest. They must be spread over the life of the mortgage, and they are considered paid and deductible over that period.

However, if the payment of any of these charges is compensation for specific services that the lender performs in connection with the borrower's account, such as the lender's appraisal fee, the cost of preparing the mortgage note or deed of trust, settlement fees, notary fees, etc., this payment is not interest.

Example. You use the cash method of accounting. You borrowed $40,000 to buy a condominium costing $50,000 to be used as your principal home. You agreed to pay the lender, in addition to annual interest of 12%, a loan processing fee of $1,200 (three points). You paid this fee to the lender solely for the use of money. The fee charged was an established business practice in the area and was not more than the amount generally charged in the area. You paid the entire loan processing fee out of your own funds in the year the loan originated and thereafter you made monthly payments on the mortgage and interest as they became due. Under these circumstances, you may deduct the full $1,200 loan processing fee as interest in the year of payment.

"Points" paid by a seller. The term "points" also is used to describe loan placement fees that the seller may have to pay to the lender as

a condition to arranging financing for the buyer. The seller may not deduct these amounts as interest. However, these charges are a selling expense that reduces the amount realized from the sale of the property.

Nondeductible Items. Items that do not affect your basis include fire insurance premiums, FHA mortgage insurance premiums, charges for the use of utilities, rent for occupancy before closing, and other fees or charges for services concerning occupancy of the property.

Basis Items. Generally, you may add all other items that are charged to you at settlement or closing to the cost of your property. They are a part of your original basis. These items include attorney's fees, abstract fees, charges for installing utility service, surveys, transfer taxes, title insurance, and any amounts that may be owed by the seller but which you agree to pay, such as back taxes or interest, recording or mortgage fees, charges for improvements or repairs, and selling commissions.

If the seller paid for any item for which you are liable and for which you may take a deduction, such as your share of the real property taxes for the year, you must reduce your basis by that amount if you are not charged for it in the settlement.

Itemizing Deductions

As a condominium or cooperative apartment owner, you may find it to your advantage to itemize deductions on Schedule A (Form 1040). The mortgage interest and real estate taxes, when added to other deductible items, may make it beneficial to itemize deductions.

Your monthly payment may consist of several parts, some of which are deductible and others which are not deductible. Your payment may include interest, an amount placed in escrow to pay real estate taxes and to buy fire or homeowner's insurance, FHA mortgage insurance premium, and an amount applied to reduce the principal of the mortgage. If you occupy and use your home as your personal residence, you may deduct only the interest and taxes.

If you use part of your property in your business, see *Using Your Home in Your Work,* later for information on what expenses you may deduct. If you rent out your property, see Publication 527, *Rental Property.*

If you own a condominium, you may deduct certain expenses if you itemize deductions.

Real estate taxes. You may deduct real estate taxes assessed by the local taxing authorities on your interest in the land and parts of the structure owned in common. You also may deduct taxes assessed on the separate dwelling unit you own and taxes on any other separate interest you own, such as a parking or storage space.

If your monthly payment includes an amount placed in escrow for real estate taxes, you may not deduct the total of these amounts included in your payments for the year. The deductible amount is the tax actually assessed and paid to the taxing authority from escrow. If the lender does not notify you of this amount, you should ask the lender or the taxing authority to tell you what was paid on your behalf.

Interest. You may deduct interest on the mortgage on your individual property. You may also deduct mortgage interest on your share of the property owned in common. If the project is subject to a blanket (overall) mortgage, you may deduct the mortgage interest for your share of the mortgage.

If you own a cooperative apartment, you may deduct your share of the corporation's deductible interest and taxes if the cooperative housing corporation meets the following conditions:

1) The corporation must have only one class of stock outstanding,

2) Each of the stockholders must be able, solely because of ownership of the stock, to live in, for dwelling purposes, a house or an apartment owned or leased by the corporation,

3) No stockholder may receive any distribution out of capital, except on a partial or complete liquidation of the corporation, and

4) The tenant-stockholders must pay at least 80% of the corporation's gross income for the tax year. For this purpose, gross income means all income received during the entire tax year, including any received before the corporation changed to cooperative ownership.

You figure your share of interest and taxes in the following way.

1) Divide the number of your shares of stock by the total number of shares outstanding, including any shares held by the corporation.

2) Multiply the corporation's deductible interest by the number you figured in (1). This is your share of the interest.

3) Multiply the corporation's deductible taxes by the number you figured in (1). This is your share of the taxes.

You are a tenant-stockholder even if you live in more than one dwelling unit in the cooperative. You do not have to live in any of the units yourself. You may rent them to others. However, you must be an individual to qualify as a tenant-stockholder, although a corporation may own stock in the project.

Shares owned or apartments leased by authorized government agencies are not considered in determining whether the corporation qualifies as a housing cooperative. These government agencies are the United States, any possession, state or political subdivision of a state, or any agency or instrumentality of these that has the power to acquire cooperative housing shares for the purpose of providing housing facilities.

If a bank or other lending institution acquires by foreclosure the stock of a tenant-stockholder, and so acquires the right to occupy an apartment or other dwelling unit, the bank or other lending institution will be treated as a tenant-stockholder for not more than 3 years from the date of acquisition. This is true even if, by agreement with the cooperative housing corporation, the bank or other lending institution or its nominee may not occupy the dwelling unit without the prior approval of the corporation.

If the original seller of the housing property acquires stock of the cooperative housing corporation from the corporation by purchase, or by foreclosure of any purchase-money security interest, and so acquires the right to occupy an apartment or other dwelling unit, the original seller will be treated as a tenant-stockholder for not more than 3 years from the date of acquisition. This is true even if, by agreement with the cooperative housing corporation, the original seller or its nominee may not occupy the dwell-

ing unit without the prior approval of the corporation. However, except in the case of foreclosure, this rule applies only to stock acquisitions that occur not later than one year after the date of the transfer by the original seller of the dwelling unit or units (including any leaseholds in them) to the cooperative housing corporation.

The original seller is the person (including a corporation) from whom the cooperative housing corporation acquired the dwelling units. This rule applies to stock acquired by the original seller after November 6, 1978.

You may not deduct taxes and interest paid by the cooperative during the construction of the project. These expenses are part of your original equity investment in the corporation. However, if you pay an amount to the cooperative housing corporation for your share of points incurred to obtain permanent financing, you may deduct this payment as interest if the points qualify as previously discussed under "Points" paid by a borrower.

You may not deduct real estate taxes assessed on a special corporation organized by your cooperative to hold and manage recreational land and facilities for the common use of all the cooperative tenants.

Mortgage prepayment penalty. You may deduct as interest the penalty payments you pay the holder of the mortgage for allowing you to prepay your mortgage.

Ground rents. You may deduct as interest payments you make annually or periodically on a redeemable ground rent. Payments on a nonredeemable ground rent are not interest. You may deduct them only if you use the property for business or rental purposes.

Amounts paid to redeem a ground rent are added to the basis of the property. You may not deduct them.

Redeemable ground rents have the following conditions:

1) Land is leased for a term of more than 15 years, including renewal periods,

2) The lease is freely assignable by the leaseholder,

3) The leaseholder has a present or future right, existing solely because of state or local law, to end the lease and acquire the entire interest in the land by payment of a specified amount, and

4) The lessor's interest in the land is primarily a security interest to protect the rental payments to which the lessor is entitled.

Other types of interest. Interest is often included in other payments, such as utility late payments, judgments, and personal loans. If you make a late payment of taxes, or are required to pay additional taxes at a later date, part of the amount due will usually be for interest. You may deduct this interest. However, you may not deduct any amount that is a penalty for late payment.

Unstated interest. Payments made under an installment contract having a sales price of more than $3,000 and containing no interest or a low stated interest may include an amount of unstated interest. See Publication 537, Installment Sales.

Your share of property taxes at settlement or closing is deductible when you buy property, as explained earlier in Division of real estate taxes, under Settlement or Closing Costs.

Assessments for local benefits that tend to increase the value of your property, such as streets, sidewalks, or water mains and sewer lines, generally are not deductible. You must add them to the basis of the property. You may deduct local benefit taxes assessed for maintenance or repair, or for meeting interest charges for such benefits.

Assessments for services, such as water, sewer, and trash or garbage collection, are not taxes. These charges are nondeductible personal expenses if you use the property solely for dwelling purposes.

If you are billed a single amount, representing a combination of service charges and assessments for maintenance, repair, or interest on a local benefit, you must be able to divide the single amount between the service charge and the assessment for maintenance. If you cannot determine what part of the amount is for maintenance, repair, or interest, you may not deduct any of the assessment.

Assessments for services also may be billed together with taxes, such as city or county garbage service billed with real property taxes. You may deduct only the amount of the taxes included in the billing.

Homeowners association assessments for promoting the recreation, health, safety, and welfare of residents and for maintaining common areas are not deductible as taxes.

Casualty and theft losses. If your property is damaged or destroyed by fire or other casualty, or if you have a theft, such as jewelry stolen from your home, you may have a deductible loss. You may deduct a casualty or theft loss of property used for personal purposes for the amount of the loss that is more than $100 for each casualty or theft.

When real property held for personal use has been damaged, you figure the amount of your casualty loss by comparing the fair market value of your entire property immediately before and immediately after the casualty. Your loss is the decrease in fair market value resulting from the casualty, but not more than your adjusted basis of the property, reduced by any insurance or other compensation that you received, or expect to receive. Your deductible loss is this amount reduced by $100.

If no better evidence of the decrease in value is available, you may use the cost of repair or replacement to restore the property to its condition just before the casualty to measure the decrease in value.

You must be able to show that:

1) The repairs are necessary to restore the property to its condition immediately before the casualty, and

2) The amount spent for these repairs is not excessive, and

3) The repairs do not care for more than the damage suffered, and

4) The value of the property after the repairs does not, as a result of the repairs, exceed the value of the property immediately before the casualty.

If you suffer a theft loss, the deduction before applying the $100 limit is the lesser of the fair market value of the property or its adjusted basis, reduced by the amount of any insurance or other recovery that you can receive.

Example 1. A fire damaged the kitchen of your condominium. You spent $300 to repair

Publication 588 (Continued)

the kitchen. You can show that these repairs meet the conditions set forth earlier. You carry fire insurance on your property and you are reimbursed $200 by the insurance company. You have no deductible casualty loss. The $200 that you collected from the insurance company plus the $100 limit for such casualty losses equals the $300 repair cost.

Example 2. A fire damaged your condominium in November 1981 and you spent $300 to have the damage repaired. You expected to recover $200 from your insurance company, but you were not actually reimbursed until June 1982. You have no deductible casualty loss for 1981 because the amount of your loss after the expected reimbursement is not more than $100. If the insurance company reimbursed you only $150 in June 1982 in full settlement of your claim, you would have a loss of $50 in 1982, and you would claim the loss on your return for that year.

If your furniture or other personal property is damaged or destroyed by a casualty, you must figure your loss for each individual item of property damaged or destroyed. Your deductible loss is the total decrease in fair market value of the individual items of property damaged, but not more than your adjusted basis of each item of property, reduced by insurance and other compensation that you received or can expect to receive, and also reduced by $100 for each casualty or theft occurrence.

Example. A fire in your home damaged an upholstered chair, and completely destroyed a rug and an antique table. You did not have fire insurance to cover your loss. The chair cost you $150, the rug $200, and the table $15. You established that the chair had a fair market value of $75 just before the fire and $10 just after the fire. The rug, which was totally destroyed, had a value of $50 just before the fire. You bought the table at an auction before discovering it was a valuable antique, and it had been appraised at a value of $350 before the fire. It was totally destroyed by the fire. You figure your loss on each of these items as follows:

	Chair $150	Rug $200	Table $15
1) Basis (cost)			
2) Value before fire	$ 75	$ 50	$350
3) Value after fire	10	–0–	–0–
4) Decrease in value	$ 65	$ 50	$350
5) Loss (lesser of 1 or 4)	$ 65	$ 50	$ 15
Total loss			$130
Less: $100 limit			100
Casualty loss deduction			**$ 30**

The chair was damaged, but not completely destroyed, so the loss on it is limited to the difference in the fair market value before and after the fire, or $65, because that decrease is less than your basis. The rug was completely destroyed, and the loss is limited to its value of $50 just before the fire, because this amount is less than your basis. On the other hand, the table had a value just before the fire that was greater than your cost basis. However, your loss is $15, because it cannot be more than your basis. Your total loss from the fire is $130 and, after reducing the loss by the $100 limit, your deductible loss is $30.

For a complete discussion of gains and losses from casualties and thefts, see Publication 547, *Tax Information on Disasters, Casualties, and Thefts.*

Items not deductible. You may not deduct any of the following, unless you use your property for rental or business purposes:

1) Condominium maintenance fees,
2) Assessments for the use of recreational facilities,
3) Expenses for repairs and maintenance of your property,
4) Depreciation,
5) Insurance, including fire and comprehensive coverage, title and mortgage insurance,
6) Utility fees, and
7) Wages of domestic help.

Excess condominium assessments refunded to you are not included in your gross income unless you previously deducted them, because you used the property for rental or business purposes.

Using Your Home in Your Work

If you use part of your home for business purposes, you may deduct certain expenses for operating a part of your home only if you use that part of your home *regularly and exclusively as:*

1) Your main place of business,
2) A place of business where your patients, clients, or customers can meet and deal with you in the normal course of your trade or business, or
3) A separate structure that is not attached to the dwelling unit that is used in connection with your trade or business.

If you are an employee you may take a deduction for business use if you satisfy the exclusive use and the regular use and the use is *for the convenience of your employer.* If the business use is only appropriate and helpful in your work as an employee, you may not take a deduction.

Example 1. Harry, an outside salesperson, is not provided with office space by his employer, but is required to write orders, make reports, etc. He does this work in one room in his apartment set aside for that specific purpose. He may deduct expenses for that part of his apartment.

Example 2. Carla, a corporate executive, can use the company's offices when she finds it necessary to work after regular hours. However, as a matter of convenience she takes this work home to do in a room she furnished as an office where she can work undisturbed. She may not deduct expenses for the office in her apartment.

Exclusive use. The exclusive use of a part of your home means that you must use a *specific* part of your home *solely* for conducting your business or in connection with your employment. If you use a part of your home as your business office and also for personal purposes, you have not met the exclusive use test. If you use the den of your home to write legal briefs, prepare tax returns, or perform similar activities as well as for personal purposes, you may not take a deduction for expenses for this business use.

Regular use. Regular use means that you must use the exclusive business part of your home on a continuing basis. The occasional or incidental business use of a part of your home does not meet the regular use test even if you do not use that part of your home for any other purpose.

Trade or business use. The business use of your home must be directly related to or in connection with your trade or business. You cannot

deduct any expenses for the use of your home in a profit-seeking activity that is not a trade or business.

Example. You use part of your home exclusively and on a regular basis, to read financial periodicals and reports, clip bond coupons, and perform similar investment activities for your own investments. You do not make investments as a broker or dealer. You cannot deduct any expenses for the use of part of your home because these activities are not a trade or business.

Storage use. You may deduct certain business expenses for the part of your home you regularly use to store goods that you sell at retail or wholesale. Your home must be the only fixed business location. This storage space can have other uses, but the space must be a specific area.

Using your home as a day-care center. The exclusive use test does not apply when you regularly use your home, or any part of your home, in your business of providing day-care services to children, handicapped individuals, or the elderly. If your state has a licensing or similar requirement, you must meet that requirement.

Dividing the expenses. If an expense is for both business use and personal use, such as heat for the entire apartment or interest on your mortgage, you must divide the expense between the business use and the personal use. If a more direct method of division is not possible, you may make the division based on the area devoted to each use.

If your business office in your condominium measures 12 × 15 feet, or 180 square feet, and your entire condominium contains 1,800 square feet of floor space, you should take 10% of your total heating expense and 10% of the interest on the mortgage for the office and deduct these amounts as business expenses. Any reasonable method of division may be used, including one based on the number of rooms in the apartment. Division based on area is usually the most accurate for these expenses.

Limit on deduction. Your deductions for business use of a home may not be more than the amount of your gross income from the business use of the home reduced by otherwise allowable expenses such as taxes, interest, and casualty losses for the business use.

Example. You use ten percent of your home exclusively for business purposes. Gross income from your business operation is $500. You had the following expenses:

	Total	10% Business Part
Taxes	$1,500	$150
Interest	2,500	250
Operating expenses	1,500	150
Depreciation	1,000	100

You figure your allowable deduction for business use as follows:

1) Business income		$500
2) Taxes (10%)	$150	
3) Interest (10%)	250	400
4) Balance		$100
5) Operating expenses (10%)		$150
6) Depreciation (10%)		100
7) Total		$250
8) **Allowable deduction (lesser of (4) or (7))**		**$100**

You must deduct the operating expenses before deducting depreciation and other basis items. In this case your $100 deduction consists of operating expenses and no deduction for depreciation is allowed.

Of course, you may deduct the remaining interest and tax expenses on Schedule A (Form 1040).

Where to Deduct

If you are an outside salesperson, you may deduct on line 23, Form 1040, those expenses that qualify as business expenses.

If you are not an outside salesperson but you are reimbursed for the expenses and you include the reimbursement in income, you also may deduct them on line 23, Form 1040. However, you may deduct the expenses in excess of any reimbursement only if you itemize deductions on Schedule A (Form 1040).

If you are self-employed, you deduct these expenses on the appropriate business schedule, Schedule C or Schedule F (Form 1040), on which you report your business income.

For additional information and a worksheet, see Publication 587, *Business Use of Your Home.*

Depreciation

You may deduct depreciation only on the part of your property used for business or rental purposes.

In general, for property that has a useful life of more than a year, you cannot deduct its entire cost in one year. Instead, you must spread the cost over more than one year and deduct a part of it each year. For property that you place in service after 1980, you generally figure your deduction under the accelerated cost recovery system. For property placed in service before 1981, you continue to figure your deduction using the same method of depreciation for that property that you used in the past. For more information on depreciation when using your home for business purposes, see Publication 587. For information on depreciating rental property, see Publication 527.

Condominiums. Your basis for depreciation of a condominium is the basis of the part of your property you use for business purposes. It does not include any part of your basis in the land, because you cannot depreciate land. If you bought your property for a single purchase price, as is usually the case with residential property, you must find what part of your total cost is for the land. If no better evidence is available, you may use the assessed values of land and improvements when you bought your property to figure the relative values of the dwelling and the land.

Example 1. You paid $64,000 for your condominium. The property tax was based on assessed values of $4,000 for your interest in the land and $28,000 for improvements, or a total of $32,000. You may consider that you paid 4/32 or one-eighth of $64,000 or $8,000, for the land and 28/32 or seven-eighths of $64,000, or $56,000, for the improvements. You then divide the basis of the improvements between the part used for personal use and the part used for business purposes. You may add the cost of improvements you make to the part of your property used for business purposes to the basis for depreciation, or you may depreciate it separately.

Example 2. You operate your business from your condominium, which cost you $72,000. You

establish that $12,000 of this cost belongs to the land and $60,000 to the improvements. The total area used exclusively for your business is one-third of the entire living space of the condominium. The basis you use in figuring depreciation is one-third of $60,000, or $20,000.

Example 3. When you moved into the condominium in Example 2, you spent $4,000 remodeling the rooms used for your business into a more convenient and attractive office suite. You also spent $1,500 replacing the heating and cooling system for the entire apartment. You may add to the $20,000 original basis for depreciation the $4,000 you spent for remodeling and $500 (one-third of $1,500) of the cost of the new heating and cooling system, so that your total adjusted basis for depreciation is $24,500.

Cooperative apartments. If you use your cooperative apartment in your business, you may deduct your share of the corporation's depreciation.

If you bought the stock as part of its first offering, you figure the amount of depreciation you, as a tenant-stockholder in a cooperative housing corporation, may deduct in the following way:

1) Figure the depreciation for all the depreciable real property owned by the corporation.

2) Subtract from (1) any depreciation for space owned by the corporation that can be rented but that may not be lived in by tenant-stockholders. The result is the yearly depreciation, as reduced.

3) Divide the number of your shares of stock by the total number of shares outstanding, including any shares held by the corporation.

4) Multiply the yearly depreciation, as reduced (from (2)) by the number you figured in (3). This is your share of the project's depreciation.

If you bought your cooperative stock after its first offering, you figure the basis of the depreciable real property to use in (1) above by:

1) Multiplying your cost per share by the total number of shares outstanding, and

2) Adding to it the mortgage debt on the property on the date you bought the stock, and

3) Subtracting from it the part of this sum that is not for the depreciable real property, such as the part for the land.

Your depreciation deduction for the year may not be more than the part of your adjusted basis in the stock of the corporation for your trade or business or income-producing property.

If you change your co-op apartment to business use, you figure your allowable depreciation as explained earlier under *Cooperative apartments.* If you bought the stock as part of its first offering, the depreciable basis of all the depreciable real property owned by the cooperative housing corporation is the smaller of the fair market value on the date you change to business use, or the corporation's adjusted basis on that date.

Do not subtract depreciation when figuring the adjusted basis. The fair market value is normally the same as the corporation's adjusted basis minus straight-line depreciation, unless this value is unrealistic.

Residential Energy Credit

The law provides tax credits to encourage energy saving and developing renewable energy

sources. The residential energy credit, which may be claimed by individuals, is discussed in this section. For information on energy credits for businesses, see Publication 572, *Investment Credit.*

The credit for renewable energy source costs for solar, geothermal, or wind-powered equipment for your home is also discussed.

Two energy credits. Two energy credits make up the residential energy credit, each with its own conditions and limits. The credit for energy conservation costs is 15% of the first $2,000 spent on items to save energy, or a maximum credit of $300. The credit for renewable energy source costs is 40% of the first $10,000 spent on solar, geothermal, or wind-powered equipment, or a maximum credit of $4,000.

The cost of the items includes the cost of installing them.

Adjustments to the basis of your home. If the items for which you take the residential energy credit increase the basis of your home, you must reduce the basis of your home by the credit you take on those items.

Grants. You may take a residential energy credit for the cost of items for which you received a taxable federal, state, or local grant. You must include the grant in your gross income.

You may not take a residential energy credit for the cost of items for which you received a nontaxable federal, state, or local grant.

Subsidized energy financing. To figure your residential energy credit after 1980, you may not use the part of the cost of qualifying energy conservation items or renewable energy source property that is financed or paid for with subsidized energy financing. In addition, the $2,000 limit on energy conservation costs and the $10,000 limit on renewable energy source costs must be reduced by the sum of:

1) The part of the costs financed by subsidized energy financing, and

2) The amounts of any nontaxable federal, state, or local government grants used to buy energy conservation items or renewable energy source property.

You *do not* reduce the limits on energy conservation costs or renewable energy source costs by subsidized energy financing and grants you received before 1981.

Definition of subsidized energy financing. Subsidized energy financing is financing under any federal, state, or local programs that are supported by tax revenues. These programs are set up to provide subsidized financing for projects designed to save or produce energy. The use of tax-exempt bonds for providing funds under such programs is an example of subsidized energy financing.

Loan guarantees. Subsidized energy financing does not include loan guarantees.

Financing from a utility company. Subsidized energy financing does not include loans made by a utility to its customers to purchase energy-saving or renewable energy source items out of funds it gets from the sale of electricity or unsubsidized borrowing from the U.S. Treasury. This is so even if the utility is a federal agency.

Owners and renters of homes are eligible for the credit, if they actually pay for the qualifying items.

Publication 588 (*Continued*)

tholders of cooperative housing corpora- and owners of condominium units may in a credit based on their share of the cost ualifying items installed by the cooperative ing corporation or condominium manage- t association for the benefit of the common ers. For a stockholder of a cooperative ing corporation, the share of the coopera- s costs is the same as the stockholder's e of the cooperative's total outstanding k.

t owners or renters. If you own or rent your e jointly with others, the overall limits on lifying costs apply to the combined costs of he owners or renters. If the actual amount nt is more than the limits, the maximum lit must be divided among the joint owners enters based on the part of the total costs each paid. The fact that one joint occupant be unable to claim all or part of the credit, er because of insufficient tax liability or be- se of not meeting the $10 minimum credit cussed later), has no effect on the computa- of the credit for the other joint occupants.

cample. You and a friend own a home and in it together. The two of you buy energy ng items that cost a total of $3,000. You pay s or 20% of the total cost of the items and r friend pays $2,400 or 80% of the cost. Be- se you are joint owners and the combined of the items is more than the $2,000 limit, maximum credit must be divided between You paid 20% of the total cost so your en- credit is figured on 20% of $2,000 or $400. r credit is 15% of $400 or $60. Your friend's lit is figured on 80% of $2,000 or $1,600. r friend's credit is 15% of $1,600 or $240. combined credit taken by you and your d is $300, the maximum credit allowable.

t purchase of qualifying property for differ- homes. If you and one or more people who in different homes share the costs of a ifying item to benefit each of your homes, n of you may take an energy credit. You fig- your credit on the part of the cost you paid. limits on the amount of the credit apply to n of you separately.

cample. John and his two neighbors each one-third of the cost of building a solar col- r that will benefit each of their separate cipal homes. Each separately pays for the s of connecting the solar collector with his er home. If the solar collector and connec- equipment otherwise qualify as renewable gy source items, discussed later, John and neighbors will have renewable energy ce costs equal to one-third of the costs of collector plus his or her separate connec- costs.

business residential use requirement. If than 80% of the use of an energy-saving or wable energy source item is for nonbusi- residential purposes, only the costs for ential use qualify for the residential energy it.

ne Energy Conservation Costs

u may take a credit of 15% of the first 00 you spend on items to save energy in home. An item qualifies when the original allation of the item is completed. The full 00 of energy-saving items does not have to stalled in a single tax year.

nge of principal home. A new $2,000 limit ies if you move to another home. This is so if you spend $2,000 for energy conserva-

tion costs on your present principal home. The $2,000 limit applies to *each* principal home in which you later live.

Example. In 1980 you spent $2,000 for insula- tion and storm windows for your principal home. You claimed an energy credit of $300.

You move to another home in 1981 and spend additional amounts for energy-saving items for the new home. You are eligible for an- other credit of up to $300 (15% of $2,000) for these costs, if you meet the other conditions. You may claim the credit for additional energy- saving costs on the new home, even though the previous owner of your new home claimed a credit for energy-saving costs on it.

Principal home (residence). Usually, the home in which you live is your principal home. If you have two homes and live in both of them, your principal home is the one you live in most of the time.

The home on which you install the qualified energy-saving items must be your principal home and must be located in the United States. It must have been substantially completed be- fore April 20, 1977. To qualify for the credit, a home is considered your principal home begin- ning 30 days before you live in it.

Substantially completed. A home is substan- tially completed when it can be used as a prin- cipal home, even though minor items must be finished or done to meet plans or specifications of the completed home.

Energy-saving items. The energy-saving items you install must be new, must be expected to last at least 3 years, and must meet perform- ance and quality standards to be set by the Secretary of the Treasury. However, items you buy before the performance and quality stan- dards are published do not have to meet these standards.

Qualifying energy-saving items are limited to the following:

Insulation designed to reduce heat loss or heat gain of a home or water heater

Storm or thermal windows or doors for the outside of the home

Caulking or weather stripping of outside doors or windows

Clock thermostats or other automatic energy- saving thermostats

Furnace replacement burners, flue opening modifications, and ignition systems that replace a gas pilot light

Meters that show the cost of energy use

Items that do not qualify for the credit include heat pumps, fluorescent lights, wood- or peat- burning stoves, replacement boilers and fur- naces, and hydrogen-fueled equipment.

Renewable Energy Source Costs

You may take an energy credit for amounts you spend on solar, wind-powered, or geother- mal property for your home. You figure this credit by taking 40% of the first $10,000 of these costs. An item qualifies when the original installation of the property is completed. As in the case of energy conservation costs, the full $10,000 limit on renewable energy source costs may be spread over several tax years.

Change of principal home. A new $10,000 limit applies for each principal home you live in dur- ing the period of the credit.

Principal home (residence). Renewable energy source property, such as solar collectors, wind- mills, or geothermal wells, must be installed for use with your principal home, which must be lo- cated in the United States. Unlike the credit for energy conservation costs, you may claim the credit for renewable energy source property for items installed for use with new, as well as ex- isting, homes. It does not matter when your home was built, as long as the renewable en- ergy source property was installed after April 19, 1977.

If renewable energy source property is in- stalled during construction or reconstruction of a home, the property qualifies for the credit when you first live in the home as your principal home. But if you reoccupy a reconstructed home that you had lived in as your principal home before the reconstruction, the renewable energy source property is eligible for the credit when it is installed. "Reconstruction" is the re- placement of most of the major structures of a home, such as floors, walls, and ceilings.

For purposes of the credit, a home is consid- ered your principal home beginning 30 days be- fore you live in it.

Renewable energy source property. The renew- able energy source property, must be new, must be expected to last at least 5 years, and must meet certain performance and quality standards to be set by the Secretary of the Treasury. However, the property does not have to meet the standards if you buy it before the standards are published *

Cost of renewable energy source property. The cost of renewable energy source property in- cludes labor cost related to the on-site prepara- tion, assembly, or installation of the property. It also includes the cost of drilling an on-site geo- thermal well, after 1979, provided you do not choose to deduct any part of the cost as an in- tangible drilling and development cost.

Renewable energy source property includes the following:

Solar energy equipment for heating or cooling the home or for providing hot water or electricity for use in the home

Wind energy equipment for generating electricity or other forms of energy for home use

Geothermal energy equipment.

How to Claim the Credit

You claim the credit on line 45 of your Form 1040 for 1981. Figure the amount of credit on Form 5695, *Residential Energy Credit,* and at- tach it to your return. You may not claim an en- ergy credit on Form 1040A. You should keep a copy of each Form 5695 that you file for your records. If you sell your principal home, you will need to know the amount of credit claimed in earlier tax years so that you can figure the basis of your home. See *Adjustments to the basis of your home,* earlier.

You must answer question 1 on Form 5695, "Was your principal residence substantially completed before April 20, 1977?" If you do not answer question 1, it will cause delays in pro- cessing your return. If you answer no, you can- not claim an energy credit for energy conservation costs. However, you still may be able to claim a credit for renewable energy source costs.

Figuring the credit for more than one principal home. If you live in one home and during the year you move to another home, you may take an energy credit for each home. Fill out Part I and Part II as applicable on a separate Form 5695 for each home. Enter the total from all Forms 5695 on line 23 of one of the forms and complete Part III of that form. In the space above line 23, write "More than one principal residence." Attach all forms to your return.

$10 minimum. Your residential energy credit for the year must be at least $10 before you can claim it. This $10 minimum applies *before* you consider the limit to tax described in the next paragraph. The minimum applies to joint and separate returns.

The credit may not be more than your tax. It is limited to the tax on line 37, Form 1040, minus the credits on lines 38 through 44.

Carryover of unused credit. You may carry over to next year an unused credit that you did not use because it was more than your tax. You may continue to carry over an unused credit to later tax years through 1987. If you are a fiscal year filer, you may carry over an unused credit through the fiscal year beginning in 1987.

You may use Part IV of Form 5695 to figure your carryover.

If your energy credit is less than $10 for this year before applying the tax liability limitation, you may not carry it over to the next year.

Alternative minimum tax. You may carry over an energy credit for which you received no benefit because of the alternative minimum tax. For information on this carryover, see Publication 909, *Minimum Tax and Maximum Tax.*

For more information on the residential energy credit, see Publication 903, *Energy Credits for Individuals.*

Keeping Records

Recordkeeping is vital to the proper reporting of income. You must keep full and accurate records so that you can support the deductions you claim. You need to know your basis or adjusted basis of property so that you can accurately figure gain or loss on a sale, and depreciation if you use the property for business or rental purposes.

You should keep records relating to the basis of your property as long as you own the original or replacement property. These records include your purchase contract and settlement papers if you bought the property, or other objective evidence if you acquired it by gift or inheritance. They also include receipts, canceled checks, and similar evidence for improvements or other additions to the basis.

Usually, you must keep records for 3 years after the due date for filing your return for the tax year in which you sold, or otherwise disposed of your home. But if you use the basis of your old home in figuring the basis of your new one, such as when you sell your old home and postpone the tax on your gain, you should keep those records indefinitely.

You should keep records to support your deductions for at least 3 years from the date you filed your return or it was due, whichever occurs later.

The form in which you keep records is not important, but they must be clear and accurate and must be available to the Internal Revenue Service.

Homeowners Associations

Condominium management associations and residential real estate management associations are homeowners associations. Both may elect to be treated as tax-exempt organizations. Cooperative housing corporations are not homeowners associations.

Tax-Exempt

If an election is made, the association is not taxed on its *exempt function income.* However, the association is taxed as a corporation with some modifications on its other income.

To qualify for this election, a homeowners association must:

1) Be organized and operated to provide for the acquisition, construction, management, maintenance, and care of association property. For a *condominium management association,* the association property must be related to a condominium project and at least 85% of the total square footage of all the units must be used by individuals for residences. For a *residential real estate management association,* the association property must be related to a subdivision, development, or similar area and at least 85% of the lots or buildings must be for residential purposes.

2) Obtain 60% or more of its gross income for the tax year from membership dues, fees, or assessments received from owners of residential units or from owners of residences or residential lots,

3) Have 90% or more of its expenses for the tax year for the acquisition, construction, management, maintenance, and care of association property,

4) Insure that no part of its net earnings will be used for the benefit of any private shareholder or individual, except through the acquisition, construction, management, maintenance, or care of association property or through the rebate of excess membership dues, fees, or assessments, and

5) Elect to be treated as a tax-exempt organization for the tax year.

Manner of election. A homeowners association must annually elect the exclusion of exempt function income. The election is made by filing Form 1120–H, *U.S. Income Tax Return for Homeowners Associations.* For details, see the instructions for Form 1120–H.

Association property includes property held by the organization, property held in common by the members of the organization, certain property within the organization held privately by its members, and property owned by a governmental unit and used for the benefit of residents of the unit.

Property held privately by members of the association qualifies as association property if:

1) It affects the overall appearance and structure of the property,

2) There is a covenant of appearance or similar requirement applying on the same basis to all property in the project,

3) There are annual assessments on all members of the association for maintaining this property, and

4) Membership in the association is a condition of every person's ownership of property in the project.

Example. A condominium management association enforces covenants that affect the appearance of the individual units and maintains the exterior walls and roofs of the individual units. Although the property maintained is private, its appearance may directly affect the condition of the entire project. The exterior walls and roof are considered association property if (3) and (4) are also met.

Exempt function income is any amount received as membership dues, fees, or assessments from owners of condominium housing units in the case of a condominium management association, or owners of residential real property in the case of a residential real estate management association.

Exempt function income includes both fixed annual membership dues or fees and assessments that vary depending upon the need of the association to pay the expenses of the common property. It also includes assessments received from owners in the project for the maintenance of exterior walls and roofs of privately owned property to the extent that such property is association property.

Exempt function income does not include assessments for work done on a privately owned residence. It does not include amounts received for use of the association's facilities from persons who are not owners of residential property and who are not association members. Amounts received from association members as customers for services provided by the association, such as payments for maid service, secretarial service, or cleaning, are not included as exempt function income. Also amounts received from members for special use of the association's facilities, the use of which is not available to all members as a result of having paid the required membership dues, fees, or assessments are not included as exempt function income. For example, if the membership dues, fees, or assessments do not entitle a member to use the association's party room over a limited amount of time, then payments received for excess use are not considered exempt function income. Interest earned on amounts set aside in a sinking fund for future improvements is not exempt function income, nor are assessments for capital improvements which would be treated as capital contributions.

Expenses related to the association's exempt function (for purposes of the 90% test) include both current and capital expenses during the tax year to acquire, construct, manage, maintain, improve, and care for association property. These expenses include salaries of managers, secretaries, and security personnel; expenses of association newsletters; costs of gardening, landscaping, paving, and street signs; property taxes assessed on property owned by the association; current operating expenses of tennis courts, swimming pools, and other recreational facilities; and expenses for replacement of common buildings, equipment, and facilities such as heating, air conditioning, and elevators.

Expenses related to the exempt function do not include expenses on privately owned property, unless the expenses are for the repair of exterior walls and roofs that qualify as association property. These expenses also do not include investments or transfers of funds to be held to meet future costs, such as transfers to a sinking fund account for the replacement of a roof.

Homeowners association taxable income is the association's gross income for the tax year,

Publication 588 *(Continued)*

other than its exempt function income, reduced by any deductions directly connected with the production of the gross income subject to tax. For this purpose, the association may not deduct net operating losses, special deductions for corporations (such as the dividends received deduction), or expenses connected with the production of exempt function income. The association is allowed an additional specific deduction of $100 in arriving at its taxable income.

For tax years beginning after 1980, all home-owners association taxable income is taxed at 30%.

Non-Exempt

If the election is not made or if the association does not satisfy the qualifying requirements, the association generally must file tax returns in the same manner as other corporations. If the management is by an unincorporated association, it may be treated as a corporation for tax purposes. See Publication 542.

Cooperative basis organization. A non-exempt condominium management corporation may operate in such a manner as to qualify as a cooperative (subchapter T) organization, thereby permitting the corporation to retain for reasonable business purposes up to 80% of its otherwise taxable income received from its unit owner-stockholders as regular assessments. This is done by distributing qualified patronage dividends for which the cooperative corporation receives a deduction. The patronage dividends may be paid 20% in cash and 80% in qualified written notices of allocation. Therefore, up to 80% of otherwise taxable income accumulated from the regular assessments may be retained by the cooperative corporation for its reasonable business needs.

A qualified patronage dividend means an amount paid to an owner-stockholder by a cooperative condominium management corporation which is:

1) Distributed pro rata based on the amount of regular assessments paid by each owner-stockholder during the year,

2) Paid under a valid enforceable written obligation (such as state law requiring such payments, corporate by-laws, articles of incorporation, or written contracts), which existed before the management corporation collected the regular assessment, and

3) Determined by reference to the net earnings (excess of amounts regularly assessed less expenses).

Owner-stockholders who do not use their condominium unit in their trade or business or for the production of income may exclude patronage dividends from their income.

Assessments. Regular assessments paid by condominium owners are income to the corporation for services rendered. The excess of this income over expenses is subject to tax.

Excess assessments over the expenses for the year do not result in taxable income to the corporation if they are either refunded to the owner-stockholders or applied to the following year's regular assessments, because of a specific vote of the membership at a membership meeting.

A special assessment is not included in the gross income of a non-exempt condominium management corporation if the assessment has been specifically voted on and approved by the stockholders, designated for a specific capital expense, set aside in a special bank account, and not commingled with the regular assessments of the management corporation.

Personal property. A special assessment that owner-stockholders vote on and designate for the replacement of personal property in the common elements of the condominium is treated as a contribution to the capital of the management corporation. Therefore it is not included in gross income, provided that the funds collected are earmarked for a specifically designated capital expense and kept in a separate bank account. This is true if the condominium management corporation is authorized by state law and its bylaws to own personal property. However, if the special assessment is to pay for services rendered by the corporation to the owner-stockholders, the funds collected from this special assessment are included in the gross income of the management corporation.

Example 1. The owner-stockholders in your condominium levy and collect a special assessment of $2 a month for 11 months to be used exclusively for the replacement of outdoor lawn furniture to be owned by the condominium management corporation. The funds collected are deposited in a separate bank account specifically designated for this purpose. These special assessments are not included in the gross income of the condominium management corporation.

Example 2. A special assessment of $3 is levied and collected from the owner-stockholders of your condominium to pay for the unexpected cost of repairing the condominium's swimming pool filter and for the increased costs of maintaining the lawns and gardens of the condominium. Because this special assessment is to pay for services rendered by the management corporation to the owner-stockholders, it is included in the corporation's gross income.

Real property. Each owner-stockholder of a condominium management corporation is considered to own an undivided interest in the common elements of the condominium's real property. If the owner-stockholders vote to levy and collect a special assessment to be used for a specific capital expense in the common elements of the condominium's real property, the corporation does not include these funds in its

gross income because it owns none of the property benefitted. If these funds are deposited in a separate bank account earmarked for a specific capital expense, and may only be expended for that designated purpose, the management corporation acts merely as an agent for the owner-stockholders because it may not use these funds to benefit any property that it owns.

Example. The owner-stockholders in your condominium at their annual meeting decide to levy and collect from each owner special assessments totaling $25 a month for 36 months. The management corporation is directed to deposit these assessments into two separate bank accounts and not to commingle these assessments with any regular assessment funds. The special assessments are to be used exclusively to replace the roof and elevator located in the common elements of the property, of which each owner-stockholder owns an undivided interest. Accordingly, since the funds are received by the management corporation as an agent for the benefit of the owner-stockholders, the special assessments are not included in the corporation's gross income.

A cooperative housing corporation is not exempt from tax and must file a corporation income tax return. It must be able to deduct taxes and interest for these expenses to be deductible in turn by its tenant-shareholders.

A homeowners association formed to administer and enforce covenants for preserving the architecture and appearance of the development, and to own and maintain common green areas, streets, and sidewalks, which does not elect, or does not qualify, to be treated as an exempt homeowners association, does not qualify for exemption as a civic league or social welfare organization. However, it may qualify for exempt status if it can show that:

1) The community served by the association is a geographical unit reasonably related to a governmental subdivision, and

2) The association does not maintain the exterior of private residences, and

3) The association owns and maintains only areas and facilities of direct governmental concern such as roadways, parklands, sidewalks, and street lights which are available to the general public, and

4) The association owns and maintains recreational areas and facilities for the use and enjoyment of the general public. The association may not qualify if it owns and maintains parking facilities only for its members.

If an association establishes a separate organization to own and maintain recreational facilities and restricts their use to members, and no part of its earnings benefit any member, it may be able to qualify for exempt status

APPENDIX B

Selected Sections from *Seller's Guide to Conventional Mortgages*

Washington, D.C.: The Mortgage Corporation, 1976.

3.203 Hazard Insurance Requirements.

†a. **General.** Each mortgage purchased in whole or in part by FHLMC must be covered by hazard insurance which, as a minimum, meets the requirements set forth in this section.

b. **Scope and Amount of Coverage Required for Home Mortgages—Other Than Planned Unit Development and Condominium Unit Home Mortgages.** Insurance coverage in the following kinds and amounts is required on the Mortgaged Premises covered by a mortgage purchased in whole or in part by FHLMC. Basic coverage must provide:

(1) The scope of coverage shall be equal to or greater than fire and extended coverage and shall be at least equal to that commonly required by private institutional mortgage investors in the area in which the Mortgaged Premises are located. The policy shall provide, as a minimum, fire and extended coverage insurance on a replacement cost basis in an amount not less than that necessary to comply with any co-insurance percentage stipulated in the policy. Except for insurance under the National Flood Insurance Act of 1968, as amended, and for deductibles, as permitted below, the amount of coverage shall be sufficient so that in the event of any damage or loss to the Mortgaged Premises of a type covered by the insurance, the insurance proceeds shall provide at least the lesser of: (i) compensation equal to the full amount of damage or loss, or (ii) compensation to the first mortgagee under the mortgage equal to the full amount of the unpaid principal balance of the mortgage loan. All buildings valued at $1,000 and over must be insured.

If the area is one identified by the Secretary of Housing and Urban Development as an area having special flood hazards, flood insurance shall be maintained in the amount of the outstanding principal balance of the mortgage loan or the maximum limit of coverage available under the National Flood Insurance Act of 1968, as amended, whichever is less.

Where Seller is aware that the Mortgaged Premises are exposed to any appreciable hazard against which fire and extended coverage does not afford protection, Seller agrees to advise FHLMC of the nature of such hazard and the additional insurance coverage, if any, which Seller has obtained against such hazard. If adequate insurance has not been obtained against such hazard, FHLMC may require Seller to obtain such coverage as a condition of purchasing the mortgage in whole or in part. Seller shall obtain a vacancy permit endorsement when necessary and available.

† (2) Policies containing a deductible clause up to the greater of $500 or one percent (1%) of the face amount of the policy applicable to either fire or extended coverage, or both, are acceptable. When policies contain a fall of building clause, such clause must be waived.

c. **Scope and Amount of Coverage Required for Planned Unit Developments.** Insurance coverage in the following kinds and amounts is required on property covered by a PUD unit Home Mortgage:

†(1) Except as provided in the following paragraph, all coverages in the kinds and amounts required for Home Mortgages Pursuant to Section 3.20a are required also for PUD unit Home Mortgages

† (2) In lieu of maintaining individual hazard insurance policies on each PUD unit, the PUD corporation, association or trust may maintain blanket hazard insurance providing, as a minimum, fire and extended coverage and all other coverage in the kinds and amounts commonly required by private institutional mortgage investors for developments similar in construction, location and use. Such coverage must be in an amount equal to the full replacement value, without deduction for depreciation or coinsurance, of all of the PUD units, including the structural portions and fixtures thereof owned by the PUD unit owners. Insurance premiums from any such blanket insurance coverage shall be a common expense of the PUD corporation, association or trust and included in the regular common assessments of the PUD unit owners. Such coverage must name as the insured the PUD corporation, association or trust for the benefit of the PUD unit owners.

(3) The PUD corporation, homeowners association or trust must have fire and extended coverage insurance for no less than one hundred percent (100%) of replacement cost of insurable PUD common property. Such insurance must name as the insured the PUD corporation, homeowners association or trust for the benefit of the unit owners in a PUD. (No mortgagee clause in favor of PUD unit mortgagees is required by FHLMC on insurance covering common property.)

(4) The PUD corporation, homeowners association or trust must have fidelity coverage against dishonest acts on the part of directors, managers, trustees, employees or volunteers responsible for handling funds collected and held for the benefit of the unit owners in a PUD if the PUD has more than thirty (30) units. The fidelity bond or insurance must name the PUD corporation, homeowners association or trust as the named insured and shall be written in an amount sufficient to provide protection which is in no event less than one and one-half times the insured's estimated annual operating expenses and reserves. In connection with such coverage, an appropriate endorsement to the policy to cover any persons who serve without compensation shall be added if the policy would not otherwise cover volunteers.

† (5) The PUD corporation, homeowners association or trust must have a comprehensive policy of public liability insurance covering all of the PUD common property. Such insurance policy shall contain a "severability of interest" clause or endorsement which shall preclude the insurer from denying the claim of a unit owner in a PUD because of negligent acts of the PUD corporation, homeowners association or trust, or other unit owners. The scope of coverage must include all other coverage in the kinds and amounts commonly required by private institutional mortgage investors for projects similar in construction, location and use. Liability coverage shall be for at least $1,000,000 per occurrence for personal injury and/or property damage.

d. Scope and Amount of Coverage Required for Home Mortgages on Individual Condominium Units. Insurance coverage in the following kinds and amounts is required on property covered by a Condominium Unit Home Mortgage:

(1) A multi-peril type policy is required covering the entire condominium project providing as a minimum fire and extended coverage and all other coverage in the kinds and amounts commonly required by private institutional mortgage investors for projects similar in construction, location and use on a replacement cost basis in an amount not less than one hundred percent (100%) of the insurable value (based upon

replacement cost). If there is a steam boiler in operation in connection with the Mortgaged Premises, there must be in force boiler explosion insurance evidenced by the standard form of boiler and machinery insurance policy and providing as a minimum, $100,000 per accident per location. If the condominium project is located in an area identified by the Secretary of Housing and Urban Development as an area having special flood hazards, a "blanket" policy of flood insurance on the condominium project must be maintained in the amount of the aggregate of the outstanding principal balances of the mortgage loans on the Condominium Units comprising the condominium project or the maximum limit of coverage available under the National Flood Insurance Act of 1968, as amended, whichever is less. The name of the insured under each required policy must be stated in form and substance similar to the following:

"Association of Owners of the _____ Condominium for use and benefit of the individual owners" (designated by name, if required).

(2) Each such policy must contain the standard mortgagee clause which must be endorsed to provide that any proceeds shall be paid to the Association of Owners of the _____ Condominium for the use and benefit of mortgagees as their interest may appear, or must be otherwise endorsed to fully protect FHLMC's interest.

(3) The association of owners must have fidelity coverage against dishonest acts on the part of directors, managers, trustees, employees or volunteers responsible for handling funds belonging to or administered by the condominium association of owners if the condominium project has more than thirty (30) units. The fidelity bond or insurance must name the condominium association of owners as the named insured and shall be written in an amount sufficient to provide protection which is in no event less than one and one-half times the insured's estimated annual operating expenses and reserves. In connection with such coverage, an appropriate endorsement to the policy to cover any persons who serve without compensation shall be added if the policy would not otherwise cover volunteers.

(4) The association of owners must hve a comprehensive policy of public liability insurance covering all of the common elements, commercial spaces and public ways in the condominium project. Such insurance policy shall contain a "severability of interest" endorsement which shall preclude the insurer from denying the claim of a Condominium Unit owner because of negligent acts of the condominium association of owners or other unit owners. The scope of coverage must include all other coverage in the kinds and amounts required by private institutional mortgage investors for projects similar in construction, location and use. Liability coverage shall be for at least $1,000,000 per occurrence, for personal injury and/or property damage.

†e. **Minimum Rating of Carrier; Other Requirements.** Each hazard insurance policy must be written by a hazard insurance carrier which has a current rating by Best's Insurance Reports of B/VI or better. Hazard insurance policies are also acceptable from an insurance carrier which has a financial rating by Best's Insurance Reports of Class V, provided it has a general policy holder's rating of at least A. (FHLMC will normally make an exception upon specific request where the insured is an assigned risk.) Alternatively, Servicer may accept an insurer that does not satisfy FHLMC's minimum Best's rating requirements, provided that the insurer is rein-

sured by a company that does have a current rating by Best's Insurance Reports of B/VI or better. This may be accomplished by having both insurance carriers execute and attach to each Borrower's policy an Assumption of Liability Endorsement. Such endorsement must provide for one hundred percent (100%) reinsurance of the policy and written notice to Borrower, Servicer and the primary insurer at least ninety (90) days prior to termination of the reinsurance.

Each insurer and any reinsurer must be specifically licensed or authorized by law to transact business within the state or territory where the Mortgaged Premises are located. Policy contracts shall provide that no assessment may be made against FHLMC (or FHLMC's designee), and that any assessment made against others may not become a lien on the Mortgaged Premises superior to the first mortgage.

f. Mortgage Clause; Endorsement. All policies of hazard insurance must contain or have attached the standard mortgagee clause commonly accepted by private institutional mortgage investors in the area in which the Mortgaged Premises are located. The mortgagee clause must provide that the insurance carrier shall notify the first mortgagee (or trustee) named at least ten (10) days in advance of the effective date of any reduction in or cancellation of the policy.

For mortgages purchased in whole by FHLMC, the mortgagee clause of each insurance policy must be properly endorsed, and there must have been given necessary notices of transfer, and any other action required to be taken must have been taken, in order to fully protect, under the terms of the policy and applicable law, FHLMC's interest as first mortgagee. Where permissible, FHLMC prefers that Seller cause the insurance carrier to name Servicer, or "[name of Servicer] or assigns," as first mortgagee under the mortgagee clause instead of FHLMC. In those deed of trust jurisdictions where it is permissible, "[name of Servicer], beneficiary" or "[name of Trustee] for the benefit of [name of Servicer]" shall be used instead of only the name of the Trustee.

However, Seller *must* cause all insurance drafts, notices, policies, invoices and all other similar documents, to be delivered directly to Servicer, regardless of the manner in which the mortgagee clause is endorsed. If Seller causes FHLMC to be named as first mortgagee, Seller must cause Servicer's address to be used in the endorsements in lieu of the address of FHLMC, e.g.,

> Federal Home Loan Mortgage Corporation
> c/o ABC Savings and Loan Association
> 100 Main Street
> Hometown, U.S.A. 14043

g. Insurance Coverage Varying from Above Requirements. Insurance coverage which does not meet the foregoing requirements will be considered on a case-by-case basis by FHLMC upon request by Seller. FHLMC may require such additional coverage as it may deem necessary in connection with any case or group of cases.

3.204 Survey Requirements.

Each mortgage purchased in whole or in part by FHLMC must meet the following survey requirements.

An improvement survey, or, as sometimes referred to, a plat of survey, must have been obtained prior to the Delivery Date. However, if private institutional mortgage investors in the area in which the Mortgaged Premises are located do not commonly require a survey, or if the title insurance policy insures against loss or damage by any violation, variation, encroachment or adverse matter which would have been disclosed by an accurate survey, a survey will not be required by FHLMC. The plat of survey must be based upon the results of an instrument survey made, dated and certified by a licensed civil engineer or registered surveyor, within one year of the date of the title insurance policy or an attorney's opinion of title obtained in connection with that particular mortgage loan, the certification of which should run to Seller and the title insurance company which is furnishing the title insurance policy, if required by the title insurance company.

The survey must show, among other things: (i) the location by courses and distances of the plot to be covered by the mortgage, the relation of the point of beginning of said plot to the monument from which it is fixed, all easements appurtenant to said plot, any established building line, and the line of the street or streets abutting the plot and the width of said streets; (ii) encroachments and the extent thereof in terms of feet and inches upon said plot or any easement appurtenant thereto; (iii) all structures and improvements on said plot with horizontal lengths of all sides and the relation thereof by distances to all boundary lines of the plot, servient easements, established building lines, and street lines. If the plot is described as being on a filed map, the survey must contain a legend relating the plot to the map on which it is shown. The survey must disclose and provide assurance that the improvements erected lie wholly within the boundaries of the plot and that no part thereof encroaches upon or overhangs any easement or right of way or upon the land of other sections, and that the improvements are wholly within the building restriction lines however established and that no adjoining structure encroaches upon the plot or upon any dominant easement appurtenant thereto. If such encroachment, overhang, or violation exists, the same must be clearly shown, and if other than permitted by Section 3.202d, written approval or waiver by FHLMC must be obtained by Seller prior to the FHLMC Funding Date.

3.205 Legal Description.

For each mortgage purchased in whole or in part by FHLMC, the legal description as set forth in the mortgage and title insurance policy or other evidence of title must be in one of the following basic forms:

a. Metes and Bounds. A metes and bounds description should comply with the following standards:

(1) The beginning point should be established by a monument located at the beginning point, or by reference to a nearby monument.

(2) The sides of the Mortgaged Premises must be described by giving the distances and bearings of each. In lieu of bearings, it is equally acceptable to use the interior angle method, provided that the beginning point is located on a dedicated public street line or a fixed line on other property or the course of the first side can be otherwise properly fixed.

(3) The distances, bearings and angles should be taken from a recent instrument survey, or recently recertified instrument survey, by a licensed civil engineer or registered surveyor.

(4) Curved courses should be described by data including: (1) length of arc, (ii) radius of circle for the arc and (iii) chord distance and bearing.

However, if commonly accepted by private institutional mortgage investors in the area in which the Mortgaged Premises are located, when a survey course is part of a dedicated public street or road line, the course may be described merely by indicating the distance and direction which the course takes along the street line from the end of the previous course.

(5) The legal description should be a single perimeter description of the entire plot. Division into parcels must be avoided unless a special purpose of the specific mortgage loan is served. Division is necessary, however, if the plot is located on two sides of a public way. (It is also customary in many areas to describe an easement appurtenant to a fee parcel by using a separate parcel description.)

b. Lot and Block Description. A description composed of lots and/or blocks which includes reference to a recorded map or plat on which said lots or blocks are delineated is usually deemed adequate.

However, when all of the lots or blocks in the description do not appear on the same recorded map or plat, the location of the apparently identical sides of lots or blocks in different recorded maps or plats, fixed in both maps or plats by the same monuments (a rare situation), is usually deemed adequate.

c. Additional Acceptable Descriptions. Although encountered in only a few cases, a description of a parcel bounded on all sides by dedicated streets or alleys can acceptably refer only to the bounding lines of the streets or alleys.

A description of registered property is acceptable, if in the form required by the local Torrens Act.

3.206 Leasehold Requirements.

For each Home Mortgage on a leasehold estate delivered to FHLMC for purchase in whole or in part, Seller warrants that the lease is a lease of the fee or a sublease which is executed by the fee owner and the sublessor, and that:

†**a.** the use of leasehold or ground rent estates for residential properties is an accepted practice in the area in which the Mortgaged Premises are located,

b. residential properties in the area consisting of such leasehold or ground rent estates are readily marketable, and

c. mortgages covering such residential properties are commonly acceptable to private institutional mortgage investors.

Seller further warrants that:

d. The lease, sublease, or conveyance reserving ground rents and their provisions is in a form commonly acceptable to private institutional mortgage investors in the area in which the Mortgaged Premises are located.

†**e.** The lease and sublease, if any, (including all amendments thereto) is/are recorded.

f. The leasehold is in full force and effect and is not subject to any prior lien or encumbrance by which the leasehold can be terminated or subjected to any charge or penalty.

g. The remaining term or exercised renewal of the lease and sublease together with any renewals enforceable by the mortgagee does not terminate earlier than five (5) years after the maturity date of the mortgage.

†**h.** The sublease payments are, at least, equal to the lease payments. The sublease payments are due no less frequently than the lease payments.

†**i.** The lease and sublease, if any, does/do not contain any provisions that:

(1) permit increase(s) in the rent (lease payment) other than a sum certain increase at a specified date(s) or time interval(s). (Increases based on cost of living or other indices or reappraisal are not acceptable unless they have the effect of limiting increased payment amounts to the *lesser* of the sum certain specified, or of the amount resulting from application of the index or reappraisal.);

(2) provide for termination for lessee's default without the leasehold mortgagee being entitled to receive written notice of, and a reasonable opportunity to cure, such default;

(3) provide for termination in the event of damage or destruction as long as the leasehold mortgage is in existence;

(4) prohibit the leasehold mortgagee to be an insured under hazard insurance policies;

(5) prohibit payment of hazard insurance proceeds to the leasehold mortgagee or insurance trustee;

(6) prohibit payment to leasehold mortgagee of any condemnation award to which lessee is entitled;

(7) prohibit the leasehold mortgagee from exercising renewal options.

j. The lease or sublease contains provisions which:

(1) permit mortgaging of the leasehold estate,

(2) permit assignment without lessor's consent,

(3) permit the leasehold mortgagee the right to acquire in its own name (or nominee) the rights of the lessee upon foreclosure or assignment in lieu of foreclosure.

†NOTE: *Notwithstanding Seller's warranties as to leasehold requirements contained in Section 3.206, FHLMC may decline to purchase a particular leasehold mortgage based on underwriting considerations arising out of a ground lease analysis. Therefore, if Seller contemplates that delivery may include a leasehold mortgage(s), Seller may elect to submit the Ground Lease Analysis (FHLMC Form 461) pertaining to such mortgage(s) prior to delivery for determination of acceptability of salient leasehold provisions.*

3.207 Condominium Home Mortgages— Special Warranties.

Condominium projects shall be divided into two categories; CLASS I or CLASS II. Whether a project is in CLASS I or CLASS II will depend, in part, upon the date on which developer control terminates, which normally will be determined by either the documents creating the condominium, or by applicable law, as applied to the facts in a particular situation.

NOTE: *If a condominium unit is located within a PUD, Seller must comply with the FHLMC condominium requirements and warranties (Part 111, Section 3.207), as well as with the FHLMC PUD requirements and warranties (Part III, Section 3.208).*

FHLMC's determination of whether a property is a condominium unit shall be conclusive.

a. CLASS I

A condominium project as to which developer control has not terminated or whose homeowners association has been controlled by the unit owners (other than the developer) for less than two years:

Seller must submit to FHLMC with the first mortgage delivered for purchase, in whole or in part, in each condominium project a certification, signed by an authorized officer of the Seller, of compliance with the warranties set forth below. In the event the Seller requests a waiver of any of these warranties, Seller shall, prior to the time of delivery of the mortgage loan, submit such certification, except for those warranties which Seller especially requests and recommends be waived or modified. This certification (and waiver request, if any) must be in the form set out in Part V, Exhibit M and must be addressed on Seller's letterhead stationery to the applicable FHLMC Regional Office. Any waiver request must list the applicable paragraph number of the warranties and the reasons why the waiver or modification is recommended.

If changes occur which affect a certification or waiver request, Seller agrees to furnish FHLMC with a new certification (with subsequent deliveries from that project) or waiver request (prior to subsequent deliveries from that project) in accordance with the procedure described in the preceding paragraph.

Seller agrees to furnish FHLMC at Seller's expense, such legal opinions addressed to Seller and FHLMC, by counsel, acceptable to FHLMC, as FHLMC may request.

Alternatively, if FHLMC so requires, Seller agrees to submit for approval by counsel to FHLMC, at Seller's expense, the Declaration of Condominium (or Master Deed, or a similar instrument), the bylaws and regulations, and such other documents that pertain to the condominium project (herein referred to as the "condominium constituent documents"), including any public disclosure report required by federal or state law.

SELLER WARRANTS that by virtue of: (i) the condominium constituent documents, (ii) a written agreement in favor of all mortgagees of units in the project with the homeowners association of the condominium, (iii) state law or (iv) a combination thereof:

(1) The condominium project has been created and is existing in full compliance with requirements of the condominium enabling statute of the jurisdiction in which the condominium project is located and all other applicable laws.

(2) Any "right of first refusal" contained in the condominium constituent documents shall not impair the rights of a first mortgagee to:

(a) Foreclose or take title to a condominium unit pursuant to the remedies provided in the mortgage, or

(b) accept a deed (or assignment) in lieu of foreclosure in the event of default by a mortgagor, or

(c) sell or lease a unit acquired by the mortgagee.

(3) Any first mortgagee who obtains title to a condominium unit pursuant to the remedies provided in the mortgage or foreclosure of the mortgage will not be liable for such unit's unpaid dues or charges which accrue prior to the acquisition of title to such unit by the mortgagee.

(4) Except as provided by statute in case of condemnation or substantial loss to the units and/or common elements of the condominium project, unless at least two-thirds (2/3) of the first mortgagees (based upon one vote for each first mortgage owned), or owners (other than the sponsor developer or builder) of the individual condominium units have given their prior written approval, the condominium homeowners association shall not be entitled to:

(a) by act or omission, seek to abandon or terminate the condominium project;

(b) change the pro rata interest or obligations of any individual condominium unit for the purpose of: (i) levying assessments or charges or allocating distributions of hazard insurance proceeds or condemnation awards, or (ii) determining the pro rata share of ownership of each condominium unit in the common elements;

(c) partition or subdivide any condominium unit;

(d) by act or omission, seek to abandon, partition, subdivide, encumber, sell or transfer the common elements. (The granting of easements for public utilities or for other public purposes consistent with the intended use of the common elements by the condominium project shall not be deemed a transfer within the meaning of this clause);

(e) use hazard insurance proceeds for losses to any condominium property (whether to units or to common elements) for other than the repair, replacement or reconstruction of such condominium property.

In the case of a condominium project subject to additions or expansions, in which sections or phases are established by the condominium constituent documents (hereafter referred to as "phasing" or "add-ons") satisfying the requirements of Section 3.207a(4)(b) and (d), and 3.207a(5) will be deemed waived to the extent necessary to allow the phasing or add-ons in accordance with the condominium constituent documents.

(5) Any proposal or plan pursuant to which the condominium project is subject to phasing or add-ons complies with the following limitations:

(a) Condominium unit owner's undivided interest in the common elements must be stated in the Declaration of Condominium (or Master Deed or similar instrument); and the conditions whereby any change in such percentage of undivided interest in common elements may take place are fully described in such Declaration (or

Master Deed or similar instrument), together with a description of the real property which will become subject to the condominium project if such alternative percentage interest becomes effective; and

(b) no change in the percentage interests in the common elements may be affected pursuant to such phasing or add-on plan more than seven years after the Declaration of Condominium (or Master Deed) becomes effective.

(6) All taxes, assessments and charges which may become liens prior to the first mortgage under local law shall relate only to the individual condominium units and not to the condominium project as a whole.

(7) No provision of the condominium constituent documents gives a condominium unit owner, or any other party, priority over any rights of the first mortgagee of the condominium unit pursuant to its mortgage in the case of a distribution to such unit owner of insurance proceeds or condemnation awards for losses to or a taking of condominium units and/or common elements.

(8) If the condominium project is on a leasehold estate, the condominium unit lease is a lease or sublease of the fee, and the provisions of such lease comply with the requirements set forth in Section 3.206.

SELLER FURTHER WARRANTS (except as to the extent that Seller requests and recommends a waiver or modification of the following):

(9) All amenities (such as parking, recreation and service areas) are a part of the condominium project and are covered by the mortgage at least to the same extent as are the common elements. All such common elements and amenities are fully installed, completed and in operation for use by condominium unit owners. If such amenities are not common or special elements under the condominium project, but are part of a PUD of which the condominium project is a part, such an arrangement is acceptable provided that the warranties applicable to PUD units are also satisfied, or waivers obtained.

FHLMC reserves the right to reject any condominium unit mortgage if FHLMC determines in its sole discretion that the number of units in the condominium project is insufficient to support the common elements and all amenities.

(10) Seventy percent (70%) of the units in the condominium project have been sold to bona fide purchasers who have closed or who are legally obligated to close. *Multiple purchases of condominium units by one owner are to be counted as one sale when counting the number of sales within a condominium project to determine if this sales requirement has been met.* (FHLMC may reduce this seventy percent [70%] sales requirement to fifty-one percent [51%] for those condominium projects where Seller can document to FHLMC's satisfaction adequate reasons for such a waiver.)

In a condominium project subject to phasing or add-ons, in which sections or phases are established by the condominium constituent documents and under a common homeowners association, a section or phase may be combined with other completed, sold and occupied sections or phases to meet the presale requirement.

A section/phase is one which is of sufficient size to contain an adequate number of units to support any common elements or recreational facilities which are included in the sale price or appraised value of the individual unit, and in a condominium project, the section/phase is generally established by the condominium constituent documents.

(11) At least eighty percent (80%) of the units sold in the condominium project are sold to individuals for use as their primary year-round residences.

(12) Condominium dues or charges shall include an adequate reserve fund for maintenance, repairs and replacement of those common elements that must be replaced on a periodic basis, and shall be payable in regular installments rather than by special assessments.

(13) A first mortgagee, upon request, will be entitled to written notification from the homeowners association of any default in the performance by the individual unit Borrower of any obligation under the condominium constituent documents which is not cured within sixty (60) days. Seller further warrants that: (i) such request has been made by Seller, (ii) as of the Delivery Date Seller has received no notice of any such outstanding default and (iii) subsequent to the Delivery Date, Seller, as Servicer, will notify FHLMC of any notice of such default, as prescribed in the Servicer's Guide.

(14) Any agreement for professional management of the condominium project, or any other contract providing for services of the developer, sponsor, or builder, may not exceed 3 years. Any such agreement must provide for termination by either party without cause and without payment of a termination fee on ninety (90) days or less written notice.

b. CLASS II

A condominium project whose homeowners association has been controlled by the unit owners (other than the developer) for at least two years, and which is not subject to phasing or add-ons which have not yet been completed.

Although Seller is not required to submit a written certification of compliance with the warranties set forth below, in the event Seller requests a waiver of any of these warranties, Seller shall submit a certification and waiver request in accordance with the procedure set forth in Section 3.207a for a CLASS I Condominium.

SELLER WARRANTS that:

(1) The condominium project has been created and is existing in full compliance with requirements of the condominium enabling statute of the jurisdiction in which the condominium project is located, and all other applicable laws.

(2) Any "right of first refusal" contained in the condominium constitutent documents shall not impair the rights of a first mortgagee to:

(a) Foreclose or take title to a condominium unit pursuant to the remedies provided in the mortgage, or

(b) accept a deed (or assignment) in lieu of foreclosure in the event of default by a mortgagor or

(c) sell or lease a unit acquired by the mortgagee.

(3) Any first mortgagee who obtains title to a condominium unit, pursuant to the remedies provided in the mortgage or foreclosure of the mortgage, will not be liable for such unit's unpaid dues or charges, which accrue prior to the acquisition of title to such unit by the mortgagee.

(4) Except as provided by statute in case of substantial loss to the units and/or common elements of the condominium project, the constitutent documents or state law provide that unless at least two-thirds (2/3) of the first mortgagees or unit owners give their consent, the homeowners association is not entitled to:

(a) by act or omission seek to abandon or terminate the condominium project;

(b) change the pro rata interest or obligations of any individual condominium unit for the purpose of (i) levying assessments or charges or allocating distributions of hazard insurance proceeds or condemnation awards, or (ii) determining the pro rata share of ownership of each condominium unit in the common elements;

(c) partition or subdivide any condominium unit;

(d) by act or omission seek to abandon, partition, subdivide, encumber, sell or transfer the common elements (the granting of easements for public utilities or for other public purposes consistent with the intended use of the common elements by the condominium project shall not be deemed a transfer within the meaning of this clause);

(e) use hazard insurance proceeds for losses to any condominium property (whether to units or to common elements) for other than the repair, replacement or reconstruction of such condominium property.

(5) The project, including all common elements and amenities is complete. All amenities are covered by the mortgage, at least to the same extent as the common elements.

(6) All taxes, assessments and charges, which may become liens prior to the first mortgage under local law, shall relate only to the individual condominium unit and not to the condominium project as a whole.

(7) No provision of the condominium constituent documents gives a condominium unit owner, or any other party, priority over any rights of the first mortgagee of the condominium unit, pursuant to its mortgage in the case of a distribution to such unit owner of insurance proceeds or condemnation awards for losses to or a taking of condominium units and/or common elements.

(8) If the condominium project is on a leasehold estate, the condominium unit lease is a lease or sublease of the fee, and the provisions of such lease comply with the requirements set forth in Section 3.206.

(9) At least ninety percent (90%) of the units have been sold and conveyed to bonafide purchasers, and sixty percent (60%) of the units in the project are occupied by unit owners as their primary year-round residences.

(10) At the time of delivery of the mortgage loan to FHLMC, no more than fifteen percent (15%) of unit owners are more than one month delinquent in payment of homeowners' dues or assessments.

3.208 Planned Unit Development (PUD) Mortgages—Special Warranties.

PUDs (which have not been classified by FHLMC as DeMinimis) shall be divided into two categories, Class I or Class II. Whether the PUD is in Class I or Class II will depend in part on the date on which developer control terminates, which normally will be determined by either the documents creating the PUD, or by applicable law, as applied to the facts in a particular situation.

NOTE: *If a condominium unit is located within a PUD, Seller must comply with the FHLMC condominium requirements and warranties (Part 111, Section 3.207), as well as with the FHLMC PUD requirements and warranties (Part 111, Section 3.208).*

FHLMC's determination of whether a property is a PUD shall be conclusive.

a. CLASS I

A PUD as to which developer control has not terminated or whose homeowners association has been controlled by unit owners (other than the developer) for less than two years.

Seller must submit to FHLMC with the first mortgage delivered for purchase, in whole or in part, in each PUD a certification, signed by an authorized officer of the Seller, of compliance with the warranties set forth below. In the event the Seller requests a waiver of any of these warranties, Seller shall, prior to the time of delivery of the mortgage loan, submit such certification, except for those warranties which Seller especially requests and recommends be waived or modified. This certification (and waiver request, if any) must be in the form set out in Part V, Exhibit M and must be addressed on Seller's letterhead stationery to the applicable FHLMC Regional Office. Any waiver request must list the applicable paragraph number of the warranties and the reasons why the waiver or modification is recommended.

If changes occur which affect a certification or waiver request, Seller agrees to furnish FHLMC with a new certification (with subsequent deliveries from that project) or waiver request (prior to subsequent deliveries from that project) in accordance with the procedure described in the preceding paragraph.

Seller agrees to furnish FHLMC at Seller's expense, such legal opinions addressed to Seller and FHLMC, by counsel acceptable to FHLMC, as FHLMC may request.

Alternatively, if FHLMC so requires, Seller agrees to submit for approval by counsel to FHLMC, at Seller's expense, the PUD Articles of Incorporation or Association or the PUD Trust Instrument, the PUD Declaration of Easements, Restrictions and Covenants or any comparable instrument which creates rights and obligations running with title to the units of the PUD, the bylaws and regulations of the PUD homeowner association, corporation or trust, and such other documents that pertain to the PUD as FHLMC shall request (herein referred to as the "PUD constituent documents") including any public disclosure report required by federal or state law.

SELLER WARRANTS that by virtue of: (i) the PUD constituent documents, (ii) a written agreement in favor of all mortgagees of units in the PUD with the PUD association, corporation or trust, (iii) state law or (iv) a combination thereof:

(1) The PUD has been created and is existing in full compliance with requirements of the jurisdiction in which the PUD is located and all other applicable laws.

(2) Any "right of first refusal" contained in the PUD constituent documents shall not impair the rights of first mortgagee to:

(a) Foreclose or take title to a PUD unit pursuant to the remedies provided in the mortgage, or

(b) accept a deed (or assignment) in lieu of foreclosure in the event of default by a mortgagor, or

(c) sell or lease a unit acquired by the mortgagee.

(3) Any first mortgagee who obtains title to a PUD unit pursuant to the remedies provided in the mortgage or foreclosure of the mortgage will not be liable for such unit's unpaid dues or charges which accrue prior to the acquisition of title to such unit by the mortgagee.

(4) Unless at least two-thirds (2/3) of the first mortgagees (based upon one vote for each first mortgage owned) or owners (other than the sponsor, developer or builder) of the individual units in the PUD have given their prior written approval, the PUD homeowners association, corporation or trust shall not be entitled to:

(a) by act or omission seek to abandon, partition, subdivide, encumber, sell or transfer the common property owned, directly or indirectly, by such homeowners association, corporation or trust for the benefit of the units in the PUD (the granting of easements for public utilities or for other public purposes consistent with the intended use of such common property by the PUD shall not be deemed a transfer within the meaning of this clause);

(b) change the method of determining the obligations, assessments, dues or other charges which may be levied against a PUD unit owner;

(c) by act or omission change, waive or abandon any scheme of regulations, or enforcement thereof, pertaining to the architectural design or the exterior appearance of units, the exterior maintenance of units, the maintenance of the common property party walks or common fences and driveways, or the upkeep of lawns and plantings in the PUD;

(d) fail to maintain fire and extended coverage on insurable PUD common property on a current replacement cost basis in an amount not less than one hundred percent (100%) of the insurable value (based on current replacement cost);

(e) use hazard insurance proceeds for losses to any PUD common property for other than the repair, replacement or reconstruction of such common property.

(5) First mortgagees of PUD units may, jointly or singly, pay taxes or other charges which are default and which may or have become a charge against any PUD common property and may pay overdue premiums on hazard insurance policies, or secure new hazard insurance coverage on the lapse of a policy, for such common property and first mortgages making such payments shall be owed immediate reimbursement therefore from the PUD homeowners association, corporation, or trust. Entitlement to such reimbursement is reflected in an agreement in favor of all first mortgagees of units in a PUD duly executed by the PUD homeowners association, corporation or trust, and an original or certified copy of such agreement is possessed by Seller.

(6) No provision of the PUD constituent documents gives a PUD unit owner, or any other party, priority over any rights of the first mortgagee of a unit in a PUD pursuant to its mortgage in the case of a distribution to such PUD unit owner of insurance proceeds or condemnation awards for losses to or a taking of PUD common property.

(7) If the PUD is on a leasehold estate, the PUD unit lease is a lease or sublease of the fee, and the provisions of such lease comply with the requirements set forth in Section 3.206. If any PUD common property is on a leasehold estate, the lease of the PUD common property is a lease or sublease of the fee and the provisions of the lease comply with the requirements of said Section 3.206.

SELLER FURTHER WARRANTS (except as to the extent that Seller requests and recommends a waiver or modification of the following):

(8) All PUD common property and amenities which are regarded as part of the value of the unit in a PUD for purposes of the appraisal upon which the mortgage loan is predicted (such as parking, recreation and service areas) are fully installed, completed and in operation for use by PUD unit owners. PUD unit owners have a right to enjoyment of the PUD common property and such property is owned in fee or in an acceptable leasehold estate by the PUD homeowners association, corporation or trust. The PUD common property was conveyed to the PUD homeowners association, corporation or trust unencumbered, except for any easements granted for public utilities or for other public purposes consistent with the intended use of such property by the PUD.

FHLMC reserves the right to reject any PUD unit mortgage if FHLMC determines in its sole discretion that the number of units in the PUD is insufficient to support the common property and improvements thereon and all amenities.

(9) Seventy percent (70%) of the units in the PUD have been sold to bona fide purchasers who have closed or who are legally obligated to close. *Multiple purchasers of units in a PUD by one individual are to be counted as one sale when counting the number of sales within a PUD to determine if this sales requirement has been met.* (FHLMC may reduce this seventy percent [70%] sales requirement to fifty-one percent [51%] for those PUD's where Seller can document to FHLMC's satisfaction adequate reasons for such a waiver.) In analysis of this requirement in a phasing or add-on PUD project, in which sections or phases are established by the PUD constituent documents and under a common homeowners association, a section or phase may be combined with other completed, sold and occupied sections or phases to meet the presale requirement.

A section/phase is one which is of sufficient size to contain an adequate number of units to support any common property or recreational facilities which are included in the sale price or appraised value of the individual unit, and in a PUD, the section/phase is generally established by the PUD constituent documents.

(10) At least eighty percent (80%) of the units sold in the PUD are sold to individuals for use as their primary year-round residences.

(11) Homeowners association dues or charges shall include an adequate reserve fund for maintenance, repairs and replacement of those elements of the common property that must be replaced on a periodic basis and are payable to regular installments rather than by special assessments.

(12) A first mortgagee, upon request, is entitled to written notification from the homeowners association of any default in the performance by the individual PUD unit Borrower of any obligation under the PUD constituent documents which is not cured within sixty (60) days. Seller further warrants that: (i) such request has been

made by Seller; (ii) as of the Delivery Date, Seller has received no notice of any such outstanding default; and (iii) subsequent to the Delivery Date, Seller will notify FHLMC of any notice of such default, as prescribed in the Servicers' Guide.

(13) Any agreement for professional management of the PUD, or any other contract providing for services of the developer, sponsor, or builder, may not exceed 3 years. Any such agreement must provide for termination by either party without cause and without payment of a termination fee on ninety (90) days or less written notice.

b. CLASS II

A PUD whose homeowners association has been controlled by the unit owners (other than the developer) for at least two years, and which is not subject to phasing or add-ons which have not yet been completed.

Although Seller is not required to submit a written certification of compliance with the warranties set forth below, in the event Seller requests a waiver of any of these warranties, Seller shall submit a certification and waiver request in accordance with the procedure set forth in Section 3.208a for CLASS I PUD.

SELLER WARRANTS THAT:

(1) The PUD has been created and is existing in full compliance with requirements of the jurisdiction in which the PUD is located, and all other applicable laws.

(2) Any "right of first refusal" contained in the PUD constituent documents shall not impair the rights of a first mortgagee to:

(a) Foreclose or take title to a PUD unit pursuant to the remedies provided in the mortgage, or

(b) accept a deed (or assignment) in lieu of foreclosure in the event of default by a mortgagor, or

(c) sell or lease a unit acquired by the mortgagee.

(3) Any first mortagee who obtains title to a PUD unit pursuant to the remedies provided in the mortgage or foreclosure of the mortgage will not be liable or foreclosure of the mortgager will not be liable to such unit's unpaid dues or charges which accrue prior to the acquisition or title to such unit by the mortgagee.

(4) The constituent documents or state law provide that, unless at least two-thirds (2/3) of the first mortgagees or unit owners give their consent, the homeowners association is not entitled to:

(a) by act or omission seek to abandon, partition, subdivide, encumber, sell or transfer the common property owned, directly or indirectly, by such homeowners association, corporation or trust for the benefit of the units in the PUD. (The granting of easements for public utilities or for other public purposes consistent with the intended use of such common property by the PUD shall not be deemed a transfer within the meaning of this clause);

(b) change the method of determining the obligations, assessments, dues or other charges which may be levied against a PUD unit owner;

(c) by act or omission change, waive or abandon any scheme of regulations, or enforcement thereof, pertaining to the architectural design or the exterior appearance of units, the exterior maintenance of units, the maintenance of the common property party walks or common fences and driveways, or the upkeep of lawns and plantings in the PUD;

(d) fail to maintain fire and extended coverage on insurable PUD common property on a current replacement cost basis in an amount not less than one hundred percent (100%) of the insurable value (based on current replacement cost);

(e) use hazard insurance proceeds for losses to any PUD common property for other than the repair, replacement or reconstruction of such common property.

(5) The project, including all PUD common property and amenities which are regarded as a part of the value of the unit for the purpose of the appraisal, is complete.

(6) No provision of the PUD constituent documents gives a PUD unit owner, or any other party, priority over any rights of the first mortgage of a unit in a PUD pursuant to its mortgage in the case of a distribution to such PUD unit owner of insurance proceeds or condemnation awards for losses to or a taking of the PUD common property.

(7) If the PUD is on a leasehold estate, the PUD unit lease is a lease or sublease of the fee, and the provisions of such lease comply with the requirements set forth in Section 3.206. If any PUD common property is on a leasehold estate, the lease of the PUD common property is a lease or sublease of the fee and the provisions of the lease comply with the requirements of said Section 3.206.

(8) At least ninety percent (90%) of the units in the PUD have been sold and conveyed to bona fide purchasers, and sixty percent (60%) of the units in the project are occupied by unit owners as their primary year-round residences.

(9) At the time of delivery of the loan to FHLMC, no more than fifteen percent (15%) of unit owners are more than one month delinquent in payment of homeowners' dues or assessments.

c. DeMinimis PUD

A PUD in which the common property has a relatively insignificant influence upon the enjoyment of the premises, or has little or no effect upon the value of the property securing the PUD unit mortgage.

†SELLER WARRANTS that the PUD is DeMinimis and that:

(i) the common property's influence and effect is as stated above;

(ii) its marketability has been proven; and

(iii) it is not subject to phasing or add-ons which have not yet been completed.

If the common property's influence and effect is as stated above, but the PUD does not meet the other two requirements, Seller may contact the Applicable FHLMC Regional Office of underwriting office to determine whether that specific PUD has been classified as DeMinimis by FHLMC. If the PUD has not been so classified and Seller believes the PUD is DeMinimis, Seller may submit to FHLMC a Request for Classification as DeMinimis PUD (FHLMC Form 488, Part V, Exhibit N).

If a PUD is warranted by Seller or classified by FHLMC as DeMinimis, Seller need not comply with the provisions in either Section 3.208a (CLASS I) or Section 3.208b (CLASS II).

3.209 Internal Consistency of Documents.

For each mortgage purchased in whole or in part by FHLMC the mortgage, title insurance policy or substitute evidence of title survey, lease, mortgage insurance policy, hazard insurance policies, and all other documents that pertain to the mortgage or Mortgaged Premises must have a description which is consistent with that in the other documents.

PART III—HOME MORTGAGES
Section 3—Property Appraisal Requirements

As to each conventional Home Mortgage purchased in whole or in part by FHLMC, Seller represents and warrants that the requirements set forth in this Part III, Section 3 have been met.

†3.301 Property Valuation.

Seller agrees to submit with each mortgage file an appraisal report on the applicable FHLMC appraisal form, which must be prepared and signed by an appraiser approved by Seller. This appraisal report must be fully completed in a manner so as to adequately support the appraiser's estimate of market value, and present to the reader a visual picture of the neighborhood, site and improvements. The appraiser must fully utilize the "comments" section of the appraisal report to make this presentation and, if necessary, attach additional documentation. The rating grids on the appraisal report must be used to rate the stability and marketability of the Mortgaged Premises as compared to other properties within the Mortgaged Premises' price range. The cost approach must include proper adjustments for any items deemed detrimental to the stability or marketability, such as physical and/or functional depreciation or economic obsolescence. FHLMC does not consider the cost approach to be appropriate in the appraisal of individual condominium or PUD units; also, realizing the complexity of estimating depreciation in the evaluation of older 1-4 family properties, FHLMC does not rely heavily upon the cost approach. The estimated land value must indicate the market value of the land, recognizing its highest and best use. The indicated value by the market approach must be supported by an analysis of sales of at least three comparable properties, preferably located in close proximity to the Mortgaged Premises, and sole within the recent past, showing a description and dollar amount of adjustments for significant variations between the comparables and the Mortgaged Premises. The indicated value by the income approach, if considered applicable by the appraiser, must be derived by the gross rent multiplier technique using economic market rent. The estimate of market value is not based upon an averaging of the values indicated by the three approaches, but upon a final reconciliation of the reasonableness of each approach and its applicability to the final estimate of value.

FHLMC does not provide minimum specifications for material and construction of 1-4 family properties. In reviewing appraisal and inspection reports, and in its inspections, FHLMC will look for properties whose material and construction are acceptable to the typical purchaser, consider those same things which private institutional mortgage investors require and will use the flexibility in making judgments which such investors exercise consistent with the price range of the Mortgaged Premises.

(FHLMC publishes "Underwriting Guidelines-Home Mortgages" to assist its underwriting personnel. Sellers may find this publication useful for its discussion of FHLMC's principles as applied to the analysis of a single family appraisal report.)

3.302 Appraisal Forms.

a. **One-Family Properties.** Residential Appraisal Report (FHLMC Form 70, as revised 7/79, Part V, Exhibit K) must be used for all appraisals of one-family properties and DeMinimis PUD units, dated on or after November 1, 1979. All appraisals of one-family properties of DeMinimis PUD units dated prior to November 1, 1979, may be on either FHLMC Form 70 (7/79) or on the appraisal form approved by FHLMC for use at that time.

b. **Two-Family Properties.** Appraisal Report-Small Residential Income Property (FHLMC Form 72, dated 7/79, Part V, Exhibit W) must be used for all appraisals of two-family properties (including two-family properties in a DeMinimis PUD), dated on or after January 1, 1980. All appraisals of two-family properties, dated prior to January 1, 1980, may be on FHLMC Form 72 or the Residential Appraisal Report (FHLMC Form 70) approved by FHLMC for use at that time.

c. **Three- or Four-Family Properties.** Either Appraisal Report-Small Residential Income Property (FHLMC Form 72, dated 7/79, Part V, Exhibit W) or Appraisal Report-Residential Income Property (FHLMC Form 71B, as revised 8/77, Part V, Exhibit QQ) must be used for all appraisals of three or four-family properties (including 3-4 family properties in a DeMinimis PUD), dated on or after November 1, 1979. All appraisals of 3-4 family properties, dated prior to November 1, 1979, may be on either of these forms, or on FHLMC Form 70 (Residential Appraisal Report).

†d. **Individual Condominium or PUD (Except DeMinimis PUD) Units.** Appraisal Report-Individual Condominium or PUD Unit (FHLMC Form 465, as revised 9/80, Part V, Exhibit KK) must be used for all appraisals of condominium (Class I and II) and PUD (Class I and II) units, dated on or after January 1, 1981. Addendum A to FHLMC Form 465 must be included if less than 70% of the units in the project have been sold to bona fide purchasers. Addendum B to FHLMC Form 465 (front only) must be included if developer control has not terminated or if the homeowners association has not been controlled by unit owners for two or more years. (FHLMC does not require the reverse of Addendum B.) Condominium and PUD appraisals dated

prior to January 1, 1981, may be on FHLMC Form 465 (9/80) or on the appraisal form approved by FHLMC for use at that time.

e. Special Flood Hazard Area Designation. The site section of the appraisal form when completed and submitted to FHLMC must contain a statement as to whether the Mortgaged Premises are located within a HUD Identified Special Floor Hazard Area. FHLMC appraisal report forms, except FHLMC Form 70, dated 5/73, have such a statement printed in the site section of each form. The following statement must be entered in the site section of FHLMC Form 70, dated 5/73:

"Subject property (is/is not) located within a HUD Identified Special Floor Hazard Area."

f. Satisfactory Completion Certificate. With respect to appraisals made subject to repairs, alterations or conditions, or subject to completion per plans and specifications, Seller agrees to submit to FHLMC, on the Delivery Date, a satisfactory completion certificate (see Part V, Exhibit O for suggested format). This report shall be made after completion of repairs, improvements, alterations, conditions or construction, and must clearly state compliance with all conditions or requirements as set forth in the original appraisal report of the Mortgaged Premises. This report, whenever possible, should be prepared by the original appraiser.

With respect to appraisals reflecting evidence of dampness, termites or abnormal settlement, Seller agrees to submit to FHLMC, on the Delivery Date, evidence or corrective action, e.g. an exterminator's certificate or an engineer's report. If corrective action was not a condition of the appraisal, the appraiser must have commented on the effects on value and marketability of adverse conditions.

g. Construction Warranty Program. If the single family home, condominium, or Planned Unit Development is covered by a warranty program, the appraiser should describe it in the space provided in the appraisal report.

h. Census Tracts. FHLMC's Appraisal Reports (FHLMC Form 70 and FHLMC Form 465) contain spaces labeled Census Tract. For all properties located within an area assigned census tract numbers, the appraiser must indicate the census tract number in the applicable space on the appropriate appraisal report form. For a property not located within a census tract area, the appraiser must insert "N/A" in the census tract space to indicate the number is not applicable. This information must be provided for all loans delivered to FHLMC on or after October 30, 1978.

3.303 Appraisers.

FHLMC does not approve specific appraisers, however, appraisers must be experienced in the appraisal of 1-4 family properties and must be actively engaged in such appraisal work. The appraiser must be approved by Seller and, normally, such appraiser will be a member of one of the professional appraisal organizations.

a. Discontinuance of Appraiser by Seller. Seller agrees to inform FHLMC immediately in the event Seller discontinues using the services of any appraiser who has made appraisals with respect to mortgages purchased in while or in part to FHLMC from Seller.

b. Discontinuance of Appraiser by FHLMC. FHLMC may, at any time, notify Seller that FHLMC will no longer accept appraisals made by a given appraiser, and Seller agrees not to use such appraiser with respect to mortgages purchased in whole or in part by FHLMC.

c. Representations to Third Parties by Appraiser. FHLMC does not approve appraisers but accepts appraisals made by appraisers who are approved by Seller. Therefore, an appraiser must not make any representation to third parties as to being approved and qualified by FHLMC.

†**3.304 Energy Efficient Properties.** An energy efficient property is one which uses cost effective design, materials, equipment, and site orientation in providing conservation of nonrenewable fuels. Implicit in this definition are proper design an installation of materials and equipment consistent with climatic conditions in the area. Items contributing to the energy efficiency of a property include, but are not limited to:

(1) insulation with adequate R-values installed in ceilings, exterior walls, roofs, around hot water heaters, under floors, covering unheated areas, and surrounding ducts and pipes in unconditioned areas;

(2) caulking and weatherstripping;

(3) double or triple pane windows;

(4) window shading or landscaping for solar control;

(5) storm fittings;

(6) automatic setback thermostat;

(7) heating, cooling, lighting systems and appliances designed specifically to be energy efficient;

(8) solar systems for water heating, space heating and cooling;

(9) wood-fired heating systems; and

(10) building designs which minimize energy use, such as smaller window area and earth sheltering.

Energy efficient items indicated on the appraisal report should be noted by Seller for their potential energy savings and possible addition to value. The appraiser should list any special energy efficient items in the appraisal report, and note the amount of their contribution to value in the market Data Analysis section. The appraiser should indicate the "Adequacy of Insulation" in the Property Rating/Unit Rating section. Seller should give special consideration to these items since an energy efficient property could affect credit underwriting guidelines (Section 3.403).

3.305 Market Value.

Market Value is defined as "the highest price in terms of money which a property will bring in a competitive and open market under all conditions requisite to a fair sale, the buyer and seller, each acting prudently, knowledgeably and assuming the price is not affected by undue stimulus. Implicit in this definition is the consummation of a sale as of a specified date and the passing of title from seller to buyer under conditions whereby: (i) buyer and seller are typically motivated; (ii) both parties are well informed or well advised and each acting in what he considers his own best interest; (iii) a reasonable time is allowed for exposure in the open market; (iv) payment is made in cash or its equivalent; (v) financing, if any, is on terms generally available in the community at the specified date and typical for the property type in its locale; (vi) the price represents a normal consideration for the property sold unaffected by special financing amounts and/or terms, services, fees, costs, or credits incurred in the transaction." (Quoted from *Real Estate Appraisal Terminology*, published 1975.)

NOTE: *In evaluation of properties, FHLMC will not consider value assigned to furniture, or any other personal property.*

3.306 Discrimination in Appraising.

The appraiser must certify that the estimate of market value in the appraisal report is not based in while or in part upon the face, color, or national origin of the prospective owners or occupants of the property appraised, or upon the race, color or national origin of the present owners or occupants of the properties in the vicinity of the property appraised. Seller's attention is also directed to Section 1.402.

NOTE: *As a matter of corporate policy, FHLMC will reject any loan supported by an appraisal report which makes reference to race or the racial composition of the neighborhood.*

3.307. Property Inspections

a. **One- to Four-Family Properties.** In addition to reviewing the documents submitted by Seller, FHLMC will make property inspections and other checks in order to assure proper underwriting of the mortgage loans offered to FHLMC.

b. **Condominium/PUD Properties.** Prior to the purchase of an initial mortgage loan within a Class I condominium or PUD project, FHLMC must inspect the project and, if the project is being constructed in sections/phases, FHLMC must inspect each section/phase.

If requested by Seller, prior to the Delivery Date, FHLMC will inspect a project if:

(i) the condominium or PUD has been created and is existing in full compliance with requirements and all other applicable laws of the jurisdiction in which the condominium or PUD is located;

(ii) the improvements, including amenities, have been completed sufficiently to provide a basis for analysis of the physical characteristics of the project and individual units; and

(iii) sufficient sales have been obtained to indicate its marketabililty.

An inspection will relate only to the physical characteristics of the project, its location and marketability, not to the acceptability of the condominium/PUD constituent documents, individual mortgage loan applications or mortgage instruments. The inspection does not constitute FHLMC endorsement or approval of the project. After the inspection has been completed, Seller will be advised only whether mortgage loans within the project or section/phase may be delivered to FHLMC. Such advice does not in any way constitute "prior approval" of any mortgage loan, an agreement by FHLMC to purchase any specific individual mortgage loans, or a waiver of any warranties required by this Guide.

If Seller requests an inspection of a project, or requests a waiver and/or modification of agreements, representations or warranties, or a classification as a DeMinimis PUD which necessitates an inspection, FHLMC will require Seller to pay an inspection fee. The inspection fee for each project or section/phase (if being constructed in sections/phases) is $350.00, plus $5.00 per unit for each unit in excess of fifty (50) units. This fee is nonrefundable and must be paid prior to the inspection. If condominium or PUD mortgage loans to be delivered under different types of Purchase Contracts are within the same project or section/phase, or if two or more sections/ phases are completed at the time of inspection, only one inspection fee will be charged.

c. Project Documentation. With the submission of the initial mortgage loan within a Class I condominium or PUD project, or with a request for an inspection prior to the Delivery Date, Seller shall submit the following documentation:

(1) completed FHLMC Appraisal Report—Individual Condominium or PUD Unit (FHLMC Form 465) and, if a prior inspection request, a separate report for each different type of unit (See Section 3.302d of this Sellers' Guide with regard to Addenda A and B to Form 465.);

(2) plat of survey, plat map or a reasonable facsimile, such as a hand drawing, showing location of improvements and common elements located upon the site;

(3) location map, identifying the location of the subject and each comparable property;

(4) sufficient photographs of the subject property, clearly showing typical buildings, all common elements and recreational amenities, and neighboring improvements (These photographs must be originals, preferably in color, and attached to separate sheets of paper.);

(5) if a prior inspection request, floor plans or sketches, with approximate dimensions of each model type;

(6) if the improvements are in legal but nonconforming use relative to zoning, documentation from the appropriate regulatory authority, outlining the conditions under which and to what extent reconstruction is permitted, if damage to the units or common elements occurs;

†(7) if individual units in the Condominium or PUD Project are on leasehold estates, a completed Ground Lease Analysis (FHLMC Form 461) as to the lease instruments or proposed lease instruments (see Section 3.501i);

(8) certification (and waiver request, if any) which complies with the provisions set forth in the applicable Section 3.207a or Section 3.208a of this Sellers' Guide, or, if a prior inspection request, a letter which states Seller's ability to submit such certification and describes any probable waiver request when the initial mortgage loan from that project is delivered to FHLMC for purchase (Each certification and letter must be signed by an authorized officer of Seller.); and

(9) cover letter from Seller, setting forth any other information which Seller feels important to convey.

d. Additional Documentation for Condominium Conversion. If the project is a condominium conversion, the following additional documentation must also be included:

(1) licensed engineer's report indicating the structural integrity of the building and the condition of the major systems including the roof, heating and cooling systems, plumbing, electrical and elevators (If the engineer's report indicates any deficiencies, the Seller must describe in the "description of the renovation and rehabilitation" those actions which the sponsor or developer has taken or will take to cure such deficiencies.);

(2) description of the renovation and rehabilitation, proposed or in process; and

(3) income and expense statements as a rental project covering the two-year period prior to conversion, and a schedule of the pre-conversion rents, received for each major model type.

NOTE: *FHLMC may request additional information or documentation on any project.*

Index